Nuance

2018 Anthology
Ventura County Writers Club

Nuance — VCWC Anthology

Copyright

Paperback: ISBN-13: 978-0-9828549-7-6
ISBN-10: 0982854978

Senior Editor and Formatter:	Carol Malone
Assistant Editor:	Judith Mathison
Graphics and Editor:	Sheli Ellsworth
Layout and Interior Design:	Carol Malone
Cover Designer:	Sheli Ellsworth
Anthology Chair Emeritus:	Lee Wade
Editing Proofreaders:	Pat Caloia
	Connie Mukherjee
	Lari Newton
Images:	Courtesy of Pixabay

VCWC Press
P. O. Box 3373
Thousand Oaks, CA 91359
Venturacountywriters.com
venturacountywriters@gmail.com

from the President...

Nuance. What a beautiful word, an intriguing title, for the Ventura County Writers Club sixth anthology! The etymology of nuance derives from the Latin root *nubes*, which means cloud. The French adapted the word to mean shades or subtle variations of color.

In the 1890s, the French artist, Claude Monet, rented rooms across from the Rouen Notre Dame Cathedral. In a series of over thirty paintings, he captured the façade of the cathedral at different times of the day and year, and in shifting atmospheric conditions. The variable light caused changes in appearance of the subject, manipulating the viewer's visual and psychological perceptions to render a distinctive nuanced character to the church in each separate painting.

Nuance in writing refers to subtle distinction in meaning. Through two elements, layers of subtext and the skillful use of vocabulary/wording to connote specific perceptions, the creative authors in this anthology are comparable to visual artists. They do not simply describe the concrete. Rather, they observe and capture the abstract; the voice, the heart, and soul of their subjects in an effort to create desired nuanced revelations.

This compilation contains winning stories and poems from 2014-2018 VCWC contests, plus juried pieces by current club members. The authors shared themselves and their unique *nuanced* view of the world. If you open yourself to the writing, you will find not only subjects, but perceptions; not simply words, but feelings; not just stories, but universal layers of the human experience.

Congratulations to all of the authors who have contributed to this work. I'd like thank Lee Wade and her volunteer committee for beginning the process. Finally, I would be remiss if I didn't end this message with deep expressions of gratitude to Carol Malone, Sheli Ellsworth, and Judith Mathison for their hard work and dedication in the creation of this remarkable anthology.

Constance Mukherjee
VCWC President. 2018-2019

From the Editor...

The editor's job is to take a raw piece of writing and with the skills developed over years of experience, turn it into a thing of sound structure and beauty for the reader. We have compiled contest winning poetry, short stories, and memoir pieces, and submitted poems and stories from our general membership from the last four years of the Ventura County Writers Club into our *Nuance* Anthology for 2018. What we ended up with is four years of splendid creative writing from amateur to skilled writers. It has been my pleasure to oversee the structuring, editing, and formatting of each piece.

Compiling the anthology has taken the sharp eyes of line editors to make sure each creative piece shines and is presented in the best way possible. This has happened through the selfless services of volunteers and I thank them for their contribution. It started with Lee Wade and her team and then finished with Judith Mathison and Sheli Ellsworth. Thank you, editors, for your invaluable assistance.

We hope as you read these poems and stories, you'll get a sense that you could write as well. You all have the right to write and should, even if it's only for yourself and your family members and descendants. Your life is special, as is the lives of those whose writing appears within the pages of this book. Share what you have learned, the experiences gained, the love lost and earned. Every life is of value and we can all share our stories, like these writers featured here have done.

The motto of the Ventura County Writers Club is to "Encourage the Craft" of writing. Let the poems, stories, and memoirs "Encourage" your craft. All those who have dedicated time, blurr eyes, and bruised fingers to the completion of this compilation, this anthology, salute those who with patience and love have crafted these pieces of creation for your enjoyment. *Enjoy!*

Carol Malone
VCWC 2018 *Nuance* Senior Editor

Table of Contents

Dedication 1

In Memoriam 1

    Remembering Victor H. Prushan 1

    2016 Short Story First Place Adult Winner: Odessa 1910 by Vic Prushan
.... 2

2014 Poetry First Place Youth Winner: Only If You Believe by Brisa Porter
Garcia 7

2014 Poetry Second Place Youth Winner: Window Talk by Erin Stoodley . 8

2014 Poetry Third Place Youth Winner: Time by Callie Blumenfield 9

Poetry: Cooking by Joan Day 10

    Poetry: Untitled Haiku by Joan Day 10

    Poetry: Crow by Joan Day 11

2014 Poetry First Place Adult Winner: Les Raboteurs de Parquet by Ron
Alexander 12

    2014 Poetry Adult Honorable Mention: Lions In The Afterlife by Ron
    Alexander 13

2014 Poetry Second Place Adult Winner: Moon Over Lima by
Nancy-Jean Pement 13

2014 Poetry Third Place Adult Winner: Knowing That All Things Must
End by Katherine Hamilton 14

    2014 Poetry Adult Honorable Mention: Morning Mirror by Katherine
    Hamilton 15

2014 Poetry Adult Honorable Mention: Rabbit Hole by Christina M. Pages
.... 16

    2017 Poetry Adult First Place Winner: A Hungarian Exile Comes Home
    by Christina Pages 17

2014 Poetry Adult Honorable Mention: A Record by Erin Moore 17

Poetry: Glendora by Bonnie Goldenberg 18

2014 Short Story Youth First Place Winner: Taken Over by Megan R.
Ragone 19

2014 Short Story Youth Second Place Winner: His January by Gabrielle Genhart....................21

2014 Short Story Youth Third Place Winner: Almost Done by Naomi Stoodley....................26

2014 Short Story Adult First Place Winner: Water's Edge by Jan Richman Schulman....................28

2014 Short Story Adult Second Place Winner: Paper Dragon by Antony Villalobos....................34

2014 Short Story Adult Third Place Winner: The Vault by Sofia Diane Gable....................39

2014 Short Story Adult Honorable Mention: Melanie's Madness by Carol Malone....................44

2016 Memoir First Place Winner: Barbie's Dream House by Carol Malone....................48

Poetry: To Sea by Wendy Rosen....................51

2014 Short Story Adult Honorable Mention: Presumption by Patricia Caloia 52

2014 Short Story Adult Honorable Mention: Under the Bed by Douglas Peyton....................57

2015 Poetry First Place 12 & Under Winner: Finally a Big Sister by Natalie Stegner....................63

2015 Poetry First Place Youth 13-17 Winner: I Am a Painting by Raya Driggers....................64

2015 Poetry First Place Adult Winner: Willa's Song: Coyote by Glenna Luschei....................65

2018 Poetry Adult Honorable Mention: WPA Dad by Glenna Luschei. 66

2015 Poetry Adult Second Place Winner: A Portrait in Raspberry by Laura Dixon....................67

2015 Poetry Adult Third Place Winner: Freeze-Up by Bruce Reynolds......68

2015 Poetry Adult Honorable Mention: Water: Written on a Balcony in Rome by Diane Mautner....................69

2015 Poetry Adult Honorable Mention: A Strand of Scarlet Yarn by Diane Caskey....................70

2015 Poetry Adult Honorable Mention: Octopus Machina by Michael Seals 71

2015 Memoir First Place Winner: Sinks and Cabbages by Karen Gorback 72

2015 Short Story Adult Second Place Winner: Beyond Measure by Karen Gorback 74

2015 Memoir Second Place Winner: Peak Attitude by Sunny Glessner 80

2015 Memoir Honorable Mention: Catechism by Louisa Angeli 82

2015 Short Story Adult Honorable Mention: Stuck Together by Louisa Angeli 84

Poetry: Weathering the Storm by Louisa Angeli 88

2015 Memoir Honorable Mention: The Topic Was Taboo by Barbara Fischer 89

2015 Memoir Honorable Mention: My Fourth Grade Baseball Career by Robb Geweniger 91

2016 Memoir Second Place Winner: Baker by Robb Geweniger 93

2015 Memoir Honorable Mention: Marching For My Brother by Thomas Pratt 96

Poetry: Downsizing (Photographs and Memories) by Judith Ayn 99

Short Story: Ringo Starr and Grampy by Judith Ayn 99

2015 Short Story Youth First Place Winner: The New Generation by Noah Sletten 101

2016 Poetry Youth Second Place Winner: The Salvation Story, Part I by Noah Sletten 105

2015 Short Story Adult First Place Winner: Coming Clean by Lee Wade 106

2015 Short Story Adult Third Place Winner: Slaying Dragons by Barbara Piszczek 111

2015 Short Story Adult Honorable Mention: Mother Load by David Panaro 116

2015 Short Story Adult Honorable Mention: Going Home by Glenn Rowe 120

2015 Short Story Adult Honorable Mention: Sounds and Motion, Motion and Sounds by William Stermer 122

Short Story: Mr. Mangy Calls the Moon by Natasha Buran 127

2016 Poetry Youth First Place Winner: Sonnet with Kitchen Sink by Lindsay Kim 132

2016 Poetry Adult First Place Winner: World Dance by Bijaya Eaton 133

2016 Poetry Adult Second Place Winner: Except to Say by Anita McLaughlin 134

2017 Poetry Adult Second Place Winner: The Rat by Anita McLaughlin 135

2017 Poetry Adult Honorable Mention: Grandfather's Photograph by Anita McLaughlin 136

Short Story: Misplaced Bride by Theresa Schultz 137

2016 Poetry Adult Third Place Winner: Girl in Blue by Karen Kinrose ... 141

2016 Poetry Adult Honorable Mention: Never Gone by Sharon Sinczewski 142

2016 Poetry Adult Honorable Mention: Meditation Frustration by Kim Reed 143

2016 Poetry Adult Honorable Mention: Toad Ode by Ron Loewe 144

2016 Memoir Honorable Mention: Apple Daises by Ron Loewe 145

2016 Short Story Adult Honorable Mention: Invasion by Rob Loewe. 147

2016 Short Story Youth First Place Winner: Completely Perfect by Sydney Edgecomb 151

2017 Poetry Youth First Place Thirteen Plus Winner: Code Blue by Sydney Edgecomb 154

2016 Poetry Adult Honorable Mention: Girlfriend Days by Channa Carter 155

2016 Poetry Adult Division Honorable Mention: The Postlude by Robert Banfill 156

Poetry: Shallow by Rhonda Noda 157

Poetry: Thunder Roars by Rhonda Noda 158

Poetry: The Player by Rhonda Noda 159

2016 Memoir Third Place Winner: The Catch by Wesley J. Ginther 160

2016 Memoir Honorable Mention: Momma Didn't Raise No Hero by Christian Spangenberg 162

2016 Memoir Honorable Mention: Three Short Mean Men by Saxon E. Sitka 164

Short Story: A Weekend In The Country by Nathan Skyer 166

2016 Short Story Youth Second Place Winner: Morning Offering by Jack Stein 170

2016 Short Story Youth Honorable Mention: Neverest by Ziv Carmi 174

2016 Short Story Second Place Adult Winner: Chirps by Wendell Lilijedahl 179

2016 Short Story Third Place Adult Winner: The Birthday Story by Mikko Cook 184

2016 Short Story Adult Honorable Mention: Real Love by Dallas Woodburn 187

2016 Short Story Adult Honorable Mention: Un-Miracle by Philip Brown 191

2017 Memoir Honorable Mention: Red Dirt Fistfight by Philip Brown 196

2018 Poetry Adult Honorable Mention: The Kindnesses by Philip Brown 198

Short Story: Hot Cross Buns by Sheli Ellsworth 199

2017 Poetry Youth First Place Winner Twelve & Under: Watching from God's Eye View by Grace Wynn 203

2017 Poetry Youth Second Place Youth Winner: The Skinny Deception by Reina Nadeau 204

2017 Poetry Youth Third Place Young Twelve & Under Winner: Mr. Xi by Lingyu Yan 205

2017 Poetry Youth Twelve & Under Honorable Mention: Simply Music by Leila Horton 206

2017 Poetry Youth Twelve & Under Honorable Mention: Daisy and the Dirt Below by Kaylee Sarah Slingluff 207

2017 Poetry Youth Thirteen+ Honorable Mention: Barbara, Marian, and the Elder by Nick Sweet 208

2018 Poetry Adult Honorable Mention Decent/Descent by Nick Sweet 209

2017 Poetry Youth Thirteen+ Honorable Mention: Objet D' Art by SR Grosslight..210

Short Story: Falling Down the Stairs by Terry O'Conner...........................211

2017 Poetry Adult Third Place Winner: Daphne by Camille Boudreau 215

2017 Poetry Adult Honorable Mention: The House Cat by Susan Chambers 216

2017 Poetry Adult Honorable Mention: But You Forgot by Nanci Woody 217

Poetry: Litany To Democracy by Maxine Landis 218

2017 Memoir First Place Memoir Winner: The Brownie Pan by Judy S. Richardson 219

2017 Memoir Second Place Winner: Of Guns, Pigs, and Flies by Christina Steiner 221

2017 Memoir Third Place Winner: Money by Susan Jones 224

2017 Memoir Honorable Mention: I Can Do This! Or Can ... I? by Shawn Simon 226

2017 Memoir Honorable Mention: Summer of Love? by Bob Calverley..227

2017 Memoir Honorable Mention: Boys and Girls by Gail Field 230

In Memoriam...232

    Remembering VCWC Member Peter Pohl...232

    2015 Memoir Third Place Winner: Freedom by Peter Pohl...................233

Poetry: Joy Dreams and Songs by Alvin Bernie Barnes 236

    Poetry: Kingdom of Light by Alvin Bernie Barnes 236

    Short Story: The Fast Forward by Alvin Bernie Barnes 237

2018 Poetry Youth First Place Twelve & Under Winner: The Mist by Elizabeth Kate Baer...241

2018 Poetry Youth Second Place Twelve & Under Winner: Reincarnation by Mathew Sun..242

2018 Poetry Youth First Place 13 to 17 Winner: The Performance by Daniel Filz 243

2018 Poetry Youth Second Place 13 to 17 Winner: Daughter by Mable Ji 244

2018 Poetry Youth Third Place 13 to 17 Winner: A Black Bird by Shakti Dutt...245

2018 Poetry Youth 13 to 17 Honorable Mention: One Man by Lola Crane Flores 246

2018 Poetry Youth 13 to 17 Honorable Mention: My Half Shell by Peter R. Appleby..247

2018 Poetry Youth 13 to 17 Honorable Mention: In The Mirror by Haley Fisher 248

Short Story: Beyond Belief by Connie Mukherjee...249

2018 Poetry Adult First Place Winner: (lover) by Caroline Erickson 253

2018 Poetry Adult Second Place Winner: Cutting on the Bias by Marcy Wingard 254

2018 Poetry Adult Third Place Winner: Stepping Back by Warren Argall 255

Dedication

This Anthology is Dedicated to
Two Long-Time Members of the VCWC
Who Left Us Much Too Early

In Memoriam

Remembering Victor H. Prushan

February 9, 1936, Bronx, NY—November 14, 2017, Thousand Oaks, CA
By Lee Wade, 2018 *Nuance* Chairman Emeritus

We got together once a month for the better part of ten years to share our writings in a VCWC workshop/critique group. A published author of marketing management books and articles, Vic turned to writing fiction after retirement. He joined VCWC to help him learn how.

Vic often said the VCWC workshop experience was an absolute bargain. He appreciated the lessons, support and comraderies. His payback was to serve VCWC as a reader, a contest judge, and on the committee for this anthology, *Nuance*.

When his story, "Odessa Steps, 1910" was awarded first place in our 2016 short story contest, he told me he was "excited and humbled" by the award. "Excited" was visible. "Humbled" spoke to the esteem he held for his fellow pen-warriors. Another story of Vic's, "A Black-Tie Affair" appeared in *Windows*, VCWC Anthology 2010.

Vic's commitment to excellence was evident. From presentation to content, there was nothing cheesy, sloppy or half-done about his work. An admired and respected craftsman, his critique and compliments were impactful. A no-nonsense attitude and wry, understated humor suffused his writing. He assiduously avoided cliché.

1

The last time Vic attended workshop he told us that he had pancreatic cancer. He was going to "beat this thing or die trying." He laughed first, and we laughed with him, wishing the cliché to not prove true. The battle lasted six months.

Florence Wernick and Victor Prushan married nine days after his graduation from the U.S. Naval Academy, Class of 1957. Vic began his naval career immediately, the majority of which was spent on submarines. Their sons Paul (1958), Marc (1960), and Robert (1962) were born during his service. That his career was keeping him from seeing his boys grow up influenced his decision to resign his commission. He loved the Navy and for some years was active in USNA alumni affairs.

In civilian life, he was a sales engineer for Honeywell Micro Switch Division in NYC, worked in product marketing for Texas Instruments in Attleboro, MA and earned an MBA from Northeastern University. He worked in navigation and controls in NYC. The Prushans came to Thousand Oaks in 1977. Vic formed VHP Associates, a management consulting firm, in 1981. In 2000, he joined one of his clients as chief marketing officer. Two years later, he retired from corporate life.

I asked Flo, his wife of sixty years. "How do you think Vic would like to be remembered?"

"As a good father and grandfather," she said, "He was a good man."

2016 Short Story First Place Adult Winner: Odessa 1910 by Vic Prushan

The Odessa Steps in the former Soviet Union, begin at the harbor and rise more than 450 feet to Primorsky Boulevard, close to the central part of the city. At the top is a statue of the Duc de Richelieu, a Frenchman and early governor of the city. In classic mode, he's dressed in a Roman toga, a wreath encircling his head. One hand holds a scroll, the other is outstretched as if welcoming travelers. In the early twentieth century there were fewer to welcome and more to wave farewell.

Avram and Leah sat halfway up the landmark steps, holding hands, looking toward the harbor. On the quay in front of them, tugs nudged the incoming steamer from Varna into its berth. Across the pier, a ship bound for Constantinople was boarding its passengers, the forward gangway for business people and the wealthy off for a holiday, the aft gangway for emigrating families leaving Odessa for a new life.

There were men with beards and frock coats, men in peasant tunics, women milling about with little girls in ankle-length dresses and *babushkas* tied under their chins. Small boys in sailor suits and knee-high stockings played tag, waiting to start the adventure of an ocean crossing. A steerage ticket might take them to New York or Buenos Aires or Montreal or somewhere, anywhere, they could go for a better life than in Odessa.

"We should be on that ship," Leah said. "So many people are leaving. There's no place for Jews here anymore."

Avram interrupted his own thoughts. "Maybe someday. First, I have to finish my degree at the university. That's what my mother and father would have wanted. With a profession, we can have a good life together, even here." He reached in the pocket of his vest for a cigarette and struck a match on the stone step.

"A good life? What's so good about a life that no matter how good it is one day, the next day some ignorant peasant can beat you to death in an alleyway like they did to your parents? We can make a good life in America. Or Palestine, if that would please you."

"If one wants to be a farmer, Palestine is a good place. But I don't want to be a farmer. Besides, my degree isn't the only reason I can't leave yet. There's other business to attend to."

Leah was puzzled. "What business?" Was there something about him she didn't know?

"It's about my family," he said, tossing the half-smoked cigarette away, lighting another as soon as the first was gone. He told her how the hurt and grief of losing them in the 1905 *pogrom* was still with him, and how much hate he felt in his heart toward those who were responsible, how much he wanted to exact revenge.

Her tone became dismissive. "I've heard you say things like this before. But after five years, whom do you want to get back at? The tsar? The police? The dock workers? Who do you take revenge on? Do you know?"

The killers themselves could never be found, he knew, but there were many surrogates – policemen, *Okhrana* agents, even a peasant or dock worker. Anyone would do. As a class, each bore some responsibility for the violence that changed his life forever.

A freshening wind blew across the harbor. He watched the cigarette stub he'd tossed away get lifted into an eddy of dust and trash. An old woman walked past, clutching her coat, trying to draw it tighter to hold out the chill. Across the basin waves topped with white caps rolled in, and the ships at anchor rocked from side to side, their masts like inverted pendulums scribing arcs in the darkening sky.

"The tsar, may he drop dead, is in St. Petersburg, out of my reach. There are too many workers to go after, but the police are here, they're reachable, and they're guilty. When the mobs came they did nothing to stop them. They deserve anything they get from us." He stopped talking and put his arm around her shoulders, pulling her to him. "Anyway, this conversation is too serious."

Leah pulled back. "So, you want to kill a policeman? Have you lost your mind? Have you thought about what they'd do to you if you were caught? To your family? To all the Jews in Odessa? And what about the morality of killing someone who may not have had anything to do with the *pogrom*?"

He grunted, avoiding her logic. "All the police here had something to do with the *pogrom*."

"Maybe, maybe not."

"There are no maybes. The police helped. They may just as well have used their own weapons against us."

She looked for a way to steer him from this madness. "Papa would be very angry if he knew I was with you today. He thinks I should give Mama more help around the house and get married and give him grandsons. And he thinks you should spend more time in *shul* and less time with crazy talk. And that's without hearing what you say now."

"Your papa lives in the past. That kind of life is for *shtetl* Jews. They sit in their little village synagogues and pray and study. When the Cossacks ride through the towns, they hide under the benches. If it weren't for the Jews in Odessa and the other cities, who would fight their battles for them?"

"I don't know, but it doesn't have to be you," she said, with rising voice. People passing turned to look. When she saw their stares she was embarrassed, but embarrassment would be the least of their problems if any official had overheard the discussion. She put an end to the talk with a light but tender kiss on the cheek. "I'm not going to let you throw your life away. You haven't heard the last of this from me," she said.

"It looks like it will rain soon. Let's go somewhere for coffee."

***

The café on Ekaterininskaya Street appealed to writers, artists and university students. The coffee and pastries at nearby Fanconi's were better and the atmosphere more elegant, but Fanconi's was for people who could spend more than Avram could afford. What little extra spending money he had, he earned by tutoring the sons and daughters of rich people. Most of the money that helped him get through school and support his brother and sister he received from his widowed Aunt Rivka in Kiev. She made sure they had food to eat and clothes on their backs, even agreeing to bring the two younger ones into her home while he finished his studies. When the money came late, as it sometimes did, he had to count on Leah for the few kopeks needed to nurse a drink or have an extra cup of coffee. This was one of those days.

With the rain coming, most of the outside tables were empty. Inside they found a place in a corner near the kitchen entrance. They'd always been able to talk to each other, no matter the subject. This time was different.

"Your parents are well?" he asked.

"Yes."

"How long will this weather continue?"

"Who knows?"

"Have you heard from you uncle in New York?"

"Not for several months."

He was running out of questions. She was upset with him. An evening together would surely help.

"Do you want to come to my place?"

He lived in a rooming house catering to university students. The rent was cheap, and the landlord tolerated most things. Bringing a woman to his room was not encouraged but accepted.

Leah declined. "I'd better go home tonight. We don't want my father to come looking for me. Right now, he still likes you. If he catches us together alone, he wouldn't like either of us."

Avram frowned. It was true Yakov Krensky was a suspicious man, especially when it came to his daughter's virtue. Most of the time his distrust brought out the best in the lovers' ingenuity for finding time and place alone together: the empty classroom in the Hebrew School, the assembly hall at the university, even among the tombstones in the Old

Jewish Cemetery. Her father had never caught them in anything but polite and chaste situations, but Leah always worried it could happen and would make it impossible to see each other again.

"Hello, Avram, Leah. You two look so serious. Today isn't a day for serious thoughts." A young man stood at their table, a smile radiating through his thick red beard. The rain had started and his clothes were wet, his hair matted down. Rivulets of water ran down his cheeks and disappeared into his beard.

"Berel, come join us," Avram said, pulling over an empty chair. "How are you? What's happening in your life?" He signaled to a waiter to take the new arrival's order. The appearance of his old friend and classmate was a welcome break from strained conversation with Leah.

"Thank you," Berel said. "I have good news. I've dropped out of the university." The smile on his face turned into laughter. His look made it obvious he had more to say.

"That's good news?"

"I'm going to America," he shouted. He stood, raising his arms in triumph. Avram and Leah stood with him, hugging their friend and offering congratulations. In a few moments all the patrons around them were laughing and cheering,

Avram lifted his coffee cup in a toast to his friend's bold step. "I'm happy for you, Berel. Where will you be going?"

"I have an uncle from Kishinev. He went to Cleveland five years ago."

"Cleveland? Where is Cleveland?"

"I have no idea, but it's America and that's all I care about."

"When are you leaving?"

"The day after tomorrow," he said, the excitement in his voice unabated. "I have to go home and pack my things and say goodbye to my family."

"God bless you. Have a safe journey and a good life." The friends hugged, hiding their tears from each other. Berel left the café waving in farewell, skipping like a happy child.

Avram thought to himself. First take care of business, then maybe America.

***

Mendel Feingold had kept a gun hidden in his shop. He told his son years earlier, it was to keep the hooligans away. How he acquired it was a mystery to Avram, who guessed that he'd bought it from someone in the army who needed money. He knew the old man had never fired the weapon; he was probably afraid to go near it. For years the old revolver and ammunition lay untouched in an office drawer, hidden until Avram found it after his father's death.

The idea of shooting a policeman came to him when he found the weapon. To acquire one on his own had been out of the question. The police would know almost immediately if a Jew were to make such a purchase. To let anyone know he was looking for a gun was also risky. There were spies everywhere and suspicion would fall on him if it were used to kill an official. But this was ideal. The weapon was old. The person who sold it had made sure there would be no way to trace it to himself or the one who bought it from him.

Avram's plan was simple. He would find a way to come face to face with a policeman on an empty street. Late at night was best. Until he identified his target, he'd conceal himself in a doorway or some such suitable hiding place. At the right moment he'd approach his victim and, to dispel suspicion, wish him a good evening. Then he'd take the gun from his pocket, shoot, and walk away. He could dispose of it by tossing it into a storm drain or into the harbor, then go about his life as if nothing had happened. There would be no fame or glory attached to the act, just the personal satisfaction of doing something to get back for the pain he'd endured so long.

Odessa was notorious for its petty criminals and crime bosses. An investigation would certainly focus on those elements. Even if inquiries were made at the university, there were known anarchists and radicals on the campus who were capable of such an act. They would come under suspicion first. With no links to him, he could marry Leah and get on with life, knowing he'd struck a blow for justice.

The gun was dirty and rusty, if his father had ever had to fire it, he thought, it would most likely have blown up in his hand. Avram spent hours cleaning the revolver, and once satisfied, he loaded cartridges in the cylinder. Test firing would be a problem. It would make too much noise and draw attention. But not testing would be worse. Suppose it wouldn't fire. He would be dead before he could blink.

He rode out to the old cemetery, the place where he and Leah had often gone to be together. He found a spot far enough from the roadway to avoid being seen, as if there'd be crowds in the cemetery in the middle of the night. He muffled the pistol with a pillow he brought from home and fired it. To his amazement it discharged without exploding.

But strange feelings gripped Avram, exhilaration mixed with foreboding. Sitting amid the gravestones and monuments, he began shaking. To calm himself, he lit a cigarette. In the match's flare he saw next to him the grave of one Esther Rabinowicz, whom the stone revealed died ten years earlier at the age of nineteen. Leah is nineteen now, he thought. How old will the policeman be whom he shoots? Would he have a family, a nineteen-year old daughter, perhaps?

"Why am I here? What should I do?" he asked, as if Esther could hear him. He told her how much he loved Leah and how much he wanted to build a life with her. He told her about his parents. For what seemed like hours he sat on the ground waiting for answers to his questions. The answers came as the sky lightened in the east.

It was time to leave. After only a few steps Avram turned back to the gravesite. He picked up a pebble from the ground. In keeping with tradition, he placed it on Esther Rabinowicz's headstone as a sign that her grave had been visited. Then he recited the mourner's prayer for her.

"Thank you for listening to me, Esther. Thank you for the advice," he said softly. He was on his way to Leah's home to spend the day with her. Reb Krensky might not like seeing him at such an early hour, but the old man would have to accept it. On the way, Avram tossed the gun into the first sewer grating he could find.

2014 Poetry First Place Youth Winner: Only If You Believe by Brisa Porter Garcia

A cherry blossom tree cannot exist on a prairie
Unless you paint the scene in your head

    Just for the sunset.
    There must be hues of
    Oranges
    Reds
    Yellows
    Pinks

Maybe even a purple
Just for the sunset.
But to light the prairie,

    You must set a fire to the sky.
    Upon this flaming landscape,
    There are two figures

Of young girls,

But the horizon has stolen their identity,
So all one sees,

Is their filled in outlines
Black shadow.

    Each outline,
    Holds a pocketful of laughter.
    One points to the left,

And they cross the field of blazing blades,
Towards a pond,

That intakes the line,

Held by a fisherman and his hat.

The line is reeled in and then once more, let out to fly.
The two girls giggle,

    Is the shadow man really trying?
    To catch a cherry blossom tree?
    I guess he could,
    If he really believed.

2014 Poetry Second Place Youth Winner: Window Talk by Erin Stoodley

Erin resides in Ventura, CA and is currently an undergraduate student at Stanford University. She has been recognized by such organizations as the Anthony Quinn Foundation, the Johns Hopkins Center for Talented Youth, and the National YoungArts Foundation. Her most recent publications include Sooth Swarm Journal, The Adroit Journal, and Belleville Park Pages.

Window Talk

Our talk resounds
past water-silled panes, the slung cut
of December's wax.

We lean, damp hair pulled
into mulch brick,
Mom's coats padding straits
of light and tobacco licks
the grocer's cigarette left. We can see
the Cross from here, thrust into holy mud.

Months before, some slick feathered crows
pecked the splints into marrow,
and we forgot to leave the storefront—

the horizon did not swell in winter,
pulse the wooden boards
as sleet ran clear.

2014 Poetry Third Place Youth Winner: Time by Callie Blumenfield

I pass by too slowly,
Or too quickly a lot,

But in the very best moments,
I am all but forgot.

I fly, I stand still,
I lift, and I drop.

But no matter what happens,
I will never stop.

I have passed through the ages,
I have seen great men fall,

And when the final sun sets,

I will have been through it all,
Whether you're rushed or you're calm
I will be at my post,

To make sure you enjoy
All that matters most.

Poetry: Cooking by Joan E. Day

A fan of both formal and free verse, Joan E. Day has read her poetry in schools throughout Ventura County. Her poems have been published online, in poetry journals, magazines and newspapers. When not writing, her interest in poetry takes her far and wide to readings and critique groups. She has also performed with the Razor Babes, a multi-generational performance poetry group, throughout California. Her love of nuances, be they seasonal or otherwise, keeps her eyes and ears alert to this world both seen and unseen. Through poetry, she creates stories and visual pictures for audiences to enjoy.

Dinner for two

Start with a strong cocktail

take one white lie
grate with suspicion
drizzle in a honey-coated story
whip in fresh shreds of evidence

let marinate one hour
transfer to pan of EVOO (extra vitriol of outrage)
add a full glass of dry whine
thicken with recrimination
cover when fully steamed

lower flame, cook till well done keeping score on back burner

remove all self blame until cool
sprinkle with salacious crumbs of retaliation
dish up past regrets
best served pickled with several dollops of sarcasm

be sure to thoroughly scour pan with sobriety before reheating leftovers

Poetry: Untitled Haiku by Joan E. Day

haiku (no title)
scattered on table
jigsaw puzzle pieces
my life undone

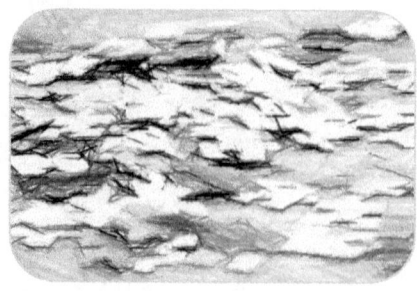

Poetry: Crow by Joan E. Day

something
      to crow
         about

the fountain sings to me
keeps me in bed after dawn
daydreaming until once again
no melodious warbler your r a u c o u s
racket drives me out from u
                           n
                           d

my   e
comforter   r
before having to rise
throw pebbles at you

I sit with a cup of tea eye
you and your feathered fiends
squawk to one another around
the fountain like wash women
in Italy at daybreak who never
liked me asking them to keep quiet

I dare not walk out onto my patio to
demand silence knowing like them
you would exact revenge mar my
clothing pelt my car because I am
on to you how you broadcast
my complaints to each other
how my face is now
ingrained in your
collective
memory

yes I am
smart to
your
ways
decide
to call
a truce
this morning
      throw blueberries

2014 Poetry First Place Adult Winner: Les Raboteurs de Parquet by Ron Alexander

LES RABOTEURS DE PARQUET,

(The Floor Scrapers) by Gustave Caillebotte, 1875

Jackets against the wall like sleeping dogs, wine bottle
to the side, hammer inert on the floor,
three wiry workmen stripped to the waist,
   frozen here as if recovered after eons from the icy gullets
  of Swiss glaciers, bodies intact, bent over like so-
these men too, long dead but still scraping; still in conversation.
     We know not who
   -a mere half-face or two between them-
  but how the subdued sunlight, miraculous, shines
   on bare skin, how straining backs glow
   like the half-stripped floor beneath them,
 decades of wax, fruit of countless hives, innumerable bees and the
    generations of families
    applying, polishing, cleaning-
     all shaved away.
   The scrapers, in harmony with the grain
 and each other, move from one end of the room to the other,
 one side to the other, shaping curls of old wax and wood, round
    like Edison's magic wax canisters.
   But the sound recorded in these waxy curls
  from the very first tenant who paced this floor,
     examining
   the room for flaws; to the lives begun here
   or ended; a child's first words, a patriarch's
  last; boys ~ shouts from games of war, dressed
in a child's version of soldiers' uniforms-wooden swords, sheets, father's
     great coat,
    their plaintive cries as they die
  for the Emperor; intimacies whispered, secrets sworn
  of crushes and fantasies, the imagination of children
    now great-great grandparents
     or gone
  No matter. While the common people of the country,
  may be romantic; those in the city, only brutish and
    coarse-unsuitable for public
     viewing.
  M. Caillebotte's painting is declined by the Salon.

2014 Poetry Adult Honorable Mention: Lions In The Afterlife by Ron Alexander

In your attic up North, you stitch quilts, stories,
until fogbound, waterlogged, you long for
sun, come visit me here in Paradise. I go
see you and recall not every town glories
in eternal spring, blooms all year round. Once
from your window we heard sea lions in the dark,
imagined they harbor old comics' souls, bark
kudos on the wharf at their churlish puns.

Twenty years we planned my looming death.
Now, U-turn: your marrow roils with cancer,
and I'm to watch *you* take that final breath?
If souls transmigrate, we'll meet up at the piers,
join those lions, seek warmer coasts to banter,
howl till we cry, fill an ocean with our gay tears.

2014 Poetry Second Place Adult Winner: Moon Over Lima by Nancy-Jean Pement

The moon has risen over Lima,
draping its luminous cloak
upon the Andean foothills

In Wakefield, she settles high
beyond the covered bridge

casting long shadows over winter fields
And in many other places there is
some version of the moon

shining full – bright over electro—
magnetic replicas of you and me
where, before we collided,

we were kindred

and our names were more
Than we could speak

For all we know, we've been
here (and everywhere) all along.

2014 Poetry Third Place Adult Winner: Knowing That All Things Must End by Katherine Hamilton

Katherine is a clinical psychologist by day, an insomniac by night, and a poet by nature. North Carolina roots, but Southern California suits her, where she lives with her forbearing husband and two jowly-howly basset hounds. She "wandered lonely as a cloud," adopted at birth by wonderful parents but raised an only child. Thanks to 23&Me, she is "surprised by joy" at the age of sixty to have become a big sister to her newfound biological brother, Kris Kaufmann, a poet as well. Props to Walt Whitman, she thanks the VCWC for the opportunity to share her work, in the hope it pleases, and reminds of essence and connection.

Throat laid bare with upturned chin,
Vulnerable exposed, breath in-
Dare to open once again.

Every joining, holding fast,

This present joy, too soon the past-
Cleaving to what cannot last.

Linger, savor, tarry, stay?

Inexorable, the end of day-
Solstice moment, parting way.

Return to one must come in time:

Unclasped, glance back, let loose of "mine"-
Silence, and the taste of brine.

2014 Poetry Adult Honorable Mention: Morning Mirror by Katherine Hamilton

Domain without dominion,
this body as I age.
    I startle at my reflection,
    in recognition of
    a "me-ness" that abides within that cage
    no longer new.
A breath-stopping moment of
shock and silence, aware
that memories now stretch longer than
the days which lie ahead
    Exhaling, holding my own gaze, I stare:
No longer young.
My passions long neglected
require now a choice.

Ancient desire sparks nascent fires,
and inchoate, arise,
seek form, and clamor to be given voice,
No longer mute.

Sight will dim and sinew thin
This hutch will rust and bend,
of little use or consequence.

I need but this breath to
sing the poem of pulse beyond body's end:
No longer bound.

2014 Poetry Adult Honorable Mention: Rabbit Hole by Christina M. Pages

Christina is an English professor who has been teaching at universities for the past thirty years. She has two poetry collections published, a children's novel, and a chapter book.

My childhood bedroom looked over lawns
cut in half-moon curves around
herbaceous borders, over a prickly hedge
that tore my sleeve when I reached for a ball,
then to a narrow lane, and fields

where I longed to run—

In a wriggle I could squeeze

Through a rabbit hole in the hedge,
into a grassy stretch of mystery

far from these heavy rooms

where our old grandfather clock
ticked in time to my father's breath
chimed each half hour of his dreams-

When I saw his face, unlined in sleep,

I knew he'd returned to his Victorian days,
through London's cobbled alleys,

immaculate in his three-piece suit,
his silver watch and chain,
drifting back to 1885

in his childhood house in Cheshire,
feeling the starch of his mother's
bodice against his cheek the lavender
of her combed-up hair, a clatter

of hooves, a carriage outside in the street -
His rabbit hole retraced the past,

while mine wound me forward
to unexplored fields, hours of magic,
a thousand dreams
the clock has never recorded.

2017 Poetry Adult First Place Winner: A Hungarian Exile Comes Home by Christina Pages

Your ashes are warm and soft inside my palm –
They cling to my skin, wait for their fall
into a soil full of seeds.

atoms of longing for slopes and trees
of a childhood land that you were forced to flee –

Here is a patch of lavender
where bees buzz their rhapsodies
in waiting shades of blue perfume,

in ground ready for the feel of you.
I open my hand, and watch your grey-blue dust
slide between sprigs and blades, powdering leaves.

You reunite with roots, stems, flowers,
with the sap that lives and runs,
that never dried in you.

2014 Poetry Adult Honorable Mention: A Record by Erin Moore

Whatever I compose
Has no hard component.
At most,
Sealed in the ink of this moment,
A sliver of me,
Grand and small,
Shivering like Hopper's man
In warm light
Hugging a trench coat,
One in the open.
At once frozen and bursting
Perpetually still.
And if I hooked up my pen like a fire hose
And depleted the ink of the world,
Alone and still would I remain.

Poetry: Glendora by Bonnie Goldenberg

Bonnie is a Thousand Oaks poet, originally from New York. She enjoys reading her poems at the open mic venues sponsored by the Newbury Park and Thousand Oaks libraries. Her poems have been published in a variety of literary journals and anthologies, including rivertalk, DAYbreak, Serendipity, *and* Remembrances. *She is also completing a WWII memoir based on her father's letters from the war. In her "free times," she helps her husband, a former Amgen scientist, run a biotech startup, GoldenBiotech, in Newbury Park.*

for Mario Savio (1942-1996)
A twinge whenever I hear the name
of this blue-collar town at the eastern end of L.A.
from some traffic reporter's mention of a crash
or backup on the 210
that runs through this place
not in any tour books.
This is where Mario Savio lived
before coming to Berkeley.
Our charismatic speaker of the FSM,
Free Speech Movement, in the 60s,
dead at 53, November '96.
When I learned that you had died,
I realized my youth had finally died, too.
> I still see you in your scuffed brown sheepskin jacket
> mingling with the crowds in Sproul Plaza,
> usually just listening, taking it in, occasionally arguing.
> But when you spoke from the steps
in front of the Administration Building,
> your back to those inside who hated your defiance,
> you were transformed into a Roman orator.
> Your curly hair framed your beautiful head,
> your profile like a classical sculpture.
Your impassioned, anguished voice told us
it was time to put our bodies on that "odious" machine.
I loved your eloquence—
like "odious"—a word I'd only learned
when studying for the SAT exams.
Years later, shortly before your death,
you were quoted as saying that our movement
was a rare moment in history when we were both
"morally right and victorious."
"Victorious"—not just that we had won.

You had been in the south the summer before
registering African-Americans to vote,
and the rumor was you were asked to leave,
because you were too passionate, too emotional—
when taunted or kicked, you couldn't resist fighting back.

Instead, they asked you to fundraise and organize
student support in the north,
which you were doing on the Berkeley campus.
University officials, Chancellor Kerr & Co.,
always called you an outside agitator.
 After we were arrested in December '64,
 we spent the year going to court.
 You ended up being sent to jail for contempt,
 in addition to the other charges they threw at you,
 because when the Judge asked you
 the routine question for those pleading *no lo contendere*,
 "Do you understand what you are pleading to?"
 you responded that the only thing you understood
 was the "hypocrisy" in this courtroom!
Mario, rest in peace—
you helped me become an adult.
My generation and I will never forget you,
 even though Glendora probably has.

2014 Short Story Youth First Place Winner: Taken Over by Megan R. Ragone

Megan recently turned fifteen and writing has always been a passion of hers. In 5th grade, she won an essay contest within her K-8 elementary school and in 7th and 8th grade she won a poetry award at her school. Her favorite way to express her words building up inside is through song and she has performed in front of many people.

"I've got it! I've got it!" I chanted, as I chased for the pop fly headed in my general direction. The hollers and excitement of the crowd kept me racing despite my body's incessant pleas to stop. My ten-year-old legs could only go so fast. In a final moment of sheer adrenaline, I reached out my glove and somehow ended up catching the ball. The team went wild, as the catch clinched the game for our neighborhood team. With adoring fans by my side, I triumphantly walked back to Tim Burik's house.

 "Greyson!" I turned at the sound of my name. The voice belonged to Johnny Lerkinson, a world class wannabe.

 Johnny was the type of kid who only seemed to notice you when others did. He always had a cocky look in his eyes, and he constantly showed off his crooked smile. "Hey Greyson, that was pretty cool." I listened to his kind words while my argument about Johnny's fake admiration grew with every syllable that poured out of his mouth.

 As the gang and I walked, we inevitably passed by my neighborhood's "Boo Radley" house. It seems that every town has one. It was owned by an elderly man known as Ellis Fielder.

 Rumor had it Ellis was crazy. He stayed inside like a hermit, driving himself to the point of insanity every day and had been for the past forty years. No family, no friends ... nobody ever went there; not even Girl Scouts or daring salesmen, for it gave off a creepy and haunting vibe. I never saw his face, and I had lived in Sandpoint since I was three. The only time the mad man ever left his house was on Monday nights, which I believe was dedicated for getting groceries and an occasional prescription medication. His rusty car's windows were tinted, and it was always parked in the garage.

No one ever saw him get in or out of it. He had things sent to him whenever possible. I always felt bad for the delivery man.

Ellis's house gave me the creeps; it gave everyone the creeps even though he'd never personally done anything to deserve that reputation. To my knowledge, he had never been to jail or hurt anyone. If anything, it was his mysteriousness that frightened everyone. The curiosity and possibilities of who he was and what he did were endless, and no one ever had the guts to find out. That is, until I heard his barbaric cry when we were walking home from the game that victorious day.

"Did you hear that?" I asked my friends. Many obviously had. When I turned to see what was happening, I saw some of them running away, screaming.

"Of course, we heard it, stupid! We have to go," Johnny said as his steps became quicker.

"Are you scared Johnny? Hey guys! Johnny's scared by old man Fielder!" one said.

"Ha! Johnny, you're such a baby!" another replied. As the taunting continued I noticed how all of them were increasing their pace. I rolled my eyes. Hypocrites!

It was then when I stopped and started to stare at the blackened abode. I listened to the faint sobbing from inside. My mind began to race. Like any child, I was curious. My head filled with wonder, and that night as I lay in bed, I recalled staring up to the ceiling trying to figure out why the elderly man cried that day. I know what you're thinking: what ten-year-old kid spends his time thinking about these things? Well, my reasoning is simple: First off, I've always been hypersensitive. I hear and see things differently than others, and second, the world sees things as black and white while I choose to live in color.

2014 Short Story Youth Second Place Winner: His January by Gabrielle Genhart

Gabrielle is a nineteen-year-old, self-published author. Her life is devoted to writing passionate poetry and prose dedicated to the affliction of the severity of mental illnesses and social injustices.

She stared into a fragmented piece of her destroyed looking-glass, the one that showed her years gone by both silently and edgily. Ceae watched her lineless, ghostly pale face in a disconnected stupor, through dull, gray eyes blown wide with prescription drugs that entrapped her in the walking corpse in which she spent all of her restless nights. She was beginning to believe that she'd never see her silhouetted boy again, and so she replaced him with a beautiful, catatonic girl with a name whispered under ruffled sheets once more: *Elena. Elena, my love.* But shivering tea cups chipped along the edges, fireplaces with scents that smother children and that parents pretend to enjoy—that isn't love.

A year passed while Ceae sat at the window timelessly: a winter of snow pressed against glass with scribbled, meaningless messages; a spring with flowers that she knew would just come to die once they had served their purpose; an autumn where crisp leaves turned beautiful colors only to shrivel up and become bothersome to those conformist, white-trimmed houses with mothers and fathers that couldn't stand to look at anything ugly, neglecting their pudgy children for their pretty ones – the ones who forced themselves to be pretty for love.

Ceae watched with glass note eyes sparked by lightning that came and went, dull and then colored with passion just to die out once more. It was winter again when he came for her. Ceae couldn't remember his name, and he couldn't remember hers; something so trivial didn't matter. He tapped on her frosted glass window, where she had been sitting and letting the seasons pass, gazing down at children who were experiencing natural wonders for the first time. She opened it with that gleam in her eyes, and together, they slid down her slicked roof and onto the patchwork of snow on her lawn.

Ceae thought it was around midnight. No candlelight or artificial colors painted the sheet of white ground before them as they ran. She had forgotten to button her coat, and it fluttered around her as icy claws wrapped her ribcage. Ceae watched the streetlights, glittering pointlessly through the growing snowstorm, and knew her silhouetted boy was a product of late January, knew that the depth of this cold was worth the heat he would inject into her thin, blue veins.

He liked the way they snaked up her arms as though they were vines that bound her from within. She was as beautiful and as deadly as the flower from which she took her full name: Solanaceae, an orchestra at its crescendo of soft, leaking violet that was poison from the first touch. Now, of course, he didn't – he *wouldn't* – remember her name, but he could never forget that permanent ink spot of purple that was etched into his memory eternally, if anything at all could be said to be eternal. Many words came to him when he thought of her: belladonna, nightshade, berries and fruit and maybe even the kind of love that Adam and Eve couldn't have known in the Garden of Eden, so long ago, if at all.

In the dead of winter, she saw the explosion of liquid fire in his stark, hidden eyes, and suddenly they were under the influence of red lights: drugs and women so forgettable, the kind of eyes one looked into with another imagined in their place.

He leaned into her ear, pale and soft with wisps lightly brushing again his pastel lips, and whispered: "Amsterdam, my love. You deserve to be free. You deserve to let the poison in your veins to run rampant, to entrap, to *destroy*. Forget everyone else, the way you couldn't forget me."

Ceae looked down, and there were ashes in her palm. *Drugs?* she thought, but no, these were no drugs at all. Her face creased in momentary confusion, full moons, half-moons, even blue moons passing in slivers across her face that was nothing but a pattern of stark silver and a sinful lungful of broken red brightening her undead features. But she shook the senselessness away and slipped her fingers through the puzzle piece slits in her silhouetted boy's hand. He smiled at her, a sly, confident smile, and he was like a picture taken in another era, reanimated: all black and white.

Days came and went, but they were nothing like her mindless seasons passed by in motionlessness beside Elena – who seemed a million miles away now, a beautiful but empty creature of imagination. Ceae could only see half of her boy's face when he asked her to wear nothing but purple, and she obliged wordlessly: a purple dress and purple shoes, face wiped clean of makeup encouraged elsewhere. She caught a glimpse of herself in a full mirror, in weak light; her eyes were still blown wide, but the drugs were of her choice this time.

Ceae's lungs were so choked with smoke that she was hardly aware of the glimpse that she caught of her boy's neck, where there was a long, dark, bolded *X* pressed against his angel-pale skin. He caught her watching and pulled on a coat that hid it, flashing her a demonic smile that ensured her that, if he were an angel at all – If those sharp shoulder blades she felt in the dead of night once had wings – he had fallen long ago.

Is this really love? Ceae's delusions whispered to her, feather-light words against her unconscious, lipless breathing. The answer was absolute, but it wasn't the kind of love that one could have in life. It wasn't the kind of love that children felt holding hands and pressing lipstick-free kisses against one another's cheeks. It was the kind of love that tore them from their bodies, their skin and blood and skeletons, and dragged them through the depths of hell, because they didn't deserve it. And yet, Ceae thought, it was worth the risk.

She hardly noticed each morning that the bits of her limbs that had chipped away hadn't yet grown back – that it had been months since she had gone home, and that she would never go home again. She didn't want to be greeted by Elena, and she lost her phone before she even received the first of many likely calls from her mother and her father.

Ceae could be an angel if it weren't for her violet poison.

And her silhouetted boy knew that as they ran across cobblestone streets with no destination, knowing that she was just as damned as he was. The stars couldn't decide whether to cross or not, and Ceae couldn't watch as they tried: They were swathed in clouds that embedded winter into the very skeletons they couldn't claim as their own any longer. *Am I dead or alive?* Ceae sometimes wondered, but it didn't really matter either way, because she was there, because he was there, because the world and the cosmic nightmares and the depth of her dull, gray eyes and the all the phases of the moon pressed into her in wait for these moments.

One more looking-glass shattered. Who believes in luck anyway?

Elena wrote letters in black, leaking ink that she didn't have an address for, and they piled up at her feet with the ends of cigarettes and all the chipped teacups that she finally shattered. On the last night, on the last day, she was so tired of waiting: she took a knife and a warm bath, and Ceae still wasn't there to find her. *C'est la vie*, tattooed across the sweet, soft curve of her neck – oh, what delicious irony no longer to be sipped from those teacups that lay in broken shards on their plain, wooden floors.

Ceae found herself in an intricate purple dress, descending into an underground grotto, where the world was false, but the wonderland was real. Her silhouetted boy protected her all the same, as she lay on the ground with closed eyes and a body too fragile for the doses it was enduring. He watched the way her eyelashes curled darkly, and her nose sloped, uninterrupted, to the gentle shape of her lips too poisonous to kiss. Her cheeks were flushed with the rush of life that she waited for at her window, and in her dreams, she wondered what meaningless messages were being scrawled across the frost now. Little visages of masked, emotionless drawings? Dirty slurs? Greetings so simple and complicated as hello or goodbye, and all of their synonymous foreign translations?

Ceae had no idea how dark that winter really was.

She walked along the streets in sobriety with her boy now, still nameless but with such a heartbreaking face, outlined sharply in the early-morning light of a dim day frosted over with winter. Ceae was wrapped in her coat, with all of its buttons now missing instead of simply forgotten, and she watched her dark shoes make light footprints as they treaded the snow beneath. She lit the cigarette in her hand, though there was already plenty of ghostly breath escaping her lips in little clouds of condensation so distant from the whole that she was reminded just how insignificant she was – and just how much she didn't care.

They stayed away from the red lights in this morning after a seemingly eternal night, and Ceae and her silhouette sat outside a little café – the only patrons willing to sit out in cold this deep, strong enough to sink far past their pale skin. But of course, they had abandoned everything within them long ago. They drank all of their coffee and smoked all of their cigarettes, content on empty stomachs to face another day that would continue forever.

Her boy reached across their little table stuck with snowflakes that seemed so identical, seemed so conformist, although they were promised even as children that everyone was unique. He pulled one of her purple gloves off finger by finger, slipping her pale hand into the exposure of the world that seemed to be a landscape of only white. He kissed her palm gently, tasting the nightshade poison that he didn't think she realized coursed through her veins. If she did, he believed, she would have forgotten him long ago – on another cold, January day that ran through their life forms on an infinite replay.

"Do you like the red lights better in winter?" she asked him quietly.

He reached over to her, pulled her closer, and murmured, "I don't like them at all. I only want you to have freedom. And those red lights are the closest you can get in life."

Something struck her agonizingly in such a simple statement that she herself believed to be true. It carved into her body, into her heart, reaching so close to that January so many years ago, too many years ago. But she forced it away with another drag off her cigarette, and idly wondered what it would be like to be bitten by a vampire or seduced by a mermaid. Maybe Elena had tried to keep her away from what paranormal was embedded in the contemporary heart-line of her life. Maybe she had done well, but Ceae was far too broken a doll to be fixed by a beautiful girl filled with joy, drained from the bite marks Ceae left on her soft skin.

Everything seemed so much more beautiful iced over by winter – children playing under a rain of snowflakes, whispers curling into air like smoke, buildings encrusted, made to sparkle when the sun managed to find a way to glint blindingly off of the stark white that seemed to envelop the world.

Ceae and her boy found a swing set almost completely buried and sat side-by-side, ignoring the cold that didn't so much bite as gnaw unstoppably at them. The metal of the chains was almost kind in its excruciating sensation against Ceae's hands when she slipped her gloves off, and she grounded herself enough to ask her boy the one question she couldn't stop from breathing aloud, under the sun and the moon and the clouds and the universe that shouldn't care about them, under destiny that shouldn't be written out for two people so deeply insignificant. Sunrise, sunset, repeat. One, two, three. It's all elementary.

"Are you going to leave me again?" Ceae said, her voice hardly even a whisper.

Her silhouetted boy turned to her, a strange and beautiful expression written across his photographic face, and said, "My love, do you want to know something?"

Bewildered, she replied with growing desperation, "I want you to answer my question."

But all he said was, "It hardly ever snows in Amsterdam."

***

Sunrise, sunset, repeat. One, two, three. It's all elementary.

Doctors' calls surrounded her, and she was terrified, her heart stuttering like a hummingbird caught in her chest. It was painful enough that she wanted to rip through her skin that she had thought she transcended, tear through her ribcage to let the poor creature free. Where was her boy? Where was Elena? Where were her mother and her father?

She was surrounded by flowers that should have been long dead. It was winter, wasn't it? Ceae thought about crying but was too bewildered to do something so simple. Finally: a familiar face. Her mother, with puffy, red eyes and tear-stained cheeks. She stepped into the room a second before her father, clean-shaven, his eyes slightly dead, but completely dry. That was how Ceae herself felt: dry, like a desert. She had always hated the desert. There was beauty in the ocean, in the rain, in the winter, in the autumn, but not where she could lay out on the sand and find herself scorched into ashes. *Ashes*. A pocketful of ashes.

"Mom, where is he?" Ceae couldn't scream.

Her mother sat down trembling, afraid of the poison she knew was in her daughter's veins as well. Her father stood leaning up against the door, looking like a corpse waiting to be told he was dead.

"Honey, you know where he is," her mother whispered through her tears, choking on them, closing her eyes so more could fall free. *Free*.

And that was true.

Ceae did know where he was. It was like her sleep in this hospital bed, in the middle of Amsterdam, had injected reality into her veins, replacing the poison. Of course, no one but the doctors and the nurses could know that. They wouldn't tell her mother and father anything, not yet, as though they wouldn't be quite as fragile when they learned their daughter had constructed such an artful, beautiful illusion in her mind, not if she was conscious when they broke the news of where she would be locked for the *next few days*, "just to make sure she was safe."

He had died that January years ago, and she couldn't let him go. He had died through some kind of means that didn't mean anything to her because he was gone, and she couldn't get him back. Ceae had moved in with her closest friend, Elena, to try to ease the pain of it, and slipped into a stupor as she pretended to fall in love again, to become all right again. No one knew that she had made herself forget that he was gone eternally, because the thought alone – even without all of its monstrous implications – was too much to bear.

Ceae, in her numbed state, had taken his ashes that she had always kept at her bedside and flown to Amsterdam to spread them somewhere not sinful but beautiful. It was mid-spring when she left, smashed her mirror and then her phone into pieces. He had promised to take her to Amsterdam someday, to let her be free.

But the only freedom was in death.

She had always known that, but he hadn't realized it until he died.

Ceae didn't know what she had done to end up in the hospital, but she had a dark inkling that it was tied to trying to find the ultimate liberty, with no more ashes beside her and a room at home—

"Where's Elena?" Ceae asked eagerly.

Sunrise, sunset, repeat. One, two, three. It's all elementary.

"She's with him, too, honey," her mother replied somberly; there was no better, no easier, way to break news like that, especially when her parents believed that was love.

—yes, a room at home full of letters and cigarette remains, shattered teacups smeared with little remnants of lipstick because no one had bothered to clean up anything past the tragedy. But it was a room Ceae never saw again.

No, where they were sending Ceae there were no locks on the doors, and she could pretend all she wanted to. She could pretend that her silhouetted boy and her silver-lined girl were still at her side, ready and willing to die, but not yet. Oh, not yet. Because dear Ceae hadn't yet learned how to live or to love, and she kept herself locked up anyway with those blue-green veins within her, trapping her in that January. No more purple, no more poison. Just reality.

Just reality.

And on her first day in that institution, all alone when the nurses stopped prodding her with questions and needles, they gave her Elena's last letter—the only one of the hundred that she would ever read. There were only five words:

Solanaceae, where is your home?

And Ceae could only find one answer buried in the depths of her drugged mind, and she spoke it aloud to her bare white, one shade, no bruise walls: "In his January and your May, away, away, from this reality in which I'm forced to stay."

2014 Short Story Youth Third Place Winner: Almost Done by Naomi Stoodley

Naomi is a student residing in Ventura, California. Recently, she received first place in Ventura County's 2014 Art Tales Contest for short fiction and was named a runner-up and finalist in Hollins University's 2013 Nancy Thorp Poetry Contest. Her poetry is published or is forthcoming in The Adroit Journal, Belleville Park Pages, *and* Cargoes, *among others.*

It tickles when the wisps of hair land on my neck and shoulders. Every so often, the hairdresser pauses and whispers to herself: "Almost done." *Almost done.*

Lydia sits crisscross applesauce at my feet. She picks up the scattered strands and plays with them distractedly. "You didn't have to do this, you know." She glances up to make sure I know she is talking to me. "Just because Mom did it doesn't mean you have to."

"I want to."

Lydia shrugs.

I pet the small patch of new-hair fuzz on her head, and she leans on my leg. Even though her head is tucked between her knees, I can tell she's crying.

"Almost done, almost done, almost done ... done! Now you look exactly like your sister. Hey, wait a minute! Aren't you two twins?" the hairdresser asks as she swivels the chair around and takes off my black smock. More hair falls. Some falls onto my shirt and pants, but I don't think about it. The hairdresser hands me a small mirror, but I don't look. I take refuge in staring at the taupe wall opposite me.

In the car on the way home, Lydia pokes my forehead. "You look funny. Like a cartoon character, because your ears are so big."

"Look who's talking, Dumbo," I respond. Then I give her the evil eye. It's fake, though. I'm not angry. I never get angry anymore. Especially not at Lydia. It's an unspoken rule in our household: Never yell or say anything that could hurt Lydia's feelings; if you do, it is an *accident*. If you call Lydia a mean name when she leaves her dirty clothes on the floor or doesn't clean her lunch dishes, pretend she is a fairy-angel-princess, kiss her feet, and apologize one hundred times a day. If you want to earn a gold star, bake cookies, too.

I make cookies every Sunday morning. My mom says that the kitchen is my church, that the oven is my altar. I've never been to church, so I don't know exactly what the purpose of an altar is. But I think Mom is right. Whenever I have unanswered questions about life or the universe or I need to complain about the annoying boy at school who draws on my locker, I bake. When I'm upset, I bake. When I *accidentally* call Lydia a mean name, I bake.

Last week, I said she was selfish because she asked me to bake cookies on Tuesday, the busiest day of the whole week – the only day that I have soccer practice, a cello lesson, and debate team. "Please? I want the house to smell nice." She widened her eyes and finished sarcastically, "But I bet you've got something better to do." The only better thing I had to do at 11:30 p.m. was sleep, but I didn't tell her that. After I baked the cookies—chocolate chip, her favorite—I left a plate for her on the table. But the plate remained full until Mom threw the cookies away a few days ago.

Before she got sick, Lydia was a pig. She ate monstrous helpings of pasta, chocolate, chips, and basically anything else she could get her hands on. But she was a gymnast, so every pound of junk food turned into muscle. Now, she eats next to nothing. She won't even taste the cookies.

"Lydia, have you seen my yellow dress? Lydia! Where is—take it off!"

"Come on, Kat! I won't ruin it. I never stain your clothes. See? I've already had it on for a couple hours, and it's spotless." She twirls and skips and curtsies. The dress swallows her tiny frame, and she reminds me of us when we played dress-up with Mom's evening gowns. "Just wear something else for the recital." Lydia flips through the array of floral, color-blocked, and striped dresses in my closet. "Like this!"

"I can't play my cello in that. It's too short." I sigh. "I've been planning on wearing *that* one since last week." I hear the *tick tick* of the living room clock. "Just take it off; I need to hurry. I haven't even made the cookies yet." Why did I commit to baking cookies for fifty parents and their baby Yo-Yo Mas?

"I know I always steal your clothes and stuff, but I—"

"Hurry up, Lyd. *Please*," I beg.

"You're not even listening. You never listen anymore. You just walk around the house and pretend I'm some baby you have to pick up after."

I haven't seen Lydia this furious since before she became sick. "What are you talking about? You *never* clean up anything. You never do what Mom asks you to do and you never—"

"That's what you don't understand. Mom doesn't ask me to do anything. She treats me like I'm some doll, like some porcelain collectible doll or something. It's like I'm not even human anymore. And it's not just Mom who tiptoes around me. You always go out with your friends, but you never invite me! You don't even ask if I want to come. What happened to going to the donut shop on Sundays? Yeah, it doesn't happen." Lydia's shoulders hunch as she sobs into her hands. She sniffs back tears and gulps air between words.

"Fine. Whatever. Just take anything you want and never give it back!" I slam the door after she walks out of my room. A year ago, Mom would storm into my room and scream at me: "What do you think you're doing? Who pays the rent? Me! Who has to pay for that door when you break it? Me! Cut it out and control yourself." But not today.

It's 4:57 PM. The concert is in two hours. I still have to run through my piece (Haydn's Concerto in C), take a shower, do my hair, get dressed…and bake cookies. As I quickly practice the most difficult shifts and sixteenth-note passages, Lydia sneaks in. Quietly. She doesn't want to disturb me, but she wants to listen. She claps softly when I finish.

"You can have it back," she tugs at the hem of my yellow dress.

"No. You can wear it. I don't even care."

"No, really, you can have it." She pulls the fabric over her head.

"Lydia, stop. Just – stop. It's okay. I'm not mad. I can wear pants and a sweater."

"I'm not mad, either. But I meant every word I said." She sits on my bed. "You have to get ready now, right?"

After I take a shower, pull my hair into a tight bun, and change, I hear clattering in the kitchen.

"Kat! Are you out? I can't find the recipe for the cookies!"

"I don't need a recipe." I smile. "Get out the sugar – brown and regular, flour, baking soda, chocolate chips, salt, butter, vanilla, and two eggs. I'll get the bowls and spatula."

We mix the ingredients and set a little bowl of cookie dough aside for later. As I spoon the cookies onto the baking sheet, she carefully places two chocolate chips on either side of the top of my head. "You look like the devil! Heheheh." She giggles.

"You're bald too, you know."

I check on the cookies in the oven. "Almost done! And I still have ten minutes to run through the Haydn."

"Yeah. Almost done," Lydia grins as she mischievously places two more chocolate chips on top of my head. I return the favor, but the chocolate chips fall on the linoleum because she's shaking with laughter.

2014 Short Story Adult First Place Winner: Water's Edge by Jan Richman Schulman

Jan Richman Schulman was born and raised in East Los Angeles and has been a resident of Oxnard, California for the past twenty-six years, where she resides with her husband, Phillip. She was previously employed by the Oxnard School District, where she worked for 18 years before retiring in 2002. She currently writes short stories and articles (most recently for The Reporter*) and volunteers at various organizations throughout Ventura County.*

Walking along the edge of the water, holding tight to her small granddaughter's hand, she breathed deeply, taking in the ocean air she loved. The day was a just a bit overcast, enough so that the heat was not oppressive nor the breezes too chilling. Her wellbeing was so dependent on the weather of California's Central Coast, where she lived, that she never felt the need to go anywhere else. Here she lived her contented life. *Safe. Loved.*

"Look Gamma. Look." Two-year-old Maxine pointed to a sand crab struggling to return to the waves from which it had been washed ashore. "Sand crab, baby. That's a sand crab. Can you say 'sand crab' for gamma?" "San Cab," the child replied pleased with herself "San Cab," she repeated, squinting up into her grandmother's delighted face. "Oh Maxie…And how did you get to be so smart?" *Oh, don't let's lose this moment.*

She released the child's hand and watched carefully as the little girl scooted along the water's edge, chasing the water and screeching in delighted bravery as the wave's pull sent the ocean to her feet and then retreated, as if in full defeat. Hard to believe, she thought. So young, so innocent, so beautiful. And so brief. For she did not dare to deceive herself into believing that this pureness of soul would last. She knew too much of life, and of the world. She knew too well of its deceptions. *Keep the now.* She stretched her back, feeling the ache and soreness, wishing she still had the youth and energy to keep up with her grandchild, wishing to throw off the mantle of old age that was slowly enveloping her. *Not so slowly now.* She stood watching her young grandchild toddle off, her hands shading her eyes, her feet planted firmly in the sand.

"Where do they get all that energy?" A man's voice came from behind.

She startled, unaware that anyone else was walking along the beach with them. "I beg your pardon?"

"Sorry. Just watching you play with your little one there. You seem to be enjoying yourself. Kind of fun to watch."

She looked at the man who was walking near to her. He was tall and slim and had thick, long white hair tied-back in a ponytail. He wore a short-sleeved light blue denim shirt and dark jeans, rolled up almost to his knees. He was barefoot; his skin was tanned and wrinkled, and he had a short, scraggly beard. It was the middle of the week, and at four in the afternoon, there were few people on the beach, none near to her. But she knew that at the house, a few hundred yards from the water's edge, caring faces were watching. She did not feel fear, only a slight discomfort. *In my space. On my beach.*

"Well, you know. My first grandchild and all. It's hard not to dote, isn't it?"

"I wouldn't know," he replied. "I've never had any grandkids. Or any kids of my own for that matter. Never felt I missed much. But couldn't help watching how … together the two of you were. Looked nice."

"I can't imagine my life without her. I think…excuse me…have we met?" She peered at him, searching for some sign of familiarity.

"No. Not to my knowledge. Just walking on the beach, like you. You live here?"

She hesitated, wondering whether to share that information with a stranger. *What could be the harm*, she thought. She was becoming so paranoid in her old…*older*…years. "Yes, we have a home here on the beach. You?"

"No. Just drove up from the valley. To get out of the heat. Wife was busy doing her stuff, whatever her stuff is," he gave a kind of half chuckle. "And I felt like getting out of the city for a few hours. Must be nice, living here."

"I wouldn't live anywhere else. I don't like to leave even to visit the kids. I let them come up here to me. I'm sorry…but you do look familiar."

He stopped and looked at her. She stared back him, all the while keeping her eyes fixed on the child. His mouth opened and closed and then he said, "I guess you look somewhat familiar also. I don't know…"

As he looked intently at her, she became aware of her age, her long grey hair, pulled back into a bun, wispy bits pulling free and blowing around her face in the breeze. Her body was slim and she was wearing a pair of tan linen pants and a white man's shirt that flapped freely. She stood barefoot in the sand. The man standing opposite her looked to be around her age, if not a few years older.

Her shoulders drooped as she accepted the inevitable. So many years. What was it: 40? 45? *No!*

"Tina? Are you … is it…?"

"Well, yes. Yes, it is, Richard." *Breathe.*

"Rick. Well, you always called me Richard; haven't been called Richard in… I don't know how long. Since … but yes, it's me. Can you believe this?"

"I'm not sure what to say. How did you find … how did you come to be here? I mean I know you said to escape the heat of the city. But here, and now, right at this moment, in this space? How is this possible?" She felt a chill at the back of her neck. This was not just implausible, it was impossible. *Not a coincidence.*

The man looked down and shuffled his feet in the sand. "I have no idea. I didn't plan this, I assure you. This is just something that … one of those horrible clichéd things that only happens in books. You know: bad fiction. Jeezus. How are you? I guess that's what I'm supposed to say." He was not trying to hide his excitement. Rather, he was giving in to the serendipitous moment.

She backed away from him a few steps, dazed and momentarily confused. She looked down the beach at her granddaughter who was moving further from her. "Excuse me. The baby … I have to…" She ran down the shore after the baby, grateful for the momentary break. She gathered the child up in her arms and walked back toward the man. "There you go, sweetheart. Stay close to gamma." She put the child down and watched as the toddler ran toward the water once more, stopping just short of the shallow, white surf. The little girl sat down in the wet muddy sand and began to splash her hands as the water washed over her legs and then retreated.

"Sorry. Didn't mean to be rude. But you can't take your eyes off them for one second."

He smiled. "That's okay. You have to do … so, how long have you lived here?"

"Almost thirty-five years now. *MY home.* My husband and I came across this little oasis of a neighborhood when we first met and we just fell in love with it. So … here we are."

She took a breath, feeling that she was talking too fast, and too much. But she continued. "Our daughter grew up here, although she and her family don't live here now. They live up in the Bay Area. San Francisco. My son-in-law's job. But we love it when they come for a visit every other month or so. It is such a joy for all of us."

There was a brief silence, broken by the sound of the ocean waves breaking and coming into shore, the screeching of the sea gulls hovering around them, the sea breezes. It was awkward, yet it wasn't; it just seemed

... appropriate. A space in time for them to regroup and settle into questioning and searching. The beach was always a good place to do that. *If need be.*

"And you?" she said. "I gather that you live in the valley. Do you work, or are you retired, or what?"

"Oh no. I still work on and off. I'm a carpenter and when something of interest comes along, I take it. It keeps the bill collectors away or something like that. Truth is, I love the work. Always have." He paused. "How about you? Are you retired?"

"A carpenter? That's terrific. I know you always liked..." She stopped. "Oh, yes. Retired eight years now. Feels wonderful. Allows me to just do ... whatever I want. I keep so busy with things that I often wonder how I had time to work. And your wife? How is she?" *I knew her. You remember that, don't you?*

"Oh, she's fine. Fine." Another pause caused her to reflect that this time the pause was not appropriate. She looked more closely at him, searching for the recognizable in the aging face. The blue eyes, yes, not big, but half hidden just as she remembered; not fully open. The stance ... still tall and slender and straight as a board. She looked at his hands and noticed that his fingers were just as she recalled: long and graceful and beautiful, the skin thinner now, more transparent. It was him. No doubt about it. Although the one thing that gave him away completely was his voice and the way in which the timber of his words pulled her in. *No.* He always sounded upbeat, never down or defeated. She pulled back again.

"Is she still working? Didn't she have children from a previous marriage? I remember..."

"Oh, yes. The boys. Well they're all grown, of course. One of them, Jake, is still living with us. Can you believe it? At his age? The other one, Bobbie, is living somewhere in the Midwest. Has a wife and kids. Our house is pretty quiet now which is the way I like it. I have plenty of time to read and study and do my work. It's nice being self-employed. I can work whenever I want for whoever I want and don't have to answer to anyone."

"Except your customers and your wife." She laughed. She noticed his reluctance to discuss his family.

He looked at her. "Well, if my customers don't like my work, they don't have to hire me. I don't make any bones about it. If you see my work and you like it, then you know what you are going to get."

'Oh. I didn't mean ... I was just joking."

"Yeah, well that's okay. But that's what I like. Not like teaching, where there's always someone breathing over your shoulder, right?"

They had both been teachers. So long ago ... *we were married once* ... she had worked for an elementary school district and he had taught at their local city college. More often than not, she did his class planning and corrected his students' work. Had that really been a life she had once lived? Suddenly she felt faded. *This is me now.*

She smiled. "Well, I never much cared for working for a school district if you recall. So much political bull and not enough real caring about the children. But the kids ... the kids..."

"Yeah, yeah. I know. I remember quite well what you were like. I'm old, not dead." The sarcasm struck her, and she recognized the defensive mood he had suddenly taken.

Tina looked up the beach and saw her daughter heading toward them. She called over to her granddaughter. "Come on sweetheart. Maxie ... run to mommy so she can get you dinner. Go on now."

She watched as the little girl ran to her mother. The woman waved to her and she waved back, indicating she would be along soon. Not wanting her to come for an introduction. Not wanting to have to explain or describe. She turned back to him. *You are not of us.*

"Well, how long have you been up here?" she asked. "Just for the day? Didn't your wife come with you?" She knew she was pushing it. Opening the conversation, she hoped, in order to alleviate some of the tension. Get past his hesitation. This *interruption*, whatever its purpose, would have to end. *Sooner rather than later.*

"So," he continued, avoiding her question. "Do you still do your illustrations? Still drawing for kids' books and stuff like that?"

Stuff like that. Stuff. She half smiled and said, "Yep. I still do 'stuff like that.' It 'keeps the bill collectors away'."

"Oh, come on. I didn't mean anything by that." He paused. "Remember that little story you wrote to go with some of your drawings? It was pretty good."

"Thanks," she said, puzzled.

"So, you never did anything with it? Never tried to get it published or anything?" He looked intently at her.

"What in the world made you think of that? Why would you even be interested now?" *You were never interested then. Dismissed all that I attempted...*

She felt it then. The beach seemed to move, as if an earthquake had occurred. Not a large one, just slight enough to send her off balance. *Betrayal.* She knew it. Years had changed nothing. She had loved him once, then did not and never again. But she had not forgotten the betrayal. The lies. The secrecy. The cheating. The resentment. The shallowness of it. All of the negative emotions from that time gone by, from so many years ago, the memory of them came rushing back upon her. She looked at him. He knew what she was thinking

"Well ... you know ... the way I was with you ... and then her ... it's not something I'm real proud of, but it shouldn't matter anymore. Not after all these years, right? You're not still harboring..." He smiled, and she remembered that his smile always contained a kind of half smirk, as if he were playing a joke on the world; a joke that only he knew, yet gleefully wanted to share. It was there for the asking. "It's just that I'd kept a copy of it for some reason and I showed it to my wife a coupla years ago. Wouldn't you know, she liked it so much, she had it published. Under her own name of course; her maiden name. It's out now and to everyone's surprise, selling pretty good for a kid's book. She's a kid's therapist, so she knew how to tweak the story a little bit more to the age group she wanted. Kept the same illustrations; she really liked those a lot. She gave it your title too, *School Days.* So ... your story, but not exactly. Who'd've thought?"

My pictures. My words. Her head was spinning now, and she felt dizzy, breathless. Her hand clasped at her chest and she stumbled. She was nauseated.

"Tina! Are you okay? Tina! Shit. I'm sorry! I'm so sorry. If I'd thought ... I didn't think. I didn't think it would matter to you. Dammit. I'm really sorry." He grabbed her and held her to him. "Tina, after all this time, I thought…"

She jerked back quickly, revolted by his touch. "No. No. It's nothing. It's just that…" She strengthened herself, pulled her body upright and apart from him. She patted her shirt down with her hands and brushed the few wisps of unruly hair out of her face. She pulled her sunglasses from the top of her head down onto her nose and covered her eyes, turning her face away from him. Then she looked back at him and saw the terror in his face. *He's a frightened old man.* The disgust she felt for him raged through her, replacing all thought and she could feel it emanate toward him. *He feels it.* She took a deep breath and allowed him to experience the results of his disclosure. *What made you think you could matter?*

"Well, Richard … Rick … it's been really … I need to get back to the house now."

"What? Tina. Don't be mad. Please. So many years have gone by. That's why I thought that by now, we … you and I could…" he stopped, realizing what he had said.

What have you become. No. It's me. I forgot what you were. Are.

"I hope you didn't spend too much time looking for me. *You could never find me, no matter how much you looked. You could never see me.* "I'm not mad. Haven't thought about it … you, her … all of it since … forever. And I'm not surprised. Everything is as it should be. And now, I must go to my family. Take care."

She turned away again and trudged through the sand, back toward the house. She knew he would not follow her. She could feel the air begin to chill as the sun set lower on the horizon. The evening fog was rolling in and she breathed in the deep dampness, allowing it to cool and refresh her. She did not look back.

Later that evening, while her family was indoors watching television, she sat on the porch, hunkered down in her chair, covered with her husband's coat and some scarves, against the chill night air, drinking her coffee and looking out at the fog covered ocean. He was still there, and she could see him, pacing a few hundred yards away, at the water's edge, his arms clasped around his own body for warmth. The silhouette of him cast a strange ghostly image in the fog and she felt his frustration, failure, and, as was always his wont, confusion about which way to go; what to do. She watched him for a while, then got up and went back inside the house.

In the morning, the fog was dense and cold, but she felt the struggle of the sun to burn through and knew that by noon the sky would be clear and the beach would warm. She could hardly see the surf now, but she could see enough to know that he was gone. A Monarch butterfly flew by, fluttering ever so slightly, coming close and then flitting away. *I must paint that,* she thought. She looked at its warm beautiful colors. *So bold,* she thought. *And so fragile.*

2014 Short Story Adult Second Place Winner: Paper Dragon
by Antony Villalobos

Antony is a high school teacher and a coach who discovered a love of storytelling later in his life. The imagination and "All things possible" mindset of his son inspires him.

Therapy—Week Seventeen. Today's my tenth birthday, also the six-month anniversary of the day my mother died. Dad'll take me to dinner at Channing's Diner. Love the fifties rock 'n roll. I hope my memories of my mom stay in the jukebox inside me.

I guess this therapy thing's okay. The waiting room smells like leather mixed with janitor's chemicals. The fountain in the corner makes calm tricklish splashes. I wish they'd change the music though, a little Chuck Berry would be nice, *Johnny B. Goode.*

That old Japanese lady, here again. Um, I think she's Japanese. Every week, same seat, sits straight, dresses real nice, like she expects the president to walk in.

All I know is, wish Mom were still here. Will work on my origami some more. I open my folder, get a piece of the square colored paper, start to make a frog.

***

"Gavin, can you tell me how your mother passed away?" Ms. Rei says.

"The monsterstatic cancer took her."

Ms. Rei giggles. "Met-a sta-tic."

"Do you know what cancer is?"

"When cells in your body go crazy."

"Where do you believe your mother is now?"

I point to the sky. "Heaven. She's an angel." *Bye Bye, Love.*

***

Therapy—Week Eighteen. I wave to the Japanese lady. She smiles, little nod of her head. I check my new origami book, my falcon gives me trouble. A tricky fold confuses me. I glance at the five crushed pieces of paper, want to make three-pointers into the fountain. Ugh, can't get this right. I don't ball this one up, just slide the folded mess away from me, like I do peas at dinner. My turn, stuff my things in my backpack, go see Ms. Rei.

***

"What else have you been up to?" Ms. Rei says.

"Well, I like to work on my origami."

"Wonderful. How long have you done origami?"

"Since my mom passed away. Trying to make a falcon."

"How's that going?"

"Frustrating. They turn into little balls."

***

I wave goodbye to Ms. Rei, step into the waiting room.

"Ready Gav? Let's grab a bite to eat," Dad says.

"Sure." Something different about the room. "Wait, Dad hold on."

The Japanese woman's gone, but she's never here when I leave.

Finished, on the table, the coolest falcon ever. I lift it like it's made of glass.

"Did you leave your origami there?" Dad says.

"Sort of." *Tutti Frutti.*

***

Therapy—Week Nineteen. I do an outside reverse fold. My third parrot this week. Maybe the Japanese lady knows more origami. I slide a piece of paper across the table, she doesn't move. Maybe not.

"Did you finish the falcon for me? You know, the bird? Paper bird?" I flap my arms.

"Douzo yoroshiku," she says.

I point at myself. "I'm Gavin."

"Anata ga omoshiroi ne."

My turn. I pack my things, wave goodbye. She must think I'm nutty.

***

"Before we end today, any questions you'd like to ask?" Ms. Rei says.

I think back to my mom, how beautiful she always looked. "A why?"

"A why? What do you mean?"

"Why'd the cancer take my mom? Some say God needed her or it was her time."

"Do you believe any of those to be true?"

"Don't think everyone's on a schedule. Like at school, bell rings, time to go."

"So, what do you believe? Is there a why?"

"With origami, I start with a piece of paper. If it doesn't work out, I get a different piece. All of us are like different pieces of paper, we start the same, a single cell. As cells sort of fold, sometimes things go wrong inside. Sometimes things go right.

"And your mom?"

I pull out my parrot, look at the folds. "Her insides had the wrong folds. Fast, Mom left too fast." *Little Deuce Coupe.*

***

Dad's ready to go. On the table, I see the sheet of paper I left the Japanese woman. On top, sits a dragon, made of paper.

"Does the dragon belong to you?"

"Yeah, Dad. It's mine." At least, I think she left it for me. *Be-Bop-A-Lula.*

***

Therapy—Week Twenty. The Japanese woman isn't here. How'd she make the dragon?

Last night I heard it growl, call to me. In my dream, I ride the dragon's back through the clouds. I lose my grip, fall, reach, can't grab anything, scream. Hit water, sink, can't breathe. Kick hard, sink further, light fades.

Hear thunder, water vibrates. The dragon swims near me, I grab its neck, we snake to the surface. If I don't hold on, I'll die. The dragon and I crash through the surface, soar upward, squeeze my eyes shut, hear the air whoosh.

We stop, I open my eyes. We're on top of a mountain, the sun shines off the snow, clouds below us. Dragon lowers his head, I slide to the ground. Dragon crouches beside me.

***

"Something on your mind?" Ms. Rei says.

"The Japanese woman who's always in the waiting room. Well, she's not here today."

"Yes, she's a bit under the weather. Did you meet Mrs. Matsumoto?" Rei says.

"Um, no, not really. She seems real nice. I was curious, that's all. See you next week."

I join Dad. I'm *The Great Pretender.*

***

Therapy—Week Twenty-One. I race through the hallway, hope Mrs. Matsumoto's there. I enter the waiting room, she's not. I plop on the sofa.

I stare at her empty seat. I don't even know her, how come I miss her?

"Good afternoon, Gavin," a woman says.

I can't answer, confused.

"Ms. Rei sends her apologies, she had a personal matter to attend to, last minute."

The music bothers me. I want to climb on the dragon's back, fly to the mountain.

She's not Ms. Rei. All my questions about Mrs. Matsumoto sit heavy in my gut, like paper left in the rain. *I Hear You Knocking.*

***

Therapy—Week Twenty-Two. Mountain fold, inside reverse fold. Where's Mrs. Matsumoto? I pull on a point, do a squash fold. Hope the toucan I work on will look like a bird. The book says to make a cut. Search my backpack, no scissors. I stuff it away for later, take out the dragon, stare into its face. I had the dream again last night. Should I tell Ms. Rei my dream?

Something different about Ms. Rei. Her eyes. Crying? Or maybe a cold?

"Hey Gavin, sorry I missed you last week. What's that in your hand?"

The dragon. "Sorry Ms. Rei, I'll put it away."

"May I see it?"

"Um, sure." She looks at the paper dragon, like I've seen Eddie McMillan look at bugs through a magnifying glass.

"Where did you get this?"

My chest begins to pound, toes tap the office carpet. "Mrs. Matsumoto. I hoped to see her. Ask her if she'd show me how to make one."

Ms. Rei takes a deep breath. She waves my dad in. "Brian, I need to share something with you and Gavin." She hands back the paper dragon, scoots her chair closer to me. "Unfortunately, my grandmother, Mrs. Matsumoto, will not be back. She passed away almost two weeks ago."

"Your grandmother?"

"Yes, Mrs. Matsumoto is my grandmother. We'd go to dinner after our session."

"But she's gone every time I leave your office."

"She likes to tidy up before we leave. She uses the restroom down the hall."

Hard to breathe, eyes feel like balloons about to pop. Dad's hand on my shoulder. I look all over the office, find Ms. Rei's eyes, we cry together. *Heartbreak Hotel.*

***

Therapy—Week Twenty-Three. "Dad, this isn't the way to therapy?"

"Rei wants us to meet her at her home."

"Her home? Why?"

"She wants to share something special with us. That's all she'd tell me."

I look at the dragon. What could it be?

Dad pulls into a driveway. Large pine trees everywhere. The sand is raked around small trees and rocks. Kinda cool, looks like a river flows

36

around everything. We take a stone path to the front door, I ring the doorbell.

"Brian, Gavin. Welcome. I hope I didn't put you through too much trouble."

"Not a problem at all. You have a beautiful home," Dad says.

"Thank you. Come in, I have refreshments on the back patio."

Pictures on the wall, I stop. The eyes of a young girl grab my attention.

"Do you recognize that girl?" Ms. Rei says. "You know her."

"I do?" Yes, I do. "Mrs. Matsumoto?"

"That's right. Nineteen forty-three, her wedding picture, she's sixteen. Doesn't look like a wedding, does it?" Rei takes the picture from the wall, hands it to me. "Look in the background."

"Rows of box houses."

"Good. My grandmother and grandfather married in Manzanar."

"Is that another country?"

Ms. Rei giggles. "No. Manzanar is here, in California, where approximately ten thousand Japanese were kept during World War Two."

"Kept?"

"Different words are used. Relocation center. Internment camp. Some say 'prison'."

"Were they criminals?"

"No, Japanese ethnicity isn't a crime."

"What do you mean?"

"On December seventh, nineteen forty-one, Japan bombed Pearl Harbor. The United States declared war on Japan, feared that the Japanese who lived here were a threat to our country's safety. They ordered all Japanese, even American born, to leave their homes and relocate to internment camps, Manzanar's the largest."

I hand the picture back to Ms. Rei.

"My grandparents left Manzanar in nineteen forty-four to start a new life together." Ms. Rei straightens the picture on the wall. "Grandfather opened two successful nurseries. Grandmother helped with the business of course, worked with flowers."

What about the dragon? Did she learn origami at the nursery? I don't think so.

"Let's join your father on the patio before all the chocolate chip cookies disappear."

***

"You live in your grandparent's home?" I say.

"Yes, when grandfather passed away in 2003, grandmother insisted Robert, my husband, and I move in. She appreciated the company and the help to maintain the house and the grounds."

"What about your mom and dad?"

"Gavin, buddy, let's not ask too many personal questions, huh? Sorry Rei."

"Not a problem. I'm happy Gavin's comfortable enough to ask me questions. My father continues to run the nurseries. My mother passed away from breast cancer when I was ten."

Breast cancer. We're connected. We lost our mothers at the same age, ten years old. Did she hurt like I hurt? Did she walk into the kitchen every morning, hope she'd wake from a bad dream? Find her mother doing the mommy things mommies do? I wrap my arms around Ms. Rei. Do we ever run out of tears? *Rescue me.*

***

"I never got to ask Mrs. Matsumoto about the dragon." I show her my gift.

Ms. Rei stares at the dragon, her lower lip begins to tremble.

"Ms. Rei, you okay?" I say.

"Can I get you anything?" Dad slides the box of Kleenex closer.

Ms. Rei wipes her eyes, reaches for an envelope. "I think it's best if I read you this letter, left by my grandmother. We found it with her will."

Rei-chan, please give Paper City to Little Dragon. I've seen in his eyes a patient and kind heart. I understand the pain in him at the loss of his mother. I, too, lived with the pain of losing a daughter. When I hurt, I always return to Paper City. To create from the heart is to understand all which is glorious in life. Little Dragon has strength. It is my wish that he be given Paper City to complete. To explore, to create, to love. Sobo.

My throat hurts, hard to swallow. "Am I... the little dragon?"

"Yes."

"What's paper city?" Dad says.

"Difficult to explain. Please, follow me. Best if I show you," Ms. Rei says.

Dad and I follow Ms. Rei into the house. She stops, places her hand on a door, "My grandmother spent a lot of time here. This is her paper room. Gavin, my grandmother requests that you be given her origami, her paper city."

I knew it. Mrs. Matsumoto did origami. I reach for the handle, freeze. The handle is a dragon's head. I look at Ms. Rei, she nods me onward. Looks like a storage room, boxes on top of tables? I see two switches. Weird. One's yellow, another black. "Which one?"

"Yellow."

Click. Don't believe my eyes, blink hard a few times.

"This is paper city?" Dad says.

"Paper city. About fifty years of my grandmother's hobby. Take a look."

Tables set in a u-shape against the walls, display an actual city. Ocean meets the shoreline, three sailboats, a pier, connected to an amusement park. A mixer, Ferris wheel and roller coaster. All made of paper... paper.

Next table. Streets, small buildings, coffee shop, donut shop, mechanic's garage, a police station. "Dad, can you believe this? How awesome."

I move to the skyscrapers, hotels, a theatre along the back wall. "Mrs. Matsumoto did all this by herself?"

"Sometimes I'd help her with a piece, like a building. But she made everything here."

I move to the last table. A small park with homes. In the park, a small platform surrounded by a fence. Why an empty platform? "Did something use to go there?"

"Yes. You noticed." Ms. Rei places her hand on my shoulder, "You have it."

"I didn't take anyth—" No way. I hold up the dragon. "This?"

Ms. Rei nods. "The guardian of paper city. The dragon represents the forces of nature. Creativity and destruction. Life is

38

strong and weak. Sometimes a person can live a full and productive life. Sometimes, the people we love, leave us unexpectedly."

"Like our mothers?"

Ms. Rei nods. "The dragon also represents wisdom. The ability to understand each."

I hug Ms. Rei. Look at Dad. How much hurt has he gone through? My mom, the love of his life, his *Special Angel.* I hug my dad, maybe I can squeeze some of his hurt away.

***

"Ms. Rei? Are you saying Mrs. Matsumoto's giving me all of this?"

"It's her wish."

"Rei, this is an incredible gift. I don't even know where to begin," Dad says.

"Yes, quite out of the ordinary. My husband and I feel that the right thing to do is to fulfill my grandmother's request. Paper city can be moved, it's built in sections."

I rub my hand over the empty table. "What did she want to put here?"

"I don't know. Whatever your heart tells you to put there'll be perfect."

"But I've never done this before. I've just worked on animals."

"There's no deadline, no time limit. You'll practice and learn. Grandmother saw something in you, Gavin. She gave you that dragon for a reason."

Something stirs in me. I can do this.

"Gavin, please turn off the yellow switch. Turn on the black one."

The city lights up. Must be little hidden light bulbs. It's beautiful.

Don't know how long we stared at the glow. Ms. Rei flips the switches. I blink my eyes back to normal. I see an old radio. "Does this work?"

"Grandmother loved to listen to her music while she worked."

The radio scratches on, "*We're gonna rock around the clock tonight…*"

2014 Short Story Adult Third Place Winner: The Vault by Sofia Diane Gable

Sofia has been writing for as long as she can remember and has several novels, novellas, and short stories published. She has been a member of the VCWC for about four years

Dr. Hannah Fields, assistant museum curator, applied a thin layer of glue to the last piece of the artifact and gingerly fit it in place. She took off her glasses, blinked her tired eyes and looked up from her worktable. It was only 10:30 pm, but it felt later. She'd been working on the same artifact all day; a two-foot long Mesoamerican figurine of Quetzalcoatl, the feather-headed serpent god. She should have gone home hours ago, but she was a perfectionist. Besides, she had no one waiting. The Quetzalcoatl was her only companion. Her stomach growled. She'd skipped dinner.

She stretched, put on her glasses, shut off the work lamp and pushed the arm of the mounted magnifying glass away. The figurine was complete, and it was a beautiful work of art. The serpent's mouth was agape, as if it was ready to strike, its fangs long and menacing. There was a small depression inside the mouth, perhaps at one time to hold an object, but it was lost in the ruins of the temple where the artifact was found. Frustrating because she'd always know it was incomplete, even if nobody else did. Her need to finish things – the main reason she could never keep a relationship

39

going for long. Every disagreement or argument dragged on and on because she could never end it until every single point had been covered.

She yawned. She needed sleep, and food. After giving the Quetzalcoatl a kiss, she draped a cloth over it and stood, stretching again.

The windowless basement that served as the artifact vault was bathed in pale yellow from the aged recessed lighting. That, mixed with the dead silence, gave her the creeps. She was used to being alone, but the vault felt like a stifling dungeon at night. During the day, when there were technicians and interns buzzing here and there, it wasn't bad, but at night it took on a different feel entirely. A chill crept over her and made her shiver.

"Come on, Hannah, you're being silly," she said aloud. "Get a grip."

With the strap of her satchel over her shoulder, she headed for the door, but startled at the sound of a metallic clank behind her. Her breath caught in her throat, but when she turned, she realized it was only the museum's archaic furnace going on. Still, it rattled her nerves nonetheless.

She turned to the door and extended her hand toward the knob but pulled it back when someone whispered her name.

"Hannah," came the soft, ethereal voice.

She spun around. "Who's there?"

Silence.

"Is someone there?" She peered into the empty space before her.

Of course, there wasn't anyone there. She was alone, always alone, even with people around. She'd spent most of her life studying and researching, delving into her career, so much so that there was never room for friends. Now apparently her loneliness was making her hear voices. She really should get out more, maybe even attend one of the museum's fundraising functions. That was a great way to meet people.

"Hannah," whispered the voice again.

That wasn't her imagination. It was definitely a voice. A strange, raspy voice echoing around the vault. She looked over at the storage drawers. There were three rows of drawers stretching the length of the vault, each five feet high, containing an assortment of archaeological artifacts. No one could have sneaked in without her noticing because the only way into the vault was through the single door that she was standing in front of. After everyone left at five, she'd locked the door from the inside, a habit she'd had since childhood when everything scared her. She remembered how she hated the night most of all. That was the time when the tree branches outside her bedroom window took on the shadowy appearance of elongated fingers stretching and reaching toward her. Locked windows and doors kept her safe from the world. Just like working in the basement of a museum kept her safe from the outside.

"Hello? Who's there? I know there's someone in here. What do you want?" Hannah shoved her trembling hands in her pockets. She didn't want whoever was there to see how scared she was.

The furnace clanked again and groaned like a wounded animal. She should leave. It had to be her mind playing tricks. That happened when someone was overly tired, didn't it? It probably wasn't a voice at all, just steam hissing from the furnace vent.

"Hannah." It was more forceful now.

She grabbed at the doorknob and unlocked it. "There's no one in here but me."

"And me, Hannah," spoke the voice, clearer and louder now.

Hannah could hardly breathe. She tried to turn the doorknob, but it wouldn't budge. It was as if someone on the other side was holding it tight. She let her satchel slide to the floor and used both hands to work at the knob.

"You cannot leave, Hannah."

"You're not real. I'm imagining you. I'm the only one here." She thumped on the door with her fists. "Hello! Is anyone out there?"

"Not out there, Hannah, in here. With you. You cannot leave."

Hannah turned and peered into the empty vault. It was still, no movement at all. The only sound was from the furnace clicking and clacking as it shut down. Had she somehow lost her mind between the time she got out of bed and right now? Was that even possible? Losing one's mind in a day? No, it was more likely that one of the technicians was playing a prank. Not a very funny prank, but they probably thought it was hilarious. There must be a speaker hidden somewhere.

She wandered away from the door and looked around the corner of a row of storage drawers. Nobody hiding, no speakers. She peeked around the next and the next and found nothing but emptiness.

"What are you looking for, Hannah? Are you looking for me?" The voice sounded like it was right next to her, whispering in her ear.

She ran to the door, grabbed her satchel off the floor and held it in front of her like a shield. "Where are you? This isn't funny. Unlock the door. I have to go home."

"You are home, Hannah."

Hannah banged on the door, over and over, tried the doorknob again and again, but it was no use. No one was coming, not even the guards. She was locked in the vault, alone. "This isn't my home. Let me out! Where are you? Show yourself."

"We have a lot in common, Hannah. You must stay here with me."

The words rang in her ears; *stay here*. Stay here? What was that supposed to mean? Was the person behind the mysterious voice a kidnapper? Why would anyone do that? She'd never hurt a soul. She came to work every day, went home, went to bed and got up the following day to start it all over again. She hardly interacted with anyone. It had to be one of the techs or an intern maybe. What if she'd said something or done something to an intern. No, she'd never spoken harshly or ordered anyone to do anything they didn't want to do.

She turned around and pressed her back against the door. "Look, just let me out. I have to go home and eat. I didn't have any dinner."

"Hannah, I have everything you need. You will see. You will never want for anything. Trust me."

She never trusted anyone. Not really. She never had. That was the reason she was alone. No friends, no family, colleagues that hardly spoke to her. What sort of life was that? And now she was hearing voices. Could it be a psychotic breakdown from being alone? But the door wouldn't open, which meant someone had tampered with it.

She yelled into the still air, "Did you lock the door? Why are you doing this? I haven't done anything to you."

Silence, except for her pounding heart.

She called out again, "Are you there?" She stepped away from the door. The vault was cloaked in an eerie hush. Not even the furnace made any noise. The quiet was worse than the voice. "Where are you?"

"We can help one another, Hannah. But I need something from you."

Hannah swallowed and wandered around the room. "What could you need from me? I don't have anything."

"You underestimate yourself, Hannah. You come here every day and have dedicated your life to your work. Loneliness is something no one should suffer. I too am alone."

"You are?" Hannah ran her hand along the storage drawers thinking of the many years she'd worked on the various collections within. There were basketry fragments, stone tools, projectile points and her favorite artifact of all, a tiny female figure carved out of granite. That little figure was found during the same excavation where they found the Quetzlcoatl figurine.

"Hannah. Come here."

"Where? Where are you?" Hannah made her way toward the voice and stopped at her work bench. "Where are you?"

"Right here."

Hannah looked down. The voice was coming from under the cloth. How could that be? She grasped the corner of the cloth and lifted it an inch, but let it go. "This isn't real. I'm hearing things. None of this is real."

"It is. I am real. You know it in your heart. Hannah, we can help one another. We are both incomplete and need to be made whole."

Hannah sat down and lifted the corner of the cloth again. "This is nothing but a pottery figurine. Inanimate. Not alive." She closed her eyes and repeated, "Not alive."

"Hannah."

"Not alive."

"Hannah. Look at me."

She opened her eyes. Slowly, she lifted the cloth higher and higher until the face of Quetzalcoatl was exposed. In the pale light, it looked like the eye blinked. But that wasn't possible. She uncovered the entire figurine. She must be more tired than she thought because the serpent's body appeared to writhe gradually, side-to-side. A forked tongue shot out for a moment before slipping back into the mouth. With her fingertips, Hannah touched the body, feeling the hardened glue where she'd carefully put each piece together. The serpent wriggled under her fingers.

"I'm imagining this."

"You're not, Hannah." The serpent lifted its head, the tongue again probing the air.

"How can this be real? I glued you together. You're nothing but clay and paint." Hannah withdrew her hand.

The serpent coiled. "But I'm not whole yet, Hannah. I need you and you need me."

"I don't understand." Hannah took off her glasses and rubbed her eyes. She felt odd, like her body was light, almost floating. She slipped on the glasses. The serpent was gone. She looked around. "Where'd you go?"

"Over here, Hannah."

Hannah followed the voice and found the serpent stretching up to one of the storage drawers. The drawer that held the little female figure. She opened the drawer and picked up the delicate piece.

"Yes, Hannah, that is the piece to make me whole." The serpent slithered between Hannah's feet. "It is nothing but a chunk of cold stone now. The spell was broken when it fell from my mouth. You have cared for me as no other, putting me back together so I may live again. I want you. You will replace that lifeless stone. You belong with me now."

"What do you mean? What are you talking about?" Hannah felt the need to protect the female figure. It was a thing of beauty, carved with amazing detail for something so small. She looked at it every day, even before pouring her morning coffee. It was like an old friend greeting her. She started to put it back in the drawer, but a sharp pain on her ankle made her drop it on the floor.

The serpent instantly coiled around it, crushing it into powder. "I was powerless until you put me together again. And now you will be the last piece. We will be together forever, Hannah."

Hannah was dizzy. The room was spinning, and she was hot. Her ankle throbbed and swelled. "What did you do to me?"

"It had to be done. Do not fear. I shall never leave you. You are mine now, Hannah. You will be with me. We will keep one another company. Neither of us will suffer loneliness. We will stay safe here in this place, together."

The serpent's words were muffled, fading away to nothing. Hannah couldn't stand any longer and slid to the floor. Her eyes were heavy, too heavy to keep open. Her arms and legs felt stiff. What was happening? Why couldn't she move? It was as if her entire body had turned to stone.

***

Hannah woke to the sound of chatter, familiar voices talking. Then light, bright light. She couldn't see clearly, there was something obscuring her vision. The voices were close. She listened.

"Where's Dr. Fields? She's never late," said Jonathan, the lead restoration technician.

"Don't know. Oh, hey look. She finished the Quetzalcoatl. Nice job." The voice belonged to Leda, one of the interns.

Hannah was suddenly jostled. She tumbled around, but couldn't get her footing. "Hey!" she shouted. "What's going on?"

Leda spoke again, "Oh, wow, Jonathan, there's something inside. I knocked it loose when I picked up the figurine. Look, it's a female effigy. I think it fits in that little depression in the mouth. Give me the forceps so I can place it back."

Jonathan groaned. "Here. I hope you didn't break anything."

Hannah felt herself lifted into the air and then put back down. "Hey! It's me, Dr. Fields! Look at me!" She screamed as loud as she could. Why couldn't they hear her?

"Hey, Leda, let's put the Quetzalcoatl in one of the drawers so it doesn't get broken."

Hannah saw Leda's face peering at her.

"Jonathan, did you look at that effigy? I swear it looks like a woman wearing glasses."

"Pre-Columbians didn't wear glasses, Leda." Jonathan's face appeared now. "Yeah, okay, it does look like she's wearing glasses. Weird. I wonder where Dr. Fields is. She probably knows all about the symbolism of whatever those ancient glasses really are."

Hannah screamed again, "I'm right here!" From her vantage point, she saw she was heading toward the storage drawers. "No!"

"Hey, Leda, there's a drawer open. I guess that's where Dr. Fields wants the Quetzalcoatl."

Hannah cried out, "No! Don't do this! Jonathan! It's me in here!" She didn't want to believe what was happening. It was a dream, it had to be. She couldn't be inside the Quetzalcoatl. That was impossible. Wasn't it?

The movement stopped, and darkness fell. Then after a moment, another voice. A voice that Hannah hoped had only been a nightmare.

"I told you we would be together, Hannah. You and I will never be alone again. We are complete now. We will be companions for all eternity."

Hannah screamed into the cold darkness of the storage drawer, knowing deep down that no one could hear her. There was no escape. She was now a part of the artifact. This was her prison, the cold, dark place she'd spend the rest of her life. Could it be this was where she was supposed to be? Her whole life had been spent searching for something, piecing things back together to make the broken whole again. But this wasn't what she wanted, to become nothing but a chunk of stone, lost to the world.

"Help me, please, somebody, help me," she whispered. "Can anybody hear me? I want to go home."

"Do not be afraid. We are one, Hannah. Rejoice in your immortality."

Immortality? She hadn't thought of that. What would it be like to spend every day in the museum, never wanting for anything, except freedom? What was freedom anyway? She'd been free her whole life, yet unhappy and afraid. There had been no one around to comfort her when she was sad or talk to her when she was lonely. Perhaps freedom wasn't what she needed after all. It made sense now, this was where she belonged; safely secluded away from the world with someone who actually cared for her. She was home and she was whole, part of something much bigger than herself.

"You *are* home, Hannah."

What beautiful words. "Yes, I am."

2014 Short Story Adult Honorable Mention: Melanie's Madness by Carol Malone

Award-winning author, Carol Malone has published three historical romance. She's been a member of the VCWC for years serving as the Social Media Manager, Editor of The Write Stuff, Recording Secretary, and the Second V.P. of Membership. Carol works as a ghostwriter/editor and lives with her husband of thirty-six years, Tim and prays that her only son, Mike, 35 will one day give her grandchildren. At night you'll find her reading a novel while watching the Dodgers or Hallmark.

Twelve-year-old Melanie woke with a start. Had she fallen asleep on her bed while reading again? She tried to shake her head, but discovered it held tightly in place. Odd. It was too dark for her to be in her room. Her room wouldn't be this black because the glow from her Mighty Thor night-light would have cut through the darkness. Shivers ran up and down her spine and goose bumps blossomed on her arms. Why was she so cold? Something was very wrong about this pitch blackness surrounding her and the heavy weight pressing her down.

I'm going to die.

The horror of her looming death and of not being able to see her parents again made her want to curl into a ball. But the heavy object on top of her, made of cloth, and stinking of stale pee and sour vomit held her down, and partially covered her face. The heaviness on her chest made it hard to breathe. She forced her head to turn to the left and gulped in stale air thick with dampness.

A cold sweat broke out on her upper lip and forehead; moisture began to pool underneath her back. The shivers from the chilly air turned to tremors of terror, and her cold hands trembled. It felt like an icy fist had closed over her heart squeezing it so tight it began to bang-thud-thud-bang in her chest.

Is this what it feels like to die underwater – damp, cold, unable to breathe?

"Where am I?" she asked, but her muffled voice bounced back at her.

She tried to scoot to the left, out from under the object pressing on her chest, but something jagged poked her just below her ribs. "Ouch," she said and shuffled back to the right. She stretched her right hand out slowly and collided with something solid and slimy. A wall? Whatever she was in, it was tiny.

She could smell fresh dirt and the solid wall under her right hand felt slick and clammy. She let out a strangled cry. "I'm in a grave!" then began to whimper.

Maybe she had gone to sleep and died, and her family had buried her. Only she wasn't dead, just sleeping, and now she was buried six feet under the ground in a slimy coffin. Her teeth started chattering as a sickening wave of dread churned in her tummy.

What was the last thing she remembered? Had she just been at Grammie's farm house for milk and cookies, or had she been across the dirt road at home reading a book? She couldn't remember and that made her cry harder.

She'd remembered seeing a movie about a lady who'd been buried alive. But she'd been rescued by the FBI guys.

Would her parents find her in time? Did they know where to look for her?

She saw a news story on TV about a little boy who'd gone missing and had never returned. His family had been awfully sad.

Melanie didn't want her parents to mourn. She battled down her terror and the icky crawly feeling on her arms. Her parents would never know what had happened to her, whether was dead or alive. She would die without seeing them again and would miss them very much.

She wouldn't miss her older brothers. All four of them were brats.

"I don't want to die." She sobbed, hot tears running into her hair. "Mommy, Daddy, where are you?"

"Don't cry, baby," her older brothers had always teased her. *"Cry baby, cry baby,"* they sing-songed.

"Never you mind those boys," Grammie said and shooed them out of her big homey kitchen. "You go on and cry all you want. It's good for the soul."

Grammie always let her cry, holding and rocking her close in the old rocker in the corner next the fireplace. Her Grammie always smelled like liniment and cookies. "Crying helps cleanse the soul, child. Makes you get out the pain so you can be stronger the next time."

"I wanna be stronger, Grammie," she'd said.

"You are, child. You are."

She was strong. Her Grammie told her she was.

"Stop it. Crying is for babies and you're not a baby." She sniffed back her tears. "You have to think."

Think. Think.

Wait!

What if she hadn't been buried alive?

What if she'd been captured by pirates and they held her captive in the ship's hold under a ton of smelly sacks of wet grain while the captain delivered a note to her parents demanding a huge ransom? Maybe what poked her side was the tip of a pirate's sword. What if the pirates didn't plan on returning her to her family, but forced her to loot and plunder just like they did? She'd be a scourge and hunted down by the British.

Would her parents cry for her, be sad she was a pirate and could never come home?

"That's it. Calm down," she said to herself. "If the pirates try to kill me, or force me to be a pirate, I'll scratch their eyes out."

She felt the cold hard floor beneath her back. "No. I don't feel the ship bobbing around."

If not a ship, what was this cold box she was in?

Maybe she fell down a well sleepwalking.

That's it. But her parents wouldn't know where to look for her. Was there a well on Grammie's farm? Maybe. She had to be the one to find it. Why couldn't one of her stupid brothers have found it?

But what was on top of her?

The dampness around her grew colder and icy air and panic started to seep into her bones. Her teeth chattered. She wrenched her head slightly, so she could breathe in and out through her mouth. She smelled dirty socks and bacon grease.

Why would someone throw bacon grease and dirty socks down a well?

Determined to know what held her down, she brought her hands up under the thing on top of her till they touched her chin. Maybe she could move what was on her so she could breathe better, discover where she was, and figure out how to escape.

The object had a soft, spongy feel. Her fingers felt along until it came to what she thought was a flat side or a edge. She wiggled her fingers around the edge. Whatever held her down was about five or six inches thick not unlike the old bunk bed mattress Dad had thrown in the basement last year when they got her a new one.

Did her brothers carry the old mattress out to Grammie's well, throw it on top of her?

Whatever it was, the stink of pee made her tummy bubble and roll.

She brought her one hand close to her face and with both hands together shoved, hard.

The big smelly thing moved.

Joy made her giggly and stopped the quaking in her hands. Maybe she wouldn't die after all.

Whatever the thick cloth object was, there was something else one top of it and weighed it down. Still she muscled it off, so it fell back landing with a thud across her legs.

She sat up slowly feeling with her hands, so she wouldn't bump her head on the top of the coffin or the pirate's hold.

She didn't feel anything above her. Her tummy tingled with happiness.

Still, her tomb was so dark, it had a little blackish blue glow to it. Maybe her eyes were playing tricks on her. She couldn't see her hand, which was free now, as she held it up in front of her face. Maybe with the object that had weighed her down gone, her eyes would finally adjust. For a moment, she didn't want to see anything because it felt like thousands of black eyes were watching her.

Silly. If she was in a well, she'd be all alone.

Her mouth felt gritty, like she'd swallowed sand. She opened it to breathe in and out and tasted the heavy air, but something else, too. Kinda like the sandwich Mom had fixed the other day when she'd forgotten to cut the green spots off the crust.

Somewhere outside her dark prison, she could hear a clicking noise, like someone tapping two wooden sticks together. Or was it the scurrying of tiny toe-nailed feet?

Above the clicking noise there was a deep rumbling, like the hovering of a helicopter or a large truck followed by a swish-thump-thump-swish-swish.

What if she'd been kidnapped by terrorists who had locked her in an old cabin back in the shadowy woods? Maybe they were outside right now in their helicopter getting ready to fly her to their country and torture her to find out what secrets she knew.

She didn't want to be tortured to death. Her parents would never find her then.

Melanie clapped a damp, dirty hand over her mouth to keep from throwing up.

She moved her legs which had started to cramp. An object dug into the back of her leg. She fingered it, brought it up in front of her face. Nothing.

"No wait. It's a cup." She fingered the rounded piece of plastic with a design molded in the side. "It's not a cup, it's the top half of a Barrel of Monkeys. What's going on?"

Reaching under her, she began to dislodge several plastic monkeys from the half-opened barrel. Feeling around some more, she picked up what she thought were dirty rags and some other plastic toys.

Realization hit like the crack of a whip. She wasn't lying in a grave, or the bottom of a well, or on the floor of a cabin, or on the wooden planks of a ship's hold, but on icy, dank cement, like the basement floor of her family's home.

"Wait a doggone minute."

With care, she reached out again and felt around for the sharp object that had jabbed her side. She ran her hand over it, then she gripped it. It wasn't a sword like she had first thought, but the broken runner of a rocking chair. It felt like a piece of Mom's chair that her two oldest brothers had smashed when they'd played tackle football in the front room after Mom told them not to.

She tugged on the broken leg, thumped it against her palm.

Her blood started to pump hard and fast, her body tensed, coiled like a snake ready to strike. So it was her own mattress holding her down. She must have been given one of Grammie's sleeping pills to knock her out. Her hands curled into fists ready to pound faces and guts.

Her fear had changed to anger and now that anger changed into raging revenge as she shimmied out from under her old mattress and struggled up on her hands and knees. She felt for the door knob of what she now knew to be the junk closet at the back of her very own basement.

If her brothers had locked her in, she was going to make their lives a living hell beginning right now.

As the doorknob turned in her hand, she plotted her revenge.

2016 Memoir First Place Winner: Barbie's Dream House by Carol Malone

My family had lost it all. The last thing I saw as we drove away from the home of my birth was my cousin clutching my precious Barbie Dream House. "You're not a child anymore, Carol Anne. It's time to grow up," Dad said, when he ripped it from my arms and shoved it into my cousin's. I embarrassed myself with a violent shock, salty tears.

"Doesn't matter," I muttered. But it mattered – to me. That Dream House was more than a child's toy left behind that day in November 1965; it was my innocence, my childish imagination, and the source of my growing storytelling creativity.

In Northern Utah during the early sixties, the big chicken raising and processing companies from out-of-state like Zacky Farms, Tyson, and Foster Farms wanted to conquer and dominate Utah's chicken distribution. They didn't want the little local growers acting as competition. Dad's business was a pimple on their progress.

I overhead my parents speaking in low tones one evening at home as I was playing with my Dream House. What I heard made my tummy rumble like I'd eaten bad cheese.

"Helen," Dad said, "It doesn't matter that our small company, or our restaurants – the best chicken restaurants in the state – employ over a hundred people. These big conglomerates just don't give a damn." Our Chick-To-Go restaurant made broasted chicken with a thin vinegar/flour coating. I've never tasted anything better – or ever would again.

Mom twisted her hands in her lap and chewed her lower lip. "What will happen to our friends who have worked for us who have young families to support?" She smeared tears from her cheeks.

"They certainly don't care about us or what we've tried to build. They don't care about the years of struggle to make a business work, or the people who sacrificed so much to see us succeed, like your parents and mine." Dad paused, but sniffed as well. "This is a pure corporate takeover." His tone lightened, but there was pepper behind his words. "Just business, I was told."

"What will happen to us, Paul?" Mom frowned. "Will we be able to keep the house?"

Dad shook his head – looked like he didn't want to answer Mom, but he knew. "I don't know. I worry about C.A. She loves her life here, her friends, and school." He paused, looked up at the kitchen ceiling. "She'll have to deal with a lot of trauma in her life, so she'd better get prepared to face it."

His words hit me like I'd run into the fence in the school yard. It smarted. I had to grind my teeth together to keep from screaming, "It's your fault."

Dad leaned back in his chair, rubbed the wooden arms. "More markets in Montana have stopped ordering. Dale saw a Foster delivery truck in the neighborhood."

Mom gasped. "What about in Wyoming and Colorado?"

"Same thing." Dad's shoulders slumped. "No more orders. Cordell saw a big delivery truck in Southern Utah. Some of our old-timer customers are holding out, but we can't beat the deals these big companies offer. I'm afraid we're … finished."

It was two days later when my married brother, Dale came running into the office at Dad's processing plant in Logan. He was breathless and kept pounding his fists against his thighs, and then on Mom's office desk.

"What's happened?" Dad asked Dale.

"Chickens – are – dead." He managed to pant out.

"What?"

"Hundreds," Dale thundered. "Thousands – all dead."

"But we just got our new feed from…" Dad's face paled, then he pounded his fist against the office wall. "That S.O.B."

Mom walked into the office then. She'd been in the building checking on some paperwork. "What's going on?"

Calmer now, Dale repeated what he'd told Dad, that thousands of our new chicks were dead and some of the older chickens were dying as well.

From my spot in the corner where I had been playing with my portable Barbie Dream House, I watched their conversation. Mom's face turned a dark scarlet. I'd never seen that before. "You don't think that … he would be in league with…."

"That's what I'm thinking." Dad said a lot of bad words. He was a master-craftsman with foul language. My little ten-year-old ears stung, and I covered them with my hands.

Mom, Dad, and Dale stood in our tiny office looking ready to murder someone, and then scared, like they would tremble out of their clothing. I started to cry and that's the first time they noticed me.

"I'm so sorry, honey. I'd forgotten you were here." Mom walked stiffly toward me and wrapped me in her arms. "It's going to be okay. I promise."

But it wouldn't be okay.

Two hundred thousand baby chicks and larger roasting chickens lay dead and rotting in our coops. I still remember the stench during cleanup and burning – the end of a twenty-five-year business which began with a couple of laying hens in an old garage at the corner of our property.

Only one of my brothers, David, lived at home, but he was involved in his own teenage drama. Wanting to prove his manhood, he'd enlisted into the Marine Corps right after President Johnson decided to send U.S. combat forces into Vietnam. It made the impossible situation my parents were enduring, a walking, breathing nightmare.

In June, my brother shipped out for Marine Corps Recruit Depot in San Diego, much to my parents' consternation and tears. Secretly, I was overjoyed. He was a thorn in my side.

However, he left me alone to deal with the rapidly deteriorating emotional state of my parents as we faced a bleak, unknown future. What would we do for work? Could we keep our home? What would happen to our employees, our friends, our family if they could no longer work for us?

Of course, the feed broker said he was sorry and told Dad the food mixer might have chosen the wrong fat for the chicken feed – on advice from an expert. But no reparations or compensation for lost business were offered. How could we prove malice or murderous intent when the feed grower was best friends with the county sheriff and the mayor?

We were done for.

Turns out it wasn't just the business we lost, but the home my parents had built, the processing building Dad built himself – brick by brick, our personal cars, businesses cars and trucks, and our restaurants. Mom lurched around, jaw clenched, her lips pulled tight, and her eyes bloodshot. A muscle in Dad's jaw would twitch and then clench up tight and he'd pound his hands together in impotence. In our home, a dark gray mask fell over the peace and happiness we once enjoyed.

Two of my brothers and two of Dad's brothers lived and worked in Southern California. They begged, "Come down here. There's plenty of work." Yeah, $2.00 an hour, for sixteen-hour a day, and six days a week.

I had to grow up fast in big city California.

Like my Barbie Dream House that fateful day, my small-town girl innocence sadly faded from view.

Poetry: To Sea by Wendy Rosen

Wendy has been living in Camarillo for the past two years. She loves the ocean and the beach. She's originally from Cleveland, Ohio. She's a recent first-time grandma to her oldest daughter's beautiful baby girl. She enjoys writing different genres and has been writing since she was in elementary school. She feels creativity and the written word are very important, as well as accuracy!

The water displayed shades of blue as it swept toward the horizon. At the shoreline it glistened a brilliant teal, developing into a deep sapphire the further out it traveled. Aside from the sound of breaking waves and seagulls chatting, the air was quiet. The birds and water intermingled as I

watched them dive into and through the waves. The sun placed itself high above the sea and

sand, emitting its warmth on everything it touched. The cloudless sky outlined the scene as it

relaxed upon the ocean. I felt the sun's rays on my shoulders and the gentle heat of it upon my

bare toes. My spirit was soothed as I sat lost in a trance, staring at the seascape. I rested on a

faded yellow blanket that had seen many beach days. It held my tired body, but the ocean

embraced my soul

2014 Short Story Adult Honorable Mention: Presumption by Patricia Caloia

Writing was a hobby but became more after Pat retired. Writing gives a different perspective on life. Pat was born and raised in Southern California, but her career, computer software, took her to many locations in the US. She even spent five years in England. Now she's back in Ventura and plans to stay for a while.

Tom, a fraternity brother, and his wife, Ellen, were early arrivals to my second annual *Celebrate the Fall* party. The event is semi-formal and always the first of the holiday season. Guests receive hand-written invitations and dress for the occasion. I wore a new dinner jacket. Gourmet appetizers, professionally prepared, were on plates placed about the living room of my new, fifth-floor apartment. The bartender had been instructed to pour generously. His bar was placed to the left of the plate glass window, so guests could look down on the lake as they waited.

I greeted them at the front door. Tom shook my hand and placed a large bottle of champagne in the crook of my arm. Ellen leaned in to kiss my cheeks and then put a protective arm back to include an intruder. Her name was Rebecca. Somehow Rebecca knew Tom and had recently moved into their apartment building. She wore jeans, no make-up to cover the flotilla of freckles that floated over her face and had wild, brassy orange hair that stood out around her head like some bizarre curly halo.

Ellen said they'd had to drag her away from her unpacking. She grinned with a mouth too large and lips too full then shook my hand with no hint of apology for her dress. Most women would be self-conscious about wearing jeans to a cocktail party. Rebecca walked with a self-assurance that startled me though I was quick to hide it, not wanting to appear inhospitable. I smiled, ushered them in and turned to the next guests.

I knew why they'd brought her. She was part of a continuing retinue of eligible young women they presented in an effort to enlist me in the ranks of blissful-coupledom. I was not unwilling, but there were two mitigating factors. While eligible women showed interest when I was introduced as a doctor, they retreated when I explained that my specialty was OB-GYN. Women loved that about me when they wanted a doctor, but not when they wanted romance. I never knew if they feared what I might see, or that I was seeing other women.

The second factor was private. I shared with no one that previously, Tom and Ellen had introduced me to The One—Sandra. From the moment I met her, no other woman could compare. She filled my heart, my head, my dreams but, sadly, not my arms.

Sandra was beautiful with blond hair flowing past her shoulders, large, wistful eyes and translucent fair skin. Her stature was petite and delicate; she moved with the grace of a dancer. There was a vulnerability about her that brought out my protective instincts but though we were attracted our timing had been off. We dated briefly but I'd known immediately I wanted a commitment. Before I could tell her, she'd met someone else. In the time since, they hadn't married so I'd continued to hope. Far too late, we found he was abusive. His latest violence had resulted in jail time.

Sandra arrived alone. I took her hands in mine and leaned in for a quick peck on the cheek. I wanted to pull her to me and wrap her into a protective bear-hug but she was still recovering from the vicious attack. I didn't think she'd want a man getting too close for a while. I tried to be sensitive to her situation. That she even came to the party surprised me. Her left eye still showed traces of purplish bruising and her face was puffy, but cosmetics and her natural beauty masked a lot. She smiled a wan smile and moved off, cautiously, to join the others. My heart hurt that she had to endure this. Our crowd knew of the incident. I felt sure they would treat her appearance with discretion.

Arrivals dwindled then stopped. I lived my profession, so it was not a surprise that most of my friends and guests were work associates—other doctors, some of the hospital nursing staff and a couple from administration. Ellen had found Sandra in the insurance department.

I made the rounds—a word here, another there—trying not to get so drawn into a conversation that I abandoned the other guests. A quick survey of the hors d'oeuvre plates showed refills were needed. In the kitchen I opened the refrigerator and tugged out one of the large food trays. Rebecca appeared at my side carrying the partially empty appetizer plates.

"I was going to..." I began.

"...refill them. I figured," she responded, replenishing from the tray.

It is what I had planned, yet her taking it over annoyed me. Struggling to figure out why, I could only think it was because she acted as though it were her kitchen—not even asking if I wanted help. Presumptuous, I labeled her. Immediately I felt chagrined. How petty of me. She only meant to help.

Holding the refreshed plates, she turned back to the living room and then paused, her head cocked quizzically. "This isn't a seasonal party – no pumpkins, no colored leaves."

"Celebrate the Fall." It's what I'd titled it last year. It had never been questioned.

"But not autumn. You mean a different kind of fall. You commemorate this, yet it's a dark celebration." Now, her small, intense hazel eyes searched mine, waiting.

How dare she? I was a very private person. Jovial and outgoing, yes, but even my best friends wouldn't tread so carelessly. They knew about my time with Sandra. They'd watched the relationship ignite, combust and shrivel to ash in rapid succession. They assumed I'd swept away the debris and moved on, but a night didn't go by that her beauty didn't dance before my eyes as I tried to sleep.

Perhaps my intensity had frightened her, so I practiced patience and distance. When I'd see her in a hospital corridor I'd give a half-smile, a nod—not even a wave. I never quickened my pace. I hoped for the day that she waited until I caught up to her. It was horrible that she'd been through this attack, but now she would see the difference between him and me. She'd realize that she could count on me, that I was one of the good guys. Soon, when she fully recovered, we'd start over. Until then, I remembered the day I met her and celebrated falling in love with her. No one had ever made the connection, not until this interloper, in under an hour, had reached out to probe somewhere else she hadn't been invited. How did she even know? I couldn't answer her unasked question. With what I hoped was an enigmatic half-smile, I shrugged.

There was concern in her voice as she implored me, "Don't carry the burden. Set it down and leave your hands free to reach out." When I still did not respond, she shook her brassy curls resignedly and exited to the party and the delivery of snacks.

I stood in the kitchen breathing heavily for a few seconds then refreshed my drink, reapplied my smile and went out to my guests.

Rebecca was speaking to Sandra. Across the room I lip-read her words. "Tell me what happened."

Sandra started to weep. Rebecca helped her into a chair and handed her a tissue. Again, this woman was sticking her nose where it wasn't supposed to go. In mere moments she'd alienated me and brought Sandra to tears. But Sandra didn't look unhappy. She mopped her eyes then their heads were bent together in deep conversation. The first smile I'd seen from Sandra all night lit her face.

She stood and embraced Rebecca then came to tell me. "Jerry, thank you so much. Sorry to rush off, but this is my first time out and I'm ready to be home." She put her hands on my arms, so I couldn't raise them and leaned in to kiss my cheek. Waving her phone, she started for the door. "Taxi's waiting."

As she left, Rebecca came to my side. I glared at her and said, "Sandra was hurt and…"

"…she's still very fragile but she mustn't think of herself as a victim."

"She needs…"

"Counseling. Yes, I recommended it."

***

Several weeks later a patient of mine, Mrs. Grove, miscarried while I was handling a delivery. The new baby boy had an easy arrival, healthy lungs and radiant parents. I cleaned up and rushed to the unfortunate woman. Rebecca was sitting on the patient's bed holding her hand and stroking her hair as the childless mother wept. I couldn't understand what Rebecca was doing there. She slid down from the bed when she saw me and turned to the woman. "Your doctor is here. I'll leave you." My patient was reluctant. "Please, can you stay with me?"

"I'll come back later." With a toss of her head, meant only for me, she gestured to the hallway. "Doctor, may I speak to you?"

I hesitated. Mrs. Grove needed me, and she'd waited too long already. Not wanting to appear churlish, I stepped into the hallway.

"She's frightened that she did something that caused the miscarriage or that she'll never be able to—"

"…carry a child. She's also afraid to ask me about it in case any of it is true." I sighed. I'd been right–presumptuous. *Now, she's trying to tell me my job.*

Later, after comforting Mrs. Grove, answering all the questions – asked and unasked – and prescribing something to calm her, I went to the cafeteria for coffee. A woman slept with her head on her arms at one of the tables. The orange hair was unmistakable. Once more I reminded myself that she'd only been trying to help. I set the mug down at the table. Rebecca peered up at me and slowly raised her head until she was finally sitting upright.

"I didn't mean to be rude," I offered. "Every woman who has ever lost a child wonders exactly those things…'

"…and you wouldn't be much of an obstetrician if you didn't know that."

She was silent, but I knew she hadn't finished. I waited.

"I miscarried at five weeks. Not really a child but I already thought of her as my baby."

"I'm so sorry. Do you know why?"

"A traffic accident. The seat-belt." She didn't look at me as she continued. "My husband was angry with me. He thought I should have been more careful. He couldn't forgive me, and he left. I lost a..."

"... child and a husband. That's rough – just when you needed him most."

"If our relationship couldn't pass its first test, I'm better off without him." She looked me in the eye and gave me a lopsided smile. "Guess I should get back to Mrs. Grove."

"She was sleeping when I left."

***

There's a Starbucks I frequent. It's near my apartment but also near the University. Sometimes it's hard to find a place to sit with students and laptops on every surface. One computer user stood out from the others – earphones, watching the screen. She didn't see me until I tapped her shoulder. She gestured to the seat opposite and, adjusting the screen so I could see, she turned up the volume and removed the earphones. The President was speaking.

Afterward we discussed or rather, vehemently voiced our opinions – at some points trying to out-shout each other within the confines of a busy establishment. I try not to offend others with my political views. Fortunately, Rebecca shared them, but her commentary showed more depth of understanding than I had considered. I was eager to research what she'd told me. At a lull I picked up her textbook–*Family Counseling*. "Is this your major?"

"I have my degree. I've practiced. There's some coursework needed for licensing in this state." She closed the laptop, gathered the books, smiled and said, "Time for my class."

It finally made sense why she'd reached Sandra and Mrs. Grove. I watched her walk away. Why didn't someone tell her how to dress or do her hair?

***

Months later, even before spring had begun to tease, Tom and Ellen had friends over for dinner. Mostly couples but some singles. My buddy Jack attended. He was the finest pediatric surgeon I'd ever seen. I was in the observation gallery one afternoon to see him work. The tiny surgery was delicate as a butterfly. When he once confided to me that he would love to dance but was a total klutz on the floor, all I could wonder was that he worried about his feet when his fingers danced with magic.

Sandra was there. Her bruises were gone, and she smiled more confidently. Maybe it was time to blow on the embers. I gazed at Sandra. She gazed at Jack.

Rebecca had changed as well. Her hair had been tamed to soft curls and the orange hue to auburn. Makeup evened the tone across her cheeks. She wore long sleeves but for a moment I envisioned the freckles rampant on her shoulders and neck and down her back. I looked quickly back at her eyes. She too gazed at Jack.

Jack was tall and lean, 6'3" or 4" with finely chiseled features and soot black hair. A few sprigs of grey matured his appearance and gave it the

55

gravity his skill demanded. By contrast, mine was a countenance mothers trusted. My features were soft with, what I thought, a winsome quality. "Baby-faced" my classmates had called me. Unmanageable, fine, light-brown hair, more often than not, fell across my forehead and had to be constantly brushed back from my eyes. It was no wonder the women preferred to look at Jack.

At the end of the evening, after my goodbyes to Ellen and Tom, Sandra caught me. "I've been going to counseling sessions at the university. I often stop for coffee at the Starbucks around the corner from your apartment. Perhaps I'll see you there."

"Perfect. I go there often. Text me the next time you're there."

She blushed as she nodded. We were both on a journey to reclaim ourselves. I wouldn't move too fast this time. A last glance around the room revealed Jack, his head bent in deep conversation with Rebecca. There was something disquieting about the scene – the strange sense that I'd forgotten something important. Jack could attract any woman he set eyes upon – a trait he seemed never to notice. Why would he take such interest in the ugly duckling? And she? Jack was apolitical. His work took all his focus. Wouldn't she find that limiting?

Sandra and I met on several afternoons. The counseling dealt with Sandra's attack. She was always raw when we met. We didn't talk about the sessions, instead tried to find common ground. Clearly, I was helping her transition back to normalcy, so I let her set the pace. I watched as Sandra strengthened toward the woman I'd known before. I was glad to see it, but sad that the spark never flamed.

Outside, buds were forming, and Sol was beginning to show us his warmer side. I decided to host another cocktail party, perhaps, to force the bloom. I envisioned the room with flowers for decoration and the women in pastel dresses. I picked the date, made the arrangements and wrote out the invitations: Please join me to Celebrate Spring.

You know how April can be, sun and flowers one-minute pouring rain the next. It was only two blocks to the post office. I wrapped the invitations in a plastic bag tight against my body as I fought with the wind trying to rip the umbrella from my hand. No one could recognize me in my raincoat and hat, bent nearly double by the wind. Ahead of me on the street a couple ran toward me, hand in hand, wet and laughing. They hurried inside a building. The couple was Jack and Rebecca; the building, a dance studio.

Celebrate Spring was a perfect party. This time I anticipated Rebecca helping in the kitchen. Perhaps it wasn't presumption; perhaps it was anticipating need. Jack interrupted my music to play something he'd brought. Holding a hand out to Rebecca she tangoed into his arms and the two of them took over the room. They moved flawlessly. He dipped her, spun her; she side-stepped, enticed him to follow – it was a grand show. At its completion, holding hands, Jack bowed low, Rebecca curtsied almost to the floor while the crowd roared and applauded.

The party continued for hours. I don't remember it. I kept seeing the way Jack and

Rebecca moved together–sometimes one led, sometimes the other–responding to the same music. I felt like weeping for a loss I still didn't understand. I looked for Sandra. She sat with Jack. I didn't care. Rebecca was headed to the kitchen with a tray of empty glasses.

I caught up with her there. "You, two..." I began.

"...are no longer together. That was our swan dance." She chuckled at her own joke.

"Why? You moved so perfectly together." I shook my head in disbelief.

"Sometimes you make a connection with someone – so close that..."

"...you know what they are thinking." I answered. "You can finish..."

"...each other's sentences." She replied. "Jack and I don't have that." She laughed.

I looked down. My hand was wrapped tightly around hers and she was smiling the most beautiful smile in the world. Her full, soft lips were everything I'd imagined.

2014 Short Story Adult Honorable Mention: Under the Bed by Douglas Peyton

Douglas has been an active musician for most of his life, touring the world, performing and entertaining, but recently he has had the desire to express his writing in more than a few lines of lyrics. "Under the Bed" represents a personal aspiration to see his prose published, rather than poetry, and much like his protagonist, it also contains his desire to do what he's afraid of. Normally a fan of dark fantasy and horror, the thought of writing something that was appropriate for younger audiences appealed to him, mainly because it challenged him to search for a new voice with which to tell a story.

Sometimes Dad gets mad. When it's late, and we're playing around and making too much noise, he can get really mad. I always hide under the bed when I hear his feet pounding on the hardwood as he stomps down the hall. When he comes in he usually yells about having to wake up early, or about not getting respect for how hard he works for the family. I'm always scared that he might yell at me. I have a problem with panting when I'm nervous, so I worry he might hear me breathing and find me hiding under the bed. I try to calm myself down by concentrating on his feet as they stomp from one end of the room to the other. He always marches in a perfect line and takes exactly ten steps each way.

Last night, well, he got really mad. I mean really, really mad. I've never seen him like that before, and I don't think I'll see him like that again.

In fact, I don't think I'll ever see Dad again at all.

It all started because of the sleepover.

I know Dad didn't want to host the sleepover that night. I could hear him through the wall, talking to Mom about it earlier that week. He kept talking about having to work "overtime". I'm not sure what that is, but he has to do it a lot. He teaches other soldiers how to use cranes. I'm not sure what they are either, but Mom says they're really dangerous. I once heard Johnny, the neighbor boy, say that they are giant metal monsters that devour the earth. They seem pretty amazing to me. I'd love to see one someday.

Well, that night Dad kept talking about how he didn't want to have a bunch of boys over at the house rough-housing and making a racket all night. He said he'd have to be up before sunrise on Saturday. I know that's true because I always hear him leaving early on those mornings. It's the only time he ever walks quietly.

Mom kept pleading with him. She said, "It'll be good for the boys to have some friends over. They've been begging me to have a sleepover and I just can't keep saying no. This will be a chance for them to make some new friends."

"What about that Johnny kid?" he asked.

"Fine, that's one. If you want to count the dog, that's two."

"Very funny. And what's wrong with the dog? At least he doesn't wake me up in the middle of the night like the boys do. If we have a bunch of them over, and they keep me up all night yelling and screaming—"

"Honey please, even if they do, can you please not storm in there and embarrass them? For me? This would really mean a lot." Mom's voice always drained the fight out him.

"Fine."

That was his way of saying, yes.

***

Friday came quick. Excitement is like a time machine. When the guests arrived after school, the air was electric. There was shouting and stomping and pounding throughout the house. Although Mom had all kinds of activities planned for the night, I think her first plan simply consisted of letting the boys run around like crazy for a while, burning off some after-school fuel. I heard her take a seat in her creaky reading chair as she watched them run circles around her. Even though it was the first sleepover I'd ever experienced, there definitely seemed to be something magical about it. I think it has something to do with the idea that you don't have to go home. It's almost as if the fun never has to end.

After a few minor scrapes and falls, Mom gathered the boys in the kitchen. She said she had a special surprise. She requested a drum roll, so they started beating their hands against the kitchen counter and cabinet doors. It went on for quite a while, slowly growing into a deafening thunder. I could barely hear Mom shouting over the thrums and bangs.

"Okay! Okay!" she said. "What a great drum roll. Now, do you want to know what it was for?"

More bangs and shouts.

"Okay, here they are!"

"Monster Mouths!" The boys all screamed in unison.

I immediately began to drool. I knew exactly what a Monster Mouth was. It consisted of two apple slices, both lined with peanut butter, pressed together to simulate a human mouth. Instead of teeth, however, there were tiny white marshmallows pressed into the peanut butter, in neat little rows. Late one night, after everyone had gone bed, I'd found a Monster Mouth forgotten on the floor of the bedroom. I licked the hardwood clean that night, it was the best treat I'd ever had.

Though the next few minutes were quiet, silence is short-lived in the company of boys. Within seconds of devouring the last Monster Mouth, the house once again erupted in bangs, crashes, and shouts. Mom's activities were no match for a room full of boys brimming with sugar, so she retired to her reading chair again, smiling and enjoying the beauty of her disaster. It wasn't until the boys magically transformed Dad's recliner into a catapult that she finally got up and redirected their energy.

I once heard Mom say that getting a group of boys to move in one direction was like herding cats. I always loved that image, mainly because I don't really like cats. They hiss at me, make me sneeze, and they act like they're better than everyone.

As I pondered the image of myself herding around all the neighborhood cats, I heard the front door creak open.

"What is going on in here?" Dad exclaimed. His voice could carry through the entire house when he wanted it to. "Why are these troops out of order? Who's in command here?"

"Honey—" Mom said.

"That's it, troops! Time for drills! Muster in the yard!" he barked. His final command hung in the air, suspended by the tension and silence of the living room.

Then he suddenly broke into a booming laugh.

The roar of Dad's laughter sent out a wave of relief. The tension dissolved as soon everyone realized he was joking, and the whole room flooded with laughter.

"Single file now! One, two, three, four, one, two, three four."

After everyone marched out of the house, it was quiet for a good while.

***

When they returned, Dad was the first one through the front door. He brought with him the line of little marching soldiers, ready for battle with the general himself. Dad was in good spirits as he gave various commands to the tiny troops, and the chants of "Yes, sir!" could be heard echoing through the house. It gave me great pleasure to hear the lightness in his voice, and I heard Mom say, "Thank you" with more love in her voice than I'd ever heard.

I felt my tail wag happily.

I didn't know everything was about to fall apart.

When the boys finished drills, it was time for pizza and video games, until Mom broke out the board game box and pulled the plug on them. She spoke loudly over the sound of their protests, telling them about the sleepovers she'd had with her friends growing up. She told them that since there were no video games, they would stay up all night playing board games instead. In fact, she said, the games in the box were the very same ones she'd owned since she was a little girl.

Mom said her favorite game was called *Adventureland*. She explained that it was based on a famous place in the magical land of Disney. I've never been there, but she always told us stories about it at bedtime. She said Main Street was paved with dreams, and there were these great big happy creatures that loved to play and take pictures with little boys and girls. I always thought they sounded a lot like me, especially Pluto. He was my favorite, and I secretly dreamed about meeting him.

By the time the game had ended it was getting pretty late, so it was up to Mom to start herding the cats again. Apparently, it's not as hard when the cats are drowsy. I heard the soft scraping of socks on the hardwood as the little troops assembled in the hall. Dad was in The Den, so no one dared disturb him. After a few minutes of splashing around in the bathroom, Mom shuffled them into the bedroom and wished everyone a goodnight. Then she turned off the light.

There were always a few minutes of silence after the light turned off, mainly because of the Closet Creature. That's what the boys called him, anyway. He didn't actually live inside the closet, but when it was really late, you could sometimes see him in the reflection of the mirrored closet door. The boys say he has red glowing eyes, leathery skin that looks like hardened tar, and arms as thick and strong as tree trunks. They say that his teeth aren't like the Monster Mouth marshmallows. They're more like stone, long and sharpened at the tips, just like his claws. I've also heard them say that he likes to eat kids or steal them away from their parents and crush up their bones for magic. The thought of him was even scarier than Dad, and although I wasn't sure if he would ever want to come after me, I somehow knew that hiding under the bed wouldn't be good enough if he ever did.

Sometimes, when I can't sleep, I stare at the mirror door and swear I can see his glowing red eyes looking right back into mine.

During a sleepover though, the dark just isn't as scary. Within minutes the boys were jumping from one bed to the other and parading and marching back and forth across the room.

Then it hit me. They were making fun of Dad.

They were imitating the way they would take ten steps, then spin on a heel, take ten more. It seemed like so much fun, I just couldn't help myself. I had to join in.

Having seen Dad's feet from beneath the bed so many times, I knew exactly how he marched. Although it was nearly pitch dark in the room and I knew they couldn't see me, I felt like they were all laughing just for me. I was certain that my imitation was perfect. As I marched back and forth, all I could hear were Dad's barks about "Respect!" in my head. I howled with laughter. I was so caught up in the fun that I didn't hear his heavy steps pounding down the hall.

The moment I saw his two feet silhouetted outside the door, pure instinct took over. I dove under the bed. I had barely made it under when I heard the door burst open and the room filled with light. All of the boys looked like they were frozen.

"What is going on in here?" His voice was like thunder. It shook the room. This wasn't a joke. The fun was over. I'm not sure why, but the thought of that brought a strange feeling over me, a feeling like none I had ever experienced before.

It was anger.

I honestly didn't know what anger was supposed to feel like. I'd never gotten past fear before, but for some reason that night, fear lost its grip. I felt my lips pull back away from my teeth, and I started to growl.

We'd been having such a good time, why did it have to stop because he didn't want to have fun? He never did. All I ever heard from him was "no," "never," "no." Mom talked endlessly about magical places like the land of Disney, but all he ever talked about was work, responsibility, and somewhere called "The Base." That place sounded dull and grey, full of other humans who had lost their fun out at sea. I'd had enough. I wanted to keep having fun.

I crawled out from under the bed.

At first everyone was silent. The boys remained frozen. They didn't even breathe. Everyone just stared at me. I was surprised because Dad had gone silent, too. No commands, no screaming. He just looked up at me, terrified.

I figured it was because I'd never stood up to him before, but as I was standing there I suddenly asked myself why I never did.

Dad was actually very small, much smaller than me.

Then it struck me. I'd never stood up in the room with the lights on before, I only came out after dark. I didn't realize that my head almost touched the ceiling when I stood up straight.

Since nobody was saying anything, I figured I'd just tell Dad that we wanted to keep having fun. So what if we were teasing him? We were just having a good time.

When I tried explaining that though, he didn't seem to understand. He just cringed. It was my first time being angry, so I didn't really know how to control my voice. I must have been shouting. Then, when I repeated myself, everyone just started screaming. The boys jumped up on the bed, and Dad ran out of the room.

I thought the party was back on. I thought I'd won.

I was so excited that I jumped on the bed with the rest of them. I'd never done it before, but it didn't seem very hard. I was wrong. As soon as I jumped on the bed, it splintered in half.

Then the boys started screaming again. At first, I thought it was because they were enjoying my little show, but their screams seemed all wrong. They sounded scared. I thought maybe I scared them when I broke the bed, so I tried to apologize. I told them that I had just gotten excited. I held up my hands as I said sorry, but they started screaming even louder when they saw the giant retractable claws come out of my fingertips. They're about nine inches long, razor sharp. They sometimes come out when I get nervous, and I was really nervous.

I tried smiling, but when they saw my long, sharply pointed teeth they started crying and holding each other. I guess my teeth look a lot different than marshmallows.

That was when Dad and Rocky came rushing back into the room. Rocky is the family dog, and Dad's best friend. He usually sleeps in Dad's room, but sometimes he comes in the boys' bedroom and I tease him from under the bed. He barks and barks, wagging his tail. I know that means he likes me, because I wag my tail when I'm happy too. However, when Rocky saw me standing there, he tucked his tail between his legs and whined.

Dad yelled at him to go get me, but Rocky didn't move, so Dad stepped further into the bedroom. He lifted up a little black toy with both his hands and pointed it at me. I'd seen one like it under the bed once. The boys sometimes pointed them at each other and ran around the house yelling, "I got you! I got you!"

As Dad was slowly walking toward me, Mom stepped in the bedroom doorway. She froze. I assumed it was because she was as nervous as I was. I'd wanted to meet her for so long, I didn't know what to say either. I decided to wave at her with one of my black, leathery hands. She let out a terrible shriek. Then Dad saw my claws, and the toy in his hand exploded.

That's when I felt something bite me in the chest.

I grabbed myself where I felt the pain, and when I pulled my hand away there was a shiny little piece of metal resting in my palm. It felt heavy for how small it was. I dropped it on the hardwood and it made a loud *clunk* as it bounced. When I looked up at Dad, his jaw dropped. We stared at each other in silence for a moment. Then his eyebrows narrowed, and he bared his teeth at me.

He took another step towards me and the toy in his hands exploded again, and again. It was the loudest sound I have ever heard. I held myself in disbelief as I felt each bite. I didn't understand why he was trying to hurt me, why he was so mad. I stumbled backwards and crashed into the closet mirror. It shattered all over the floor. I looked down at the broken pieces of mirror, horrified by the amount of trouble I had gotten myself into, but what I saw in that fragmented reflection scared me even more.

I saw two flaming red eyes staring straight back at me.

They were my eyes.

I was so confused by the sight that I leapt across the room, straight out of the bedroom window. It was closed, so I crashed through it with an eruption of glass. My skin is really thick though, so it didn't cut me.

I hit the ground on all fours, stood up, and looked back up to the window on the second floor, to the place I'd been living for years. Dad was perfectly framed in the window, looking back at me. He wasn't screaming, he wasn't yelling. We just stared at one another in silence for a while. Faintly, I could hear Mom sobbing and Rocky barking from inside the bedroom.

It wasn't until the neighbors screamed that I snapped back to reality.

I was so embarrassed that I just started running.

I ran as fast as I could. I ran as far as I could. At first I was overwhelmed by fear and remorse, but the further I ran the better I started to feel. It had been so long since I'd gone outside I'd forgotten what it was like to be out in the cold night air. I could feel my muscles burn with life as I ran faster and faster. My claws dug into the cement with ease, pushing me further and further ahead as I raced away from home. I'd forgotten how strong I was. I'd forgotten how fast I was too. After spending so many years afraid of Dad, hiding under that bed, I had forgotten how much I loved the moonlit sky and feeling of wind in my face.

I had forgotten who I was.

***

I don't feel afraid anymore. I've discovered an entirely new world, full of wonder and awe. I spent so long living in fear of someone I'd never even seen, I'd let my world shrink down to the space beneath a child's bed. I know I can't go back now, and I wouldn't want to even if I could.

I scared a few neighbors on my way down the street that night, but now that I'm out I can stay up all night jumping from roof to roof, chasing the stars. I have also officially decided where I'd like to go next. I'm going to start off by meeting a crane monster, and then it's off to visit the magical land of Disney.

I'm finally going to walk down Main Street and meet Pluto.

2015 Poetry First Place 12 & Under Winner: Finally a Big Sister by Natalie Stegner

Natalie is twelve-years-old and lives in Camarillo. Her favorite things to do are play with her baby sister, dance, read, and write. She loves to make other people happy and has a very big heart. If she could be anywhere in the world, she would choose Disneyland every day.

Finally a Big Sister
My sister's name is Scarlett
and she is only half a year
Though she sometimes cries a lot,
She is still such a dear
Her favorite things to eat are carrots, peas, and more
So it doesn't make her happy when she spits them on the floor
She squeals and screams in delight Every morning, day, and night
I have been a little sister the past nine years of my life
And that has been pretty okay
Even dealing with my brother's strife
But being a big sister is by far the best prize
Every time I look into those big blue sparkling eyes.

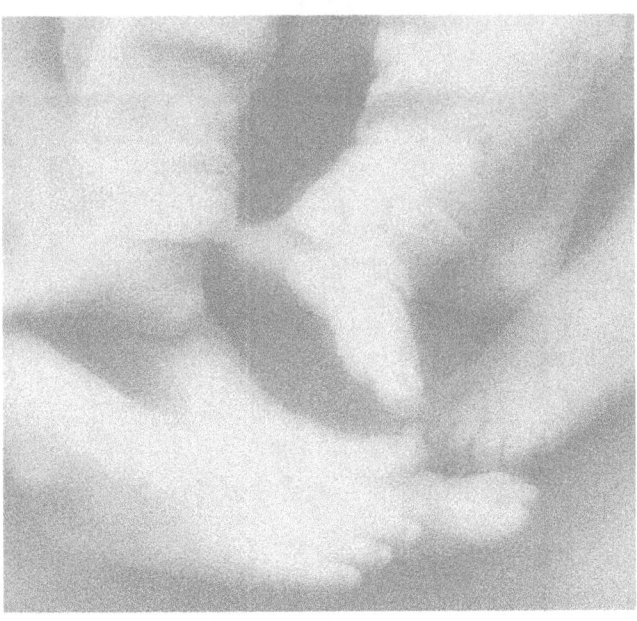

2015 Poetry First Place Youth 13-17 Winner: I Am a Painting by Raya Driggers

Rayna is thirteen years old and has written poetry and short stories for about six years now, not only about what interests her, but about what is in her heart and what is important. She's always been pulled to write about slavery and the unfairness of inequality. That's not to say that she doesn't write about other things as well. She writes for herself in hopes that others will enjoy it too.

I Am a Painting
I am a painting that wants to say
I am a beautiful girl with light and dark curly brown hair
I am a painting that wants to say
I have light milk chocolate skin that always absorbs intense heat
I am a painting that wants to say I know
what it is like to be put down or bullied by people that were your friends
I am a painting that wants to say I feel
great when I sing and I am passionate about it too
I am a painting that wants to say I can
do anything that I put my mind to
I am a painting that wants to say I might
become a famous singer and go on a world tour
I am a painting that wants to say I'm lucky
that one side of my family is black and the other is white
I am a painting that wants to say
look, stare, admire, relate, cry, smile, and say
that is one beautiful painting.

2015 Poetry First Place Adult Winner: Willa's Song: Coyote by Glenna Luschei

Glenna was named the Poet Laureate for San Luis Obispo City and County in 2000, has taught poetry workshops throughout California and at the University of Nebraska. She has been active in small press for over 50 years as a poet/publisher with her own Solo Press. She was the recipient of the DH Lawrence Ranch Fellowship. Her book The Sky Is Shooting Blue Arrows *was published by the University of New Mexico Press. Glenna has published Solo Press magazines for fifty years. Luschei is the author of many chapbooks, special editions and trade books. In 2016, she released* Singing and Dying, *published by Penciled In. Three of her artist books have received prizes from the Rounce & Coffin Best Western books from Occidental College. Recently, she was named a "Literary Treasure of the Mid-Coast" by the Ventura County Arts Council. She has received a National Endowment of the Arts Fellowship and many individual California Arts Council grants. She was recently inducted to the Cal Tech Half-Century Club.*

Willa Cather migrated to the prairie
with her parents when she was 10.

In a covered wagon, my family took me,
from the Blue Ridge,
from Shenandoah to Nebraska.
I was ten.

We left behind the white pine
and the hickory. I found the birch
and cottonwood. I found the coyote,
heard him howl all night and dreamt of him,
his eye a glint
of red.

We hoisted the chicken crate onto our bed.
I stayed awake until the rooster crowed. Safe!
But he followed our wagon and at night circled the team.
Days I walked the trail to pick the blue flax named for Meriwether
Lewis, who crossed before us.

In Nebraska,
I found the plains and yes, the coyote.
I picked the scarlet poppy,
the back to school flower.
Like the farmers' children, I wore overalls.
School days mother said to wear a skirt.
Father said pants were safer on the prairie.
Friends showed me the cactus and mushroom that grew in the ravine.
They called it "coyote lair."
Once Coyote crossed our path.
He was grand but father shot him.
Still I dream of him at night, the glint.

2018 Poetry Adult Honorable Mention: WPA Dad by Glenna Luschei

My teacher asked what our fathers did. When children said, "WPA,"
I asked my dad, "What's the WPA?"
To explain, he took me to our post office. A man on a step ladder was painting tunnels of wheat on the wall and farmers with fat legs. The man climbed down and handed me a paint brush.

"The wheat needs a little more ochre," he said. I had never heard "ochre" before.
It was the most beautiful word for the most beautiful golden color. That's what I wanted to be, an artist for the WPA.
I fell in love with the smell of paint,

and one day, with the murals of Coit Tower in San Francisco.
Cowboys and orange pickers painted on walls meant escape from poverty, dad said.
It meant soup for the first grade.
I paid a quarter for soup and a nickel to see Roy Rogers at the Saturday picture show.

A friend gave us a loaf of bread she cooked
with bacon grease. My mother's bread was the best.
We shared it with men who came looking for work.
Baked in coffee cans, the loaves looked like a farm of toadstools cooling on the windowsill.

That's what I loved about the Depression. We all helped each other. One day a classmate came into my brother's law office.
"Your father bought me my first suit of clothes. He took me off the street. I wanted to thank you."

"We could not have lived through that winter without your father. He sent us a truckload of coal."

What I loved most about the WPA was my dad.

2015 Poetry Adult Second Place Winner: A Portrait in Raspberry by Laura Dixon

Laura is a Sacramento native who studied English Education at CSU, Chico. After semesters of encouraging her students to enter writing contests, she felt compelled to do the same. Laura now lives in Ventura with her husband, Cody, and her infant son, Theo.

In her dry palm is a raspberry, plump and purple.
She offers it to me, extending her weathered hand:
A taste from her time.
Her smile shines through her eyes-
glacier melt grey, satiny and deep.
As her face becomes wreathed in wrinkles,
like streambeds in the desert,
I listen to her laugh, the warm bubble of a brass kettle.

She stoops, dropping each fruit into bright green baskets.
Hunched over, she clasps her hands to the pinch of her back,
more annoyed with age than plagued by pain.
She tells me she's a "silly old lady,"
But her fingers are as nimble as copper wire,
her mind as sharp as glass,
and her words concrete:

"Never forget
you are just as good as the other guy,
even if your socks don't match."
Under the shade of evergreens,
I watched her pick raspberries off a summertime vine.

2015 Poetry Adult Third Place Winner: Freeze-Up by Bruce Reynolds

Bruce's love of poetry descends from family, family friends, and teachers, in particular, George Bennett. Retired from a career as a college teacher, he now winters with his wife, daughter, son-in-law, and two inspirational granddaughters in Potomac, Maryland. He defines summer expansively and enjoys every drop of it living in a lakeside Wisconsin farmhouse, on land settled by his grandfather's grandparents.

Their marriage was as lovely as a lake
merged with the sky. Playfully, he'd
ripple up a cats' paw on her skin, then
storm up white-cap waves, roll her from
shore to shore, the circling shores their bed.
They made a sweet girl-child the same way
sunsets pour pink into water: a single
huge rose-glow conjured her up.

Then serpent-words invaded paradise:
Why can't you tell me what you're feeling?
And You're always so demanding. As if water
could learn to be air, or air
turn into water. He'd taken her to be
the wind, like him; she'd looked up
to her lover, embracing the sky, and seen
a lake. Talk slowed, chilled, froze.

Lake ice, as it thickens, groans: a low lament,
the sound skittering from shore to shore, like
scavenging coyotes half-seen amid brush,
or a wave barely breaking the lake's plane.

Then the ice splits – the sharp crack hanging like
a gunshot in the thin, dry January air.

2015 Poetry Adult Honorable Mention: Water: Written on a Balcony in Rome by Diane Mautner

Diane is author of Draw Me a Story *and* Word Flips: Spanish. *She has authored two workbooks for the Cartoon Network. Diane also wrote curriculum for the Los Angeles Unified School District and Disney English Language Learning Schools in Shanghai, China. She enjoys writing poetry and sharing poems with other writers.*

At dawn on a balcony in Rome,
I sit in the stillness of early morning,
Listening to the faint sounds of rippling water,
That soon dissipate into a trickle, as tears.

Hannah crying for her seven sons,
Milton crying with sightless eyes in his prison cell,
Anne, in hiding, crying for the miseries of the world.

And yet, Hannah kept the faith,
Milton wrote his finest poetry,
And Anne affirmed her belief in humanity.

And I, on my balcony in Rome,
Hear the soft sighs of the river,
Feel drops like tears from the sky.
I welcome the tears.
I rejoice in the rain.

2015 Poetry Adult Honorable Mention: A Strand of Scarlet Yarn by Diane Caskey

Diana Caskey has been writing and painting since childhood. Poetry helps her process what goes on in her life. Unfortunately, many of her earliest poems have been lost during moves, bad moods and cleaning sprees. In addition to her family she is passionate about art and poetry.

Imagine the terror
of the second bird,
captured with his brother.

The first bird is torn apart,
flesh and feathers over a vessel of water.
The second watching with his tiny bird eye
as brother bird's blood

flows into a vessel
of clear clean water.

His bird beak nose
smelling the sharp
iron of blood
into which
he finds himself thrust.

Along with sweet
cedar wood,
fragrant hyssop

and strangely enough
a strand of scarlet yarn.

And just when death
soils and shakes
his feathered skin
he is set free, free
to fly from
shared death,

free from disease
free from man's sin.

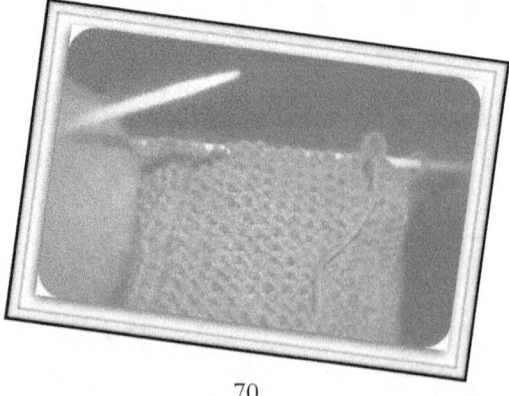

2015 Poetry Adult Honorable Mention: Octopus Machina by Michael Seals

Michael is a sailor in the United States Navy from Carrollton, Georgia. He lives with his wife, Jesse, in Camarillo, California. Currently a student at Coastline Community college, in his free time he also enjoys hiking, reading, or playing his guitar.

Archaic stars are grains of sand
He drifts throughout the abyss
Sifting debris with all eight limbs
Octopus Machina

Brightly lit are the scattered motes
He, the lone guardian.
Shepard of the solar systems
Millennial Sheriff

Celestial demons howling
Cursing imprisonment
Inky black holes absorbing evil
Cephalopod Justice

Kicking up his galactic spurs
Peaceful jurisdiction
The suns never set for his watch

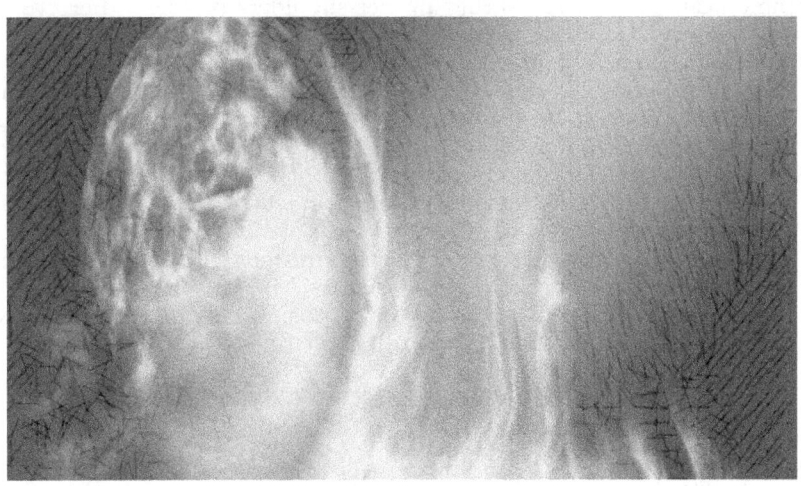

2015 Memoir First Place Winner: Sinks and Cabbages by Karen Gorback

Karen Gorback has been a VCWC member since 1999, serving on the board as the membership chair, treasurer and president. A memoir titled "The Jackpot" was recently published in Chicken Soup for the Soul – My Amazing Mom *(March 2018). Karen's debut picture book,* Nathan and Nana Cassandra – Superheroes, *will be published this fall by Waldorf Publishing. Her novel* Freshman Mom *(2014) is based on a short story which won second place in the 2000 VCWC Short Story Contest. Karen enjoys teaching at Conejo Valley Adult School and speaking to groups on a variety of writing topics. Contact Karen through her web site at* www.karengorback.com.

The fall semester began the day after Labor Day and it was hot – the type of hot that compels precocious fourth graders and news reporters to fry eggs on the sidewalk. A noisy box fan in the corner of the classroom did little to relieve the suffering of my thirty-six high school students, fanning themselves with notebook paper accordions. Air conditioning in public schools was a luxury in 1975 when I began my first teaching assignment in California's San Joaquin Valley; so the old, brick building did without. I could not have imagined on that first day that the scorching heat would be the least of my challenges that year.

Marissa was in my fifth-period English class, following lunch, when the kids were high on Snickers and sugary sodas. She dressed in dark chinos and white tee shirts nearly every day, moved with a defiant swagger, and wore a perpetual scowl that warned others to keep away. Despite my best efforts to encourage her participation, the lanky sophomore would have no part of group discussions, reading assignments, or homework. She communicated mostly by shrugging her shoulders or rolling her eyes with teenage angst.

One day, Marissa trudged into my classroom dragging a sink – an old, white, bathroom sink, scared with the stains of age and abandonment. Perhaps she found it near a dumpster on her way to school, a discarded vessel needing some attention. Marissa had drawn a heavy chain through the open drain hole, looped it around the longer end and tugged it into the classroom. The other students loved the distraction. Raucous laughter filled the air, along with a few unflattering remarks about Marissa.

Once the commotion subsided, I suppressed a grin and deadpanned, "Marissa, I see you've brought a sink to class."

The teenager nodded and adjusted the position of the bathroom fixture to fit under her desk. "Isn't there a stupid rule or something about not being allowed to bring your dog to school?"

"That's correct. No dogs at school."

"But I never heard nothin' about sinks," she said.

"Me either. Nothing about sinks." I should have dropped it right there, but I couldn't resist. "Will it sit quietly during our lesson on *To Kill a Mockingbird?*" The class giggled, and I was immediately sorry about the cheap shot.

"It's a SINK, okay?" she said, spitting out each syllable.

"Point taken. I'm sure it will be fine." I paused and picked up the novel, "What does Atticus mean when he tells Scout that in order to understand another person, you need to walk around in their skin?"

***

Gang violence had left an ugly stain on the pastoral community in recent years. Turf battles in the neighborhood park were not uncommon, and I began to worry when Marissa was absent from class for several days.

"She got her arm broke in a fight," one of her pals told me on a Friday afternoon. Although I knew she must have been miserable with a broken arm, I was grateful she hadn't suffered a more serious fate and mailed a get-well card on my way home.

Marissa didn't show up again until late the following week, sporting an impressive cast, covered with autographs of her friends. She resumed her position of quiet discontent in my English class, *sans* sink, and never mentioned receiving my card.

On Friday evening, my husband and I grabbed a couple of front row seats on the crowded bleachers in the high school football stadium. Friday night football was a religion in a place where everyone showed up to cheer on the hometown team. At some point during the halftime festivities, while the band belted out a Sousa march and cheerleaders romped on the sidelines, I saw Marissa and a bunch of her buddies sauntering down the sidewalk toward my husband and me. Knowing that teenagers generally do not appreciate being acknowledged by teachers and other adults during private times with their friends, I pretended not to see her and picked at my week-old manicure instead.

Then a miracle occurred, right there in the front row of the football stadium. I didn't notice at first, but Marissa had fallen back from the pack and without saying a word, gently tapped my knee. By the time I looked up, she had already begun to catch up with her friends, but she looked back and nodded her head, like Fonzy in *Happy Days*. I could almost hear that famous *Heeeey*. Then, she blended back into her group and was gone. "I'll be damned," I said to my husband. Communication between teacher and student had just ratcheted up a notch. I was elated.

Later that fall, the school district advertised a late afternoon, home-teaching position with the daughter of migrant workers, and I jumped at the opportunity. The girl had refused to attend classes because she was embarrassed about changing schools so often. Driving down a rutted dirt road beneath a canopy of old growth walnut trees, I found a small, wood-framed bungalow and knocked on the door. An older woman in a cotton dress and flowered apron answered, *"Si."*

I smiled and took a moment to enjoy the spicy aromas coming from the kitchen. "Hello, I'm Mrs. Gorback. I'm going to be Rosa's home teacher."

"No inglés," she said.

***

A pre-teen with large brown eyes joined us at the door. "I'm Rosa. Are you the new teacher?"

"Yes. Nice to meet you."

"This is my grandmother Juanita."

"Buenas tardes," I said. "Please tell your grandma that I don't speak much Spanish, but I'm very happy to be your new home teacher."

Rosa showed me to the bedroom she shared with her siblings. I sat at the foot of the neatly-made bed and quizzed my attentive student on the spelling and vocabulary lessons she had been assigned by the previous instructor. Rosa was bright and eager to learn. It was a shame she wouldn't go to school. At the end of the hour, I started for the door when Juanita attempted to hand me a paper sack filled with cabbages. "*Gracias*," she said.

"Oh, my gosh," I said, refusing the gift. "Rosa, please tell you grandmother that the vegetables are lovely, but she doesn't need to pay me. The school district takes care of that."

After my student translated for her grandmother, Juanita handed me the sack again. This time I accepted, smiled, and regretted my earlier rudeness. "*Gracias*," I said, knowing that I had learned more that afternoon than my student.

***

I enjoyed working with students like Marissa, Rosa and others for whom school presented unique challenges. And although I loved teaching expository and creative writing, journalism, and literature, it wasn't enough – whether in a classroom or a bungalow. I wanted to help students acquire the life skills they would need to become happy, healthy adults. I needed to learn how to empower young people with resiliency and the self-confidence to make decisions that were in their best interests. But other than acting upon instinct, as with sinks and cabbages, I had no tools with which to work.

I knew I had a lot to learn and began a course of study in the field of counseling psychology at California State University, Fresno. Four years later, I had earned a master's degree in counseling and knew that my career in education was about to change forever.

2015 Short Story Adult Second Place Winner: Beyond Measure by Karen Gorback

"Are you certain?" Benjamin asked his eighteen-year-old daughter the night before she embarked for Skagway in early September 1899. The frontier town would be Hannah's port of entry to Alaska, where she would board the White Pass and Yukon Railroad to Lake Bennett, then travel by freighter up the Yukon River to the Klondike gold fields.

"I've thought about nothing else for months," Hannah said. "I can't explain it. It's as though the Northern Lights themselves are drawing me toward the Yukon Territory."

Benjamin shook his head. "Klondike fever," he said, a trace of his Russian accent still noticeable.

"That's ridiculous," Hannah said, "I have no such thing."

Glancing around the bedroom that Hannah shared with her younger sister in a third-floor walkup on Post Street, Benjamin said, "You have everything a young woman could want. What more do you need?"

Hannah didn't answer. She could never describe the intoxicating appeal of solitary adventure or the desire to bring unimaginable wealth back to her parents.

Propping open a trunk on the floor, Hannah produced a tattered newspaper article titled "From [A] Woman's Standpoint – Hints to Women" by Annie Hall Strong. Originally published in the December 31, 1897 issue of the *Skagway News*, it had been reprinted in newspers throughout the country, advising women about the practicalities and perils of making the journey to the Klondike. Hannah had torn the article out of a local paper in Benjamin's general store and read it a hundred times; but she was blinded by the glitter of gold, unable to appreciate the words of caution.

"Please listen," Hannah begged her father who sat on the bentwood rocker where he had cradled his first-born as an infant. "The article says, Women have made up their minds to go to the Klondike, so there is no use trying to discourage them. It includes a list of what to bring: heavy-soled walking shoes, one pair house slippers, two skirts of heavy duck to wear over bloomers. . . and many other items. I've bought nearly everything; and what I don't pack, I'll purchase in Skagway. I'm sure it's a lovely town, and I'll be able to find ample provisions in an outfitters' shop near the dock."

When Benjamin shook his head with disapproval, Hannah dug deeper and produced a travel brochure from the Pacific Coast Steamship Company. "Listen to what this one says: During the excursion season of 1895, many thousand tourists visited Alaska. To say they were pleased conveys but a faint impression of their enthusiasm. They were delighted – harmed. Do you want to hear more?"

Silence filled the space in the small room like a thick fog rolling through the city. Benjamin rubbed his forehead, summoning forth memories of his parents' immigration to San Francisco in '49. He winced at the painful remembrance of his father going off to seek his fortune at Sutter's Mill and never returning, leaving his mother to raise three babies alone. Benjamin rejected his father's pipe dreams and worked hard to purchase a small mercantile to support his wife and children. He feared his older daughter was stricken by the same blind ambition from which his father suffered.

"No, you don't need to read any more," Benjamin said, removing his wire rimmed glasses and wiping his eyes with a handkerchief. He leaned toward the four-poster bed on which Hannah sat and bit off each word. "Someday you will discover that a person's wealth is measured by the compassion in his heart and not the coins in his pocket."

Hannah's hazel eyes filled with tears. She curled her long legs up beneath a white-washed muslin dress, drew the chestnut curls behind her ears, and wiped her nose on the back of her hand, certain her father would never understand.

When Hannah's mother entered the bedroom with seven-year-old Elizabeth, the child jumped onto her father's lap. Miriam sat on the edge of Hannah's bed, fingering the familiar stitches on the patchwork quilt she had sewn for her older daughter's nuptials.

"When are you leaving?" the younger girl asked.

"In the morning. Pier 10. Will you come to see me off?"

"Of course, I will. We'll all go. Right, Papa?"

With a sideways glance at her husband, Miriam answered, "Yes, of course we'll all go to see Hannah off."

"You'll be a good girl and help Mama with the canning this fall, won't you, Lizzie?" Hannah said.

The younger girl thought for a moment. "I guess so, but you won't be gone forever, right?"

"Right. I won't be gone forever." Hannah caught her father's eye, saw his pain, and looked away.

"Here," Miriam said, handing Hannah her own knit scarf. "Take this babushka to keep the wind out of your ears so you don't catch cold."

Hannah hugged her mother. "I'll keep warm. I promise."

"And I've baked a nice *challah* for you to take on the boat to say the blessing and make the Sabbath on Friday night."

"Ship, Miriam. It's called a ship, not a boat," Benjamin said.

"Ship, boat, what's the difference?" Miriam shot back, sliding a package into the open trunk.

Hearing the familiar, gentle banter between her parents, Hannah smiled weakly and knew that everything would be okay. When she returned, she would buy them a house atop Nob Hill. Their lives would be grand.

***

Hannah was grateful that the three-week voyage was nearly over. Rough seas, meager rations and drafty quarters had left Hannah with relentless sea sickness and a nagging fever. In fitful dreams, she was back home, lying atop her feather bed, pulling the patchwork quilt up snugly beneath her chin.

"Can I bring you a bowl of nice, hot chicken soup?" her mother called from the kitchen in Hannah's delusion, only to fade away before Hannah could answer.

As the freighter *North Fork* edged up the Lynn Canal toward the Port of Skagway, Hannah stood amid the crush of a hundred weary passengers jockeying for a glimpse of their destination. Bumped and bruised by the jostling crowd, Hannah finally reached the railing for her first view of Skagway.

But something was wrong. Had the ship taken a different route while Hannah slept, or was this a feverish aberration? Although the travel brochures touted pristine, arctic air, Hannah pulled the *babushka* over her nose and mouth to ward off the noxious fumes of a dozen other steamships and freighters filling the channel. As the *North Fork* nudged the moorings on the congested wharf, Hannah looked down onto a dock teeming with hundreds of newly-arrived settlers. Some wandered aimlessly; others shouted in a dozen languages and swarmed like flies over piles of sleds, tools, trunks and sacks of provisions, which had been carelessly thrown about the landing.

Assorted livestock bellowed in distress, large dogs howled from cramped cages and nervous horses whinnied and reared up over men unable to handle the anxious animals. Even with the scarf, Hannah gagged from the stench rising from rivulets of muddy sewage. She tasted the soot wafting through the air from dozens of open fires stoked by newcomers desperate for warmth in the late September chill. Cinching together the top of her woolen coat, Hannah's eyes filled with tears. "Oh, my God, what have I done?"

After the ship docked and the passengers began moving toward the gangway, Hannah turned and trounced the toe of another traveler.

"Ow," a small voice squealed.

"Excuse me," Hannah said, looking down on a young girl, a few years older than Lizzie.

"That's okay," the girl said, shivering in a stained, gray flannel dress.

"I'm sorry. I didn't mean to step on your toe. My name's Hannah. What's yours?"

"Charlotte," the younger girl said, looking up with frightened blue eyes. Her damp, blond hair hung in tangles over her forehead and cheeks, pink from the cold.

76

"How do you do, Charlotte? You're not traveling alone, are you?"

"No," the child said.

"Where are your parents?"

The young girl didn't answer, fidgeting with her collar, attempting to stave off the biting wind.

"If you'll tell me where your parents are, I'll walk you back to their compartment," Hannah offered.

Charlotte hesitated. "My mother's in bed. She's sick. My father's not on the ship."

"Where is he?"

"A place called Klondike. He's a gold miner. He's going to buy us a big house when we get home. He sent for my mother and me to meet him."

Seeing the child shivering from the cold, Hannah removed her mother's *babushka* and wrapped it around Charlotte's head, tucking in the wet, blond curls. Then she gently drew the girl into her arms beneath her coat, shielding her from the wind. The trembling child did not resist, so Hannah rubbed her back as though she were a newborn pup, drawing warmth into the frail frame.

When the sun broke through the clouds and the deck began to clear, Hannah and Charlotte sat down on a pile of mooring ropes and huddled together beneath the coat. Though strangers, they began talking as old friends, each hungry to find companionship in the other. Charlotte explained that her father had left for the Yukon Territory a year ago, after word of the gold rush spread throughout Seattle. She and her mother, Giselle, were traveling to a long-awaited reunion; but Giselle became ill after a few days at sea, leaving Charlotte to fend for herself.

As they continued to talk, a long shadow fell across the girls, cast by an older man in a boatswain's uniform. In an instant, he reached down and grabbed the younger girl's arm, yanking her off the rope. Charlotte screamed.

"So, here's our little thief," the intruder grumbled through an unkempt beard. "Captain's been lookin' for ya. Let's go," he said, tugging at Charlotte's arm.

The young passenger resisted. "No, I didn't do it! It wasn't me."

Hannah stood up and swallowed hard, desperate to hide her fear. "What's the problem, sir?"

"This little rat's been stealing rations from the ship's larder. You'd better watch your valuables, missy. We got us a thief here."

"No, wait," Hannah said. "If you'll leave her with me, I'll be sure she's punished."

"Can't, missy. Captain's promised a fiver for bringing her in."

Hannah thought quickly and reached beneath her coat for the purse strapped securely around her waist. "Here," she said, offering the seaman a ten-dollar bill her mother had slipped to her back at Pier 10, in the event of an emergency. "This should take care of it, okay?"

The boatswain snatched the money from Hannah's hand. "Yeah. Okay." He shoved Charlotte back onto the ropes. "Nothin' but sea vermin." The crew member leered at Hannah and lowered his voice. "You need someone to show you around? Gets awfully cold at night, missy."

"Ah, no thank you. My husband's waiting in our cabin. Come along, Charlotte." Hannah took the girl by the hand, pulled her up off the ropes and strode toward the ship's stairwell, her confident demeanor belying a racing heart.

Once the boatswain was out of sight, the two sprinted down the steps to Giselle's cabin, where the child tumbled onto her mother lying in bed. "Mama, Mama, you should've seen it. You should've seen what Hannah did. She's the bravest person on the ship. Maybe in the whole world."

Hannah shook off the hyperbole and spoke to the woman lying in a heap of rumpled bedding. "I'm pleased to meet you, Ma'am. Your daughter's delightful, but I've kept her out too long. I hope you won't be angry with her. It was my fault."

Giselle sat up. "Please don't apologize. I'm glad Charlotte's found a friend. I'm afraid I've been ill and unable to provide proper supervision."

"I don't need supervision. I'm a big girl. Almost eleven. I can take care of myself," Charlotte said.

"We'll see about that," her mother said, managing a weak grin.

"Mama, I have a wonderful idea. Since Hannah's traveling alone, can she come with us to the Klondike? Can she come along to see Father? Wouldn't it be fun?"

Hannah responded louder than she intended. "What?"

Giselle took Charlotte's small hand into her own, feeling so much love that her heart nearly burst. "While that does sound like great fun, I don't think I can travel much longer."

"What do you mean?" Charlotte asked, kneeling at her mother's berth.

Giselle hesitated, then looked into her daughter's eyes. "I've decided we'll remain on the ship for the return trip to Seattle."

Charlotte panicked. "No, we can't. You promised. Father's waiting for us. We can't go home yet. We can't."

Feeling an intrusion, Hannah turned to leave, but Giselle said, "Please don't go."

Charlotte sniffed back tears. "We're already in Skagway. We're almost there, right?"

Giselle shook her head, too weary to argue with the willful child.

Hannah spoke to Charlotte. "I know you want to see your father very badly, but it's still a long trip from Skagway to the Yukon Territory. The weather's going to worsen as the nights get longer. It's going to be very cold and could become dangerous."

"I don't care. Father's waiting. I'm not afraid."

Giselle looked at Charlotte and then at Hannah, sensing that the two had become fast friends. The mother thought quickly and spoke to Hannah, "I have a little money that Cecil sent me for the trip. I know I have no right to ask this of you, but if I give you the money, can you take her? Can you take Charlotte to see her father?"

Charlotte yanked off the *babushka* and buried her head in her mother's lap, sobbing. "No, I won't leave you! You have to come with us."

"Shhhh," Giselle murmured, stroking her daughter's hair as she had done a hundred times before. The mother looked into Hannah's eyes and said, "It's okay. You have your own plans. I understand."

Crouching on a stool in the corner of the damp cabin, Hannah's heart nearly broke. It was Friday afternoon. She pictured her own family, safe and warm, preparing for Shabbat dinner. Aromas of spicy brisket and freshly-baked challah would soon fill the third-floor walk-up. Lizzie would set the table, putting the candlesticks in front of her mother's place setting and positioning the utensils around each plate, just as Hannah had taught her.

Back in cabin, Hannah looked at the mother and daughter huddled in the bedding. Then, she heard her father's admonition as clearly as if he were sitting before her. *A person's wealth is measured by the compassion in his heart and not the coins in his pocket.* And in that moment of clarity, she knew what she needed to do. She knew that she wanted to help this family more than she desired adventure, or wealth, or a majestic home on Nob Hill. Hannah looked at Giselle and answered, "Yes. I shall be honored to accompany Charlotte on the journey to see her father."

With sudden strength and purpose, Hannah sprinted to her cabin where she gathered her belongings and scribbled a note that she would ask Giselle to mail upon returning to Seattle.

> *Dear Mama, Papa, and Lizzie:*
> *I miss you very much. By the time you receive this letter, I shall be on my overland journey to the Yukon Territory. But even if I never stake a single claim, I have already found wealth beyond measure, as I help reunite a young girl with her father.*
> *All my love,*
> *Hannah*

2015 Memoir Second Place Winner: Peak Attitude by Sunny Glessner

Sunny loves travel, reading in bed, parties, and tasty cuisine. She treasures the fine friends she's made all over the world and loves being a grandparent. Sunny aspires to be a writer when she grows up and is having some success. Published in anthologies, print and e-zines, she has also won contests with her short stories.

When the Tokyo U. S. Army base cancelled my flight reservation and left me stranded in August, 1988, Rick happened by the desk and overheard my dilemma.

I'd met Rick, a teaching colleague, the year before when I flew in from the States to Tokyo, but barely knew him. I'd just finished teaching troops in Korea and now was excited about working in Japan, an even more mysterious country. He told me he'd be lodging at Camp Zama Friday night and climbing Mt. Fuji Saturday. "Want to share my room?" he asked.

I needed a place to stay, so do I try to find the Salvation Army as I had in Hong Kong or hike Mt. Fuji? No contest. A thirty-year-old compared to my mature fifty, he seemed safe.

I jumped at what might be my only opportunity to climb the icon. Prime climbing season is July and August when way stations are open, and the weather is most cooperative. "Sure, why not," said my spontaneous self. I also had an adventurous self – why else would I live in Asia alone? I wasn't even worried about being a novice trekker.

Was my delayed military flight serendipity or fate, creating this opportunity? Either way, it was further evidence that my decision to jump into Asia was the best one of my life.

The night went by quickly as I anticipated the adventure. The tour bus deposited us at the 5th Station, halfway up the massive 12,400-foot mountain. Its top reminded me of whipped cream, and Fuji was the crème de la crème of my Asia stay. By 6th Station, as the climb became steeper, I thought my decision might be foolhardy. Thank goodness, without a car in Korea, I was used to walking long distances with a heavy backpack.

Because I hurt my toe in Bangkok the week before, I hadn't worn shoes for several days. I started climbing in thongs, but the sharp, unstable, volcanic rock soon changed my mind. I donned my trusty tennies and ignored the pain to focus on the summit. The icy rain and cold winds made Rick and me miserable, despite rain ponchos and layers of clothes.

Only 1% of Japanese actually climb this treasure. For some Japanese it's a spiritual experience, and we saw generations of families on the slopes. As we passed climbers, we exchanged *"Konichiwa"* with a slight bob of the head. Otherwise, I limited conversation to conserve breath. Even though Rick was younger, he assured me he had to stop and catch his breath as often as I did – a real gentleman.

I trudged uphill, greedily drinking water, barely able to go six steps before resting, but I never considered quitting. This trek required the same endurance that life sometimes does – one foot in front of the other – slow and steady. It boosted my ego to see the military guys, who I expected to be in better shape, puff and drag. Some cocky Marines, however, jogged up and down the whole mountain in one day.

Some people make the complete climb at night, but I needed to see where I was going. During breaks in the *undai* (sea of clouds), the view was breathtaking – as though seen through the openings of a white lace tablecloth covering the valley.

At each station we paid to have the traditional "chop" or special symbol we earned burned into our wooden pilgrim's pole. We also warmed up by the bed of coals used to heat the branding iron. A Japanese flag waved at the top of our stick, along with the anti-bear bells that explained why no bears attacked us.

Rick and I made it to the 8th Station, our lodging that night, in a respectable six hours. We huddled over the fire to trade tales and sympathy with other hikers, discussing the challenge of the last two stations. Then we all crammed like sardines into an unheated loft, lying fully clothed on futons. When we woke at 1:30 a.m. to finish the climb before sunrise, I just wanted to roll over, but there was no way to stay warm without the other bodies. Besides, I'd have heard from Rick if I didn't make it to the top.

That morning we clambered in the dark over large boulders with small flashlights, but at least it wasn't raining. Each step was a chore as we used traditional cotton gloves to get a safe handhold. That difficulty, combined with the higher altitude and even less oxygen, caused the queue to move slowly.

And then – the top! We'd made it.

Exhilarated, I looked down the mountainside at the twinkling line of flashlights. As the other climbers switched back and forth across the slope, I felt a magical connection, no matter what language we spoke. We shared the same determination to attain our goal, the sought-after ideal of *goraiko* – to see sunrise from the apex of Fuji-san. And our timing was perfect.

Since climbing Mt. Fuji started as a spiritual practice, a large *tori* (gate) greeted us at the peak. We passed through it to symbolize our triumph. The Japanese climbers snapped group shots with the sunrise in the background – proof they had accomplished the once-in-a-lifetime destination. I wasn't sure how they felt about *gaijins* (foreigners) being there, but proud to share the magnificent event, they pushed me forward, so I could also capture the majestic orange and yellow ball as it breached the horizon. I felt honored to share the top of their world.

I gulped for air. "Look how far I've come. From small-town Iowa to the peak of Mt. Fuji, half a globe away," I said to Rick, "I'm so jazzed."

He grinned. "I know what you mean. We still need to get that last chop to prove we tamed the peak."

The glorious sun shone through the clouds as I peered into the iconic crater. However, the lack of oxygen did more than just affect my stamina while climbing. I now felt nauseated and had a headache. Altitude sickness struck me for the first time. That, plus the 40° temperature, meant no dallying at the top. "Let's roll," I said, hoping it wouldn't really happen.

With the sun out and little cloud cover, sunscreen replaced yesterday's rain slickers. The inspiring views of the valley and Tokyo, 60 miles away, were as crystalline as the air.

Surely the descent would be easier, but it wasn't, although it took only half the time. The small, rust-colored rock covering the backside of the mountain presented a danger to my own backside. In spite of my trusty walking stick, I was forced to slalom the steep path to avoid gaining too much speed. This used different muscles from the day before and produced multiple aches in both legs. Sometimes hikers slid several feet, and others would ask "*Daijobu*?" Are you ok?

I agree with the Japanese saying, "A wise man climbs Fuji once, but only a fool does it twice." I'm jubilant I did it but have no desire to repeat the experience. The snow-capped cone with its serene look, as captured in classic woodblock prints, doesn't deceive me. I know better.

Years later, I reflected on the question friends had asked, "Why move to Asia?" I answered, "Why not?" Now I knew I explored other cultures to understand myself. My beloved stick and woodblock prints are visible evidence of a "peak" experience, reminding me of other figurative mountains I've conquered and how my horizons have broadened—literally.

2015 Memoir Honorable Mention: Catechism by Louisa Angeli
Louisa was born in San Francisco but grew up in Southern California. She has lived in Santa Barbara and Ventura Counties for most of her life. Louisa was an educator for over 30 years before retiring in 2013. During that time, she also pursued a Master's Degree in clinical psychology and is a licensed therapist. After many years of focusing on her profession, pursuing further education and raising children and pets, Louisa has decided to enjoy lots of unstructured time in her garden, with friends, traveling, seeking adventures, and some volunteer service. She is a member of Women's Artistic Network and VCWC. Louisa has been writing for many years, but it has only been during the last decade that she has begun to explore poetry. Over the years, Louisa has seen the spark of creativity change lives and inspire infinite possibilities in children and adults. So she continues to seek adventure, the unusual, and loves living spontaneously.

I was nearly ten when I met my father. I heard a firm knock on the front door. When I looked up from my puzzle, I could see a man through the glass. He smiled at me when I opened the door, and then he asked to see my mother. In those days we weren't worried about strangers or ax murderers. Mom was in the bathroom, so I politely told him to wait, and I would get her.

Mom taught my brother, Manny, and me not to tell people she was in the bathroom because it wasn't polite. As I walked to the bathroom, I tried to figure out how I was going to tell her. She did not like to be disturbed when she was on the toilet which was often because she was always constipated.

I knocked gently on the door and said, "There's a man at the front door who wants to talk to you."

With irritation in her voice, she asked, "Who is it?"

Since I didn't know, she made me go back and ask. So I did, and boy was I ever surprised. He told me he was my father! Mom had told us earlier in our lives our father had left us when Manny and I were just babies, so I really didn't remember him at all. I couldn't wait to tell her, "Mom, it's Dad!"

I heard the toilet flushing. Mom came out in her tattered pink terry cloth bathrobe. Her lips were pinched real tight and her eyes were like slits – not her happy look. I decided to follow behind her at a safe distance.

When she got to the living room, I heard her gasp. As I peered around, I could see her neck start to turn dark pink like her bathrobe. The pink spread to her chin, cheeks and ears. It turned out that the man wasn't my father, but Father Ignacio, the parish priest.

He had been visiting the neighborhood looking for wayward Catholics like us.

Later, Mom told me that the church needed money, so he was trying to drum up business. I had never been to church before, so I wondered what kind of business this was. After that visit, Mom said my brother and I would have to start going to Catty Kissim. I wasn't sure who she was, but I was friendly and liked meeting new people. When Manny and I found out that Catty Kissim wasn't a person but a place you go to learn and memorize stuff, we were not happy campers.

At catechism we learned about the Ten Commandments, rules that God made. I was in trouble already because I had lied, stolen candy from Woolworth's and killed cockroaches. I even covered another man's wife, Grandma, when she fell asleep on the sofa and looked cold. I did not like catechism. I also didn't want to tell Mom that Manny and I had seen pictures of an almost naked man and woman because she would probably make us stop going. The man and woman got in trouble by the way, and it was the woman's fault. There was one good thing about catechism, and that was the punch and cookies we got after it was over.

There were some other problems too. It seems that ever since Manny and I started catechism, Mom would get sick every Sunday, so we had to go to church without her. Mom would smile, give us a big hug, some money for church and tell us to say a prayer for her. She was probably constipated. As my brother and I walked to church, me in my black patent leather shoes and red polka dot dress and Manny in his brown polished shoes and corduroy trousers, we used to think of ways to get constipated. I decided to ask my friend, Cynthia. She was really smart and knew everything.

Every time we got back from church, Mom would ask, "How was church?" I would say fine. I didn't want her to think that all the money she was paying was being wasted. The truth was that we couldn't understand a single word. The priest did not speak English. We just copied what everyone else was doing. We didn't get too bored because there were exercises and music.

Sometimes we waved our arms in front of our chest and face. That was called the "Sign of the Cross." Other times we stood up, kneeled and sat. We never sat in the front row, because then we wouldn't have been able to copy anyone. One thing was not fair. In the middle of the meeting, some people got to go up front for snacks. They got a white cookie and something to drink. All I know is that we weren't allowed to, maybe because we were not old enough. Later in catechism, the nuns, ladies who wore long black dresses and hoods, said we had to make our "Holy Communion" first. They said that was why we were going to catechism.

Well, the day finally arrived when we were supposed to make our confession. That's when you told the priest all of the bad things you had done since you were born. We had to wait in line for our turn. I remember watching my friends go into the box where Father Reardon was, and one-by-one, kids came out crying. I could hear Father Reardon shouting, "How many times!" over and over and over. My turn was coming up fast so I did some quick thinking. The door opened and Amelia, who lived next door to me, came out with wet swollen eyes, flushed cheeks and quivering lips. She wiped her dripping nose and sniffled as she walked past me.

My turn. I went in, sat down, said a short speech, "Bless me Father..." and waited. Father Reardon was looking down. He didn't bother to look at me. We were told that the priest could never see you, but you could see him. So I had decided to make my voice deeper, hoping he wouldn't recognize me. When he asked me what sins I had committed or what bad things I had, done, I started listing them. I could swear I saw him smile. This wasn't so bad after all, and then came the moment. He asked me how many times I had fought with my brother. I blurted out eighty-four. He jerked his head up, turned and looked towards me. *Dear God, don't let him see me.* He turned his head back to his original gaze downwards and told me to say ten "Hail Marys" and ten "Our Fathers," prayers for penance or forgiveness.

I walked out triumphantly. Next Sunday, Manny and I would finally be able to have the white cookie and juice.

2015 Short Story Adult Honorable Mention: Stuck Together by Louisa Angeli

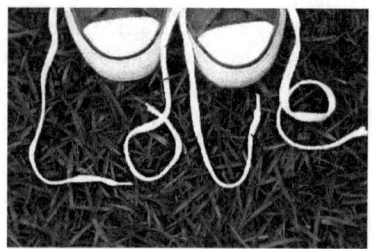

"Hurry, Ethan. It's late, and we still have to get Sissy to day care!" There was no response as Liv continued brushing her long thick wavy hair with quick tense strokes. She used to take time, making sure she carefully took out the tangles so there would be minimal breakage.

Derrick used to love watching her brush the golden-brown strands that shone in the morning light when she sat by the window. He would often come up behind Liv and wrap his arms around her as he kissed her slender neck and delicate shoulders. It seemed so long ago, before Sissy was born and Ethan was still a toddler. No use dwelling on the past. Nothing will ever change the fact that he's gone. She sighed as she put the brush down and shouted one more time, "Ethan, let's go! I can't be late for my first day. You don't want to make Mommy late, do you?" Still, no reply.

She quickly picked up Sissy who had been calmly dozing in her crib until now. Liv grabbed the day care bag and her purse, then hurried into Ethan's room, "We're leaving now. Get your lunch and backpack." Liv didn't mean to shout, but she couldn't help it. All she could see was Ethan, fiddling with his shoelaces. He kept pushing his fine straight brown hair away from his forehead, so he could see his shoes. His hair wasn't even combed. Why couldn't he be more prepared? *I have enough on my plate. I can't do this all by myself, but, I have to. No one else is going to do it for me.* Liv took a deep breath, "That's it, shoelaces tied or not, get in the car." *I can't worry about shoelaces right now. I showed him how so many times!*

She left the room and headed towards the garage. Passing through the kitchen, Liv gasped as she saw Sissy's morning bottle on the counter. She had forgotten to put it into the daycare bag. *Why can't I be more prepared!* She sighed with frustration. Liv put her sleepy seven-month-old daughter on the family room sofa, then grabbed the bottle and put it into the bag. She looked back towards the hallway, hoping that Ethan was on his way. Liv picked Sissy up, then headed for the car.

All that could be heard was quiet stillness. No garage door noise. Still closed. Ethan wiped the tears from his eyes and sighed heavily. People used to say he had his father's eyes, dark brown and penetrating with long curly lashes. He tried not to cry too much in front of Liv when he was sad because it would just make her remember. Ethan carefully but reluctantly put the photo of his father back on the nightstand and tucked his shoelaces into the sides of his shoes. He had tried all morning to remember how Liv had shown him how to tie shoelaces, but he just couldn't get his fingers to move the way hers did. *If I walk carefully, my shoes might not slip off.*

When he got into the car, Ethan could tell Liv was already in that other place, the one that made him feel like she was gone even though she was less than three feet away. He had on his new school clothes, black and white plaid baggy shorts and a crimson red polo shirt. With his backpack on his lap, he sat in quiet anticipation wondering what the first day of school would be like, if his teacher would be nice and would he make new friends easily in first grade. Sissy dozed in her car seat next to him.

Liv drove first to the daycare. She was a cautious driver, her eyes continually checking the rear and sideview mirrors for the unexpected. Some might say that she became obsessive because of Derrick. He had been a Seabee stationed in Afghanistan and loved the work he was doing, always building, creating. He was driving on a road that had been declared "safe" when two young children darted across the road. He had to swerve to miss them, and that's when his Jeep struck a land mine. "A senseless death," was what his commanding officer said. None of it made any sense. Liv's world had switched gears and taken her in a completely different direction.

Liv and Derrick had been married in a modest ceremony. Their wedding reception, a potluck affair, was held in her parents' home in Moorpark, a large town in Southern California. Both Liv and Derrick had decided to save money to buy a home instead of having a lavish wedding. They had their lives planned out in detail. Liv became pregnant and had Ethan right away. Derrick was going into the Navy as a Seabee, and Liv would continue at Moopark Community College, later transferring to California State University in Northridge. Derrick was to have continued on in the Navy at least until Liv had graduated and earned her teaching credential. Liv became pregnant a second time, as they had planned, after completing her credential work, towards the end of her student teaching. Even though Liv's parents thought they should wait to have children, Derrick and Liv wanted to start their family as soon as possible.

They were young, invincible, and goal-oriented with nothing to deter them or so they thought.

Sissy was still asleep at 7:00 a.m. when Liv handed her to Christine, the day care provider. Liv had been practicing the routine for two weeks before school started so her first day of teaching would go smoothly. Christine was just the person Liv had needed to relieve the stress of having to leave Sissy for most of the day. Christine was gentle, soft-spoken, and had two young children of her own. She had come highly recommended.

The next stop was Ethan's school. They arrived twenty minutes early, but Liv had made arrangements with the school secretary that would allow Ethan to sit in the front office until the playground gates opened. So far, everything was going like clockwork.

Liv breathed a calming sigh of relief because she felt she could let her mind begin to shift to the teaching day ahead as she drove the short stretch of country road to her school in Camarillo, a small city about fifteen minutes north of Moorpark. Camarillo was where Derrick and Liv had originally lived while in Navy housing. It was the best of both worlds because there was a school with daycare for Ethan located next to the housing development. He walked to school with older neighborhood children when he started kindergarten, and the freeway access was close by so Liv could get to Cal State easily to finish her credential work. She would be finished with her course work and student teaching before Sissy was born.

All of that changed after the accident. Sissy was born three months after Derrick's death.

Liv temporarily moved in with her parents and later bought a modest house with the survivor benefits from the Navy. The plan was for her parents to help with the children. However, shortly afterwards, Liv's mother was diagnosed with a terminal brain tumor. After the funeral, her father was in no condition to help with anything. None of this was part of Derrick's and Liv's plan.

Pulling into the parking lot of Maple Elementary, she felt a surge of excitement, anxiety, and then a bit of fear. *I wonder if Ethan is on the playground at his school now?* He looked a bit flushed. *I hope he's not getting sick.* These and other thoughts about Sissy raced through Liv's mind as she made it to the front office, picked up her mail, and then headed into the lounge to check for any updates in the first day bulletin. She spotted donuts and a "Have a successful first day" sign on the table from Mrs. Tarkington, the principal. *Thank goodness I don't have any first day morning playground duties*, thought Liv. All she had to do was make sure she picked up her students on time. Liv dashed to her classroom, pulling her wheeled school case. She left the school case by her desk and quickly scanned the room, then headed to the work pod to greet her grade level teaching partners. They had all been amazing and supportive throughout the month before school started.

The bell rang. It was time, the beginning of her teaching career. As Liv walked down the outdoor corridor towards the scraggly line of first graders on the playground, she had the same feeling as being up on a swing and coming down with butterflies in her stomach. She practiced slow steady breathing as she began to greet her students. Liv noticed one red-faced boy with a mop of curly blond hair. He wiped his nose with the back of his hand and shuffled along slowly.

Why is he dragging his feet? I hope he's not sick on the first day.

As the boys and girls entered the classroom and looked for their name tags on desks, Liv noticed the curly blond-headed boy stoop down and fiddle with his shoes. He didn't seem in the least bit interested in finding his name tag. She went over to him, "Honey, what's your name?" Thinking that he was unable to read or write his name, Liv thought he would need help, so she took him by the hand. She could feel wetness on his palms and realized he had been wiping his nose. A bit repulsed and worried about germs, Liv took a closer look, and that's when she noticed that he had been crying. "What's the matter, sweetie? Everything is going to be okay." She quickly grabbed a tissue from the box on a nearby table and gently dabbed his eyes.

"Zack, my name is Zack," he sniffled out the words. Holding her hand, he followed Liv. Then stumbled. His left shoe had fallen off. Zack bent down to put his shoe on, and that's when Liv noticed that the shoelaces on both of his shoes were untied. "I don't know how to tie my shoelaces. Mommy got mad at me because she was late for work and—" Sobbing and more tears followed. Liv froze. Her mind flashed back to the early morning at home. *Oh, Ethan, I'm so sorry. Please forgive me.* That was all that she could think about as she hugged Zack.

Liv stood up, "Good morning boys and girls. Go ahead and write your name on the page in front of you and draw a nice picture of yourself for me." In the meantime, she bent down to tie Zack's shoelaces. She wiped his tears and took him to his seat. The guilty feeling in the pit of her stomach grew. Later as the class recited the "Pledge of Allegiance," Liv read the poster near the flag: "It's okay to make mistakes. That's how we learn." The letters were royal blue, underlined in red with cartoon-like smiling characters below the phrases. *I made a mistake. I will make it better. I'm not a bad mother.* She took a deep breath and blinked several times to hold back the tears.

***

The rest of the school day went by quickly. After preparing for the next day, she left at four o'clock, hoping to beat the traffic on the drive back to Moorpark. Ethan would have been picked up by Christine who also did afterschool care for him and two other children. During the drive back, Liv thought about what she could do to show Ethan how sorry she was for her impatience and sharp words this morning. Then her thoughts shifted to the activities and lessons of the school day. She remembered how later in the day, Zack went from a six-year-old boy with a puffy tear-stained face to an energetic super star in his neon yellow soccer vest with blue Velcro ties. The Velcro made it easy for a six-year-old to get the vest on and off without difficulty. That's it! "Thank you, Zack!" she said aloud. Liv was pleased with herself and couldn't wait to pick up Ethan and Sissy.

"Hi, sweetie, how was your day?" she asked as she wrapped her arms around Ethan and lifted him up. After covering his face with kisses, she said, "I have a surprise for you! Two actually." Liv glanced at his shoes as she lowered him to the ground. She picked Sissy up and kissed her plump rosy cheeks. Liv held Sissy with her right arm and held Ethan's hand with her left hand as she headed to the car with renewed energy. Ethan wondered why his mother was so happy and not tired like she usually seemed. She was full of questions. "How was your first day? Did you make any friends? Tell me about your teacher." He enjoyed the attention and answered all of her questions. Where are we going? he wondered.

Liv pulled into Town Center Plaza in front of the Payless shoe store. A few minutes later Ethan was trying on gray shoes with Spiderman sprawled across the sides of both shoes. "What do you think, honey? These are going to be much easier to put on in the morning. No shoelaces." Liv beamed. *Velcro, why didn't I think of it before? Thank you again, Zack!*

87

"Mommy, these are awesome. I just have to stick them together." Ethan kept pulling the straps apart and sticking them back together as Sissy sat in her stroller looking on with fascination. Ethan liked his new shoes, but even more, he liked seeing his mother happy and full of energy. "What's the other surprise?"

"Follow me." Liv let Ethan push the stroller as they headed further down the walkway and ended up in front of Baskin-Robbins Ice Cream. "I hope you know what flavor you want. I'm having chocolate." Again, Liv enjoyed the look of pleasure and surprise on Ethan's face.

As they sat outside eating their ice cream cones, it was quiet. Sissy sat in her stroller watching for a bit, but mostly giving her attention to the toy rattle attached to her stroller. She had not yet tasted the delight of ice cream. Ethan had been licking the bubble gum flavored ice cream dripping down the sides of his waffle cone when he stopped, looked at Liv and said, "I guess we're stuck together like my shoes."

Smiling, Liv said, "Yes, Ethan, stuck together."

Poetry: Weathering the Storm by Louisa Angeli

You know I love you.
I know you love me.

Our love is like a small puddle of water that grows after a steady
   rain

I see you
You see me

Like the reflection of the water from the puddle to the sky

And when the sun comes out
The water begins to evaporate
Sending vapor into the atmosphere

When our love is having a warm sunny day
Its vapor surrounds our delicate sphere

In the water cycle, droplets condense to form clouds
When dense heavy clouds can no longer hold, precipitation
occurs

The precipitation can be
      Sudden fierce hailstones
            Soft chilling snowflakes
                  Even steady quiet drizzle

Sometimes I just need an umbrella

2015 Memoir Honorable Mention: The Topic Was Taboo by Barbara Fischer

Barbara's interests include people's lives, and a love for animals and nature. Her published work includes interviews, personal experience and feature articles. While shepherding five kids, she worked as a technical writer and pursued the craft of writing with college classes at night. A second marriage expanded her flock to seven teenagers and an opportunity to delegate responsibilities. Thus freed, she completed her AA at Moorpark College, and took advanced writing classes at CLU. She's now focused on a memoir of her New England roots.

Bundled up in a bulky snowsuit I felt like an overstuffed pillow. But I didn't care. At age three and a half, I was deemed old enough to go ice skating with my mother, dad and sister. I chattered in excitement. My dad hoisted me on his shoulders with my legs forward and I tightened them against his chest.

We walked a short distance down a gravel road, in brilliant sunshine, one afternoon in Connecticut. From my perch, I saw the gleam of ice on the neighbor's pond amid tree-shrouded banks.

Daddy sat me down on a lichen-covered log. He squatted in front of me, strapped on my double-bladed skates and tightened the clamps onto my boots.

Mother sat next to us, laced up her skates and streaked off across the ice in long, graceful strokes. My sister, Joan, who was four years older than me, quickly followed and I heard the ice creak faintly under their weight. Moments later Mother swirled to a stop near me, sending a little shower of ice crystals onto the grassy edge. "You ready, Bubsy?" Her cheeks glowed a ruddy pink.

My dad finished lacing up his skates and both parents took my hands. I clumped onto the ice.

Mother said, "Don't walk. Glide. Push like this." She shoved one foot in front of the other and grinned at me. "You can do it. Just hang onto your daddy. I'll be right back."

I gripped my dad's finger and inched onto the pond. Mother skated backwards, watching us. She stopped a short distance away, got on her knees. With her nose a few inches from the ice, she cupped her face with her gloves. "Bubsy, look!"

I let go of my father and staggered over to where she knelt.

"Look, what do you see?"

I dropped to my knees. At first, the ice looked black, but as soon as I shielded my eyes with my mittens, I saw little fish swimming around.

"Oh. How can they swim through the ice?"

"They're swimming under the ice. It's only a few inches thick."

I watched, fascinated, as they swam through a wonder world of ferns and slender red and green plants.

"Do you see the frog?"

"Where?" And then I saw something – a silvery grey shape partly hidden in the mud. Brown dots speckled his back. "Oh! Is he dead?"

"No, he's hibernating."

"What's hibernating?" I brushed icy flakes off my nose and peered at the frozen fairyland and the poor little frog.

"He's sleeping. Remember in our book how bears curl up in caves in the winter? That's hibernating."

***

Three years later, in the spring of 1936, we moved to Dover, Delaware where my dad had a new job. That July, on my sixth birthday, Mother told me I'd be starting school. I shrieked with joy, hugged her, and we danced around the room together.

Several weeks passed. My dad told us our mother needed to stay in the hospital for a while. Grandmother Morris came from Connecticut to take care of us.

I sensed something was very wrong but when I asked questions, they said, "She'll be home soon." One night, after I went to bed, I heard Grandmother and my dad downstairs, talking. I tiptoed to the banisters and tried to hear what they were saying, but they spoke softly.

Once Grandmother raised her voice, "Woodbridge, my son, don't blame yourself for Jean's depression. You've done everything you could since the last miscarriage. That was when? Almost two years ago."

I didn't know what "depression" was, but it sounded bad and scared me.

In September, Grandmother Morris left and I was delighted when my mother's parents came from Scotland. I ran down the brick walk to greet them, tripped and fell. Gram'pa Muir lifted me up, "Oh, lit'l get'l."

I loved the way he said, "little girl."

He reached into his pocket and held out a red lollipop. "Kahndie?"

We went into the house. Granny enveloped me in her soapy-clean smell, "Come, lit'l one, let's get you patched up." Her words, richly tinted with her Scottish burr, soothed as much as the bandage she gently applied.

A few days later, Daddy told us we could visit our mother. The hospital smelled funny, like our medicine cabinet at home and it looked very white and shiny. And what was all that bonging for? I clung to my dad.

When Mother saw us, she looked very happy and chuckled. "My darlings." She stretched out her arms to hug Joan and me. She didn't smell the way I remembered, not the good out-of-doors smell I was used to.

After Daddy kissed and hugged her, I gave her a bundle of daisies. I thought I saw tears in her eyes when she said thank you.

A nurse abruptly grabbed the flowers from right under my mother's nose and said, "I'll put them in some water." She seemed rude and I didn't like her.

Joan and I told Mother about helping Daddy in the garden. He told her that while we worked, we sang a couple of the Scottish songs that she'd taught us.

It seemed liked we'd only been there a few minutes when my dad said Mother was tired and we should go. When I hugged her, I realized with a shock that I could feel her bones. She really was sick.

We started to walk out to the corridor, but I stopped. "Daddy. The flowers? What happened to them?" I burst into tears and ran back to Mother.

I tried to get up on her bed, but Daddy caught my arm. "Bubsy! Come along now. The nurse will bring them back. They are busy ladies."

***

Several weeks later, my sister and I got ready for school and started downstairs where Granny would be making breakfast in the kitchen. I was surprised to see her standing by the newel post in the entry hall. She said our dad wanted to see us in the living room.

When we walked in I saw him sitting on the davenport with his head thrown back.

"Daddy?" We ran to him.

Tears flooded his face.

My sister and I said, "What's wrong?"

He opened his arms to embrace Joan on one side, me on the other.

I felt his body tremble.

He sobbed. "Your mother is dead. She shot herself."

He cried harder, howling like a wild animal.

Scared, I started to cry. I'd never seen my daddy like this.

Words scraped from his throat as though against a jagged metal edge. "She left a note – she said she didn't want to be a burden anymore."

Dead? Like the bird that I once found, its feathers a muggy grey? No! Not like that!

"Where is she?" I screamed. "I want her! I want my mommy!"

***

Somehow, I knew the way she died was a secret.

The months after her death faded into an eclipse but that taboo remained with me and I kept wondering why she said she was a burden. Why did she abandon us?

Twenty years later, I learned that in 1936 people did not talk about suicide. I began to ask questions. My sister was abrupt and tight-lipped. When I saw my dad's pain, evidenced by his inability to recall the devastating spiral of events, I talked with relatives. I learned that the burden Mother referred to wasn't her daughters or husband it was bipolar disease.

2015 Memoir Honorable Mention: My Fourth Grade Baseball Career by Robb Geweniger

Robb aka Robert Michael has been writing his entire life. He also been busy with many life adventures. When he was in first grade he sold more Christmas cards than anyone else in the school. He once walked across Abbey Road before it was famous. One of his uncles fought Rocky Graziano, twice. While working at Chicago's O'Hare airport, Robb shook hands with Harry Belafonte and later flirted with a woman who turned out to be Lee Trevino's wife. He earned a BA in English and studied Communication Arts at the University of Maryland. His career was primarily as a radio announcer and news-person at small stations in the Midwest. When he retired he began writing memoirs, short stories, and poetry. Other than that, Robb's granddaughter thinks he is the second most famous man in the world.

When I was in fourth grade an uncle asked me if I liked baseball.

"Yeah, sure," I said in order to end the conversation right there. The day would come when I could tell him about my big catch, but at that time, I had nothing to talk about. The fact was I didn't like baseball at all. I was terrible at it. I couldn't catch. I couldn't hit, and I didn't care. I knew there were two teams in Chicago, because my classmates talked about them all the time, but ask me to name a single player and I'd be guessing.

There were 19 boys in my class, which meant unless somebody was absent, one boy had to sit in the bleachers and watch. That boy was always me. I savored the days when I didn't have to play. Rather than sit in the bleachers watching, I walked around the playground looking at things: a footprint left in dried mud, a butterfly (which I would track about as far as it would let me), a dandelion with an ant carefully working its way across

91

the flower, a dust devil (which I would try to step into so I could feel the bits of dust spinning around me), a window with a spider and web on one side and the remains of a dead spider on the other.

On those days when I knew I would have to play I had problems paying attention in my classes and I felt sick all morning. I'd never say anything because I didn't want to be sent home. My mother was working. I didn't want her to take time off just because I didn't want to play baseball.

Finally, it was the last full day of the school year. It was going be a good day. One boy was absent, so I wouldn't have to play. I tallied my stats for the year: Sixteen games (give or take a game or two), one hit, no catches, lots of errors. It didn't matter anymore. My fourth-grade baseball career was about to come to an end. With a little luck one of the guys in my class would move away during the summer or better yet, another fifth-grade boy would move into town and there would not be a fifth-grade baseball career to worry about.

Getting close to lunch time I was thinking about flowers. I knew where all the flowering weeds were around the playground, so I was planning to check on some of them.

Needless to say, that wasn't going to happen.

"Hey, sissie," someone shouted as I headed across the playground. I recognized the voice. It was one of my classmates, one who always called me "sissie." I ignored him and continued toward the basketball court. It was my plan to look at some little blue flowers at one end of the cement slab.

"Hey, sissie, Jenkins went home sick. You have to play."

"No, no, no," I thought. "He's got to be kidding, playing some kind of joke on me."

When I realized he wasn't kidding, I started doing what I always did in that situation, I prayed. I didn't pray for a hit, not that it was asking too much of God. I simply didn't see any reason to bother God with such a little problem. Having a ball hit toward me in right field. Now, that was a problem, a very please-God-help-me-and-don't-let-them-hit-the-ball-to-me kind of problem. Most of the guys weren't bothered much when I struck out, most likely because they struck out plenty of times, too. What bothered them was that when I finally tracked down a ball hit my way, even though I threw it as hard as I could toward the infield, it often didn't go anywhere. A good throw of mine would land about twenty feet away.

So I trudged over to the ballfield. My team batted first. We got two runs. I was going to hit in the next inning, but first I had to get through a half inning in right field. One ball was hit in my direction, but lucky for me, the first baseman caught it before it got close.

When it was my turn at the plate I surprised everybody. The ball hit the bat and trickled passed the second baseman into right field. "Not bad," I said to myself, "two hits in seventeen games." Our games rarely lasted more than three innings. By the time we got to that third inning my team still led by two runs.

In their half of the third, the other team got two hits. With runners on first and third and two outs their best player, their team captain came to the plate. Out in right field, I wasn't paying much attention to him. Instead, I was watching the playground monitors. One of them was walking toward the doorway to ring the bell, calling everyone back to school, ending the lunch hour.

In an instant these things happened:

Instinctively, I started walking toward the school.

My classmates started screaming my name.

Someone was yelling, "Catch it! Catch it!"

I spun back toward the commotion.

The baseball zipped past my face and slammed into my chest, knocking the wind out of me and knocking me to the ground.

The school bell started ringing, but the playground seemed strangely quiet. Something seemed very wrong.

I lay on the ground gasping for air. My chest hurt.

Out of the corner of my eye, I saw the centerfielder running toward me.

As I sat up, something rolled off my chest into my lap. I grabbed it before it hit the ground.

"He's got it!" the centerfielder screamed. "He caught the ball."

It was the first time all year that my team had won the game and it couldn't have come at a better time, the very last game of fourth grade.

That summer my wish came true, a new boy, a fifth grader moved into town, right down the street from me. He was baseball crazy. All he wanted to do was play baseball, so that's about all we did and I got pretty good at it. Good enough that when it came time for the first lunch hour of fifth grade, I was looking forward to heading out to the ball field.

2016 Memoir Second Place Winner: Baker by Robb Geweniger

After I dropped out of Western Illinois University, I volunteered for a while at the St. Joseph Catholic Worker House, a homeless shelter in Davenport, Iowa. We served breakfast, lunch, and dinner to as many as fifty people and offered shelter to about twenty of them every night.

One night the Director, Margaret, hung up the phone, and said, "That was the Moline police. They want us to pick up Baker*."

"What's the problem?" asked Bob, one of the volunteers.

"Found him sleeping on a park bench," Margaret said.

Bob, Tom, and I – the three male volunteers – drove over to get Baker. Bob was happy to have me along in case Baker was passed out. Baker was a big man and it might take more than two people to wrestle him into the car if he was passed out.

As it turned out, Baker was not unconscious, maybe a little drunk, maybe not. When the Moline police found him, he said he lived at the Catholic Worker and asked if they could give him a ride there. The police were familiar with the Catholic Worker house. It was on their list of homeless shelters to call, so they called us.

We walked Baker to the car. He sat in the back seat with me.

"Baker what were you doing all the way over here," I asked, just trying to make conversation. Usually the men who stayed at the shelter never strayed too far, rarely more than a mile away.

"Personal business," Baker said as Bob started the car.

"You okay back there, Baker?" Bob asked, as Baker fidgeted in the seat apparently trying to get comfortable.

"Oh yes, fine, jes fine," Baker said.

Actually, he looked like something in his back pocket was bothering him and he was reaching around trying to straighten out whatever it was.

"Did you walk or take a bus over here?"

"Walked," Baker said.

"Well, I can understand…"

I was about to comment about the four miles between where we were and where we were going when Baker waved his hand in front of my face and a switchblade knife snapped open.

To say that scared me was an understatement.

"You know…" he said in a very hushed voice, "you know, I could kill you, real quiet like."

The car was moving now. Bob and Tom were talking; unaware of what was happening in the back seat.

"You know, Baker," Bob said, turning his head a little toward the back, "Margaret's going to check, make sure you're not drunk."

"I know," Baker said, not sounding like someone with a switchblade who'd been talking about killing me.

"And if you're not sobered up by the time we get back, you can't stay."

"I ain't drunk, so you can keep goin'."

"Sounds good," Bob said. A while ago Bob told me he empathized with most of the guys who stayed there because it was just a matter of luck he wasn't one of them.

When Tom and Bob resumed their conversation, Baker turned back to me. "What you gonna do if I stick you with this?" he said softly.

"Not much I could do. Outside I could jump away, but here, there's no place to go. So, I think you'd have me dead before I could do much of anything."

"You ain't afraid?"

"I don't know," I said as calmly as I could. *Afraid? I'm terrified. I'm sitting here shaking, wanting to scream, but he might kill me if I do. I can hardly breathe.*

Long before, when I was in the army I learned how to have a poker face. Unless I was extremely happy, meaning I had an unbeatable hand, the other players couldn't tell if I was bluffing or if I wasn't. They almost never knew by looking at my face if I thought my cards were good or not, so I won more often than I lost.

What Baker was looking at was my poker face. It automatically locked into place whenever I was in a difficult situation. I didn't look like I was afraid.

"You don't know? Damn, you ain't afraid."

Maybe I wasn't afraid. The knife scared me, that's true, but this wasn't making any sense to me. There was no reason for Baker to be doing this. Although he and I weren't friends, we also weren't enemies. In the food line, where we'd had the most contact, I served him just like everyone else, even giving him extra food when he asked.

We'd talked a couple times and I knew a little about him.

Originally from Nashville, he'd lived in Chicago for awhile so we had talked a little about the city, the L-trains, and the Chicago sports teams. I thought he was an intelligent, gentle man who didn't belong in a place like this, that he was here more because he was Black than any other reason. That didn't seem like enough reason to be threatening me.

"You know I could kill the three of you and take this here car to Mexico. Never been to Mexico, but I'd get by."

"You speak any Spanish?"

"See Senyoour," he said and laughed, "gimme some tacos."

"What are you planning to do when you get there? Eventually you'll need some money."

"Well, I got this blade. I'll get what I need."

"You're talking crazy, Baker. Maybe you should learn some Spanish first. You're smart enough you could learn in a few months, then you could go and you wouldn't have to be killing people."

"Man, you be nasty. You sposed to be beggin' for your life, squealin' 'Baker don't kill me and Baker put that knife away.' You sposed to be cryin' and screamin' but you talkin' 'bout learnin' Spanish. Man, you takin' the fun outta this."

As we turned the corner onto 5th Street, just a few blocks from the Catholic Worker, Baker said, "You know, Robb, I like you. You okay." Then he folded the switchblade and put it back in his pocket.

I breathed a sigh of relief and said, "Baker, you are a mean, mean man."

"Yeah, maybe so. Had you goin' a little there, didn't I?"

"More than a little," I said.

"Yeah?"

"Yeah, to tell you the truth, I was petrified."

Baker stared at me as if either he wanted to remember my face or there was something wrong with me.

"Now you the one bein' mean," he said.

Bob parked the car and we went into the house. Margaret met us at the door.

"How're you feeling Baker," she said. This was how she determined if someone was drunk or not, a short conversation was all she needed. "These guys treat you alright?"

"Jes fine," he said, winking at me. "Me and Robb here, we had a nice conversation about Mexico."

"Mexico." I heard Margaret saying as I walked away. "Have you ever been to Mexico, Baker?"

I climbed the stairs up to my room and eventually managed to fall asleep. In the morning, I saw Baker sitting around with the other guys waiting for breakfast.

He smiled at me and I nodded back. I never told anyone about his knife and never talked about that night in the back seat until now. There was no need to talk about it. Baker was killed a few weeks later crossing a busy street in Moline.

* Baker is not his name.

2015 Memoir Honorable Mention: Marching For My Brother
by Thomas Pratt

Thomas is a retired Engineering Systems Analyst. Writing, and especially reading are his hobbies. He's in the process of writing his memoirs with the help of family and friends. He's had a few letters to the editor published over the years and had one story about a trip to an orphanage in Nicaragua published in a Christian magazine. Other than that, he's just an ordinary great-grandpa who likes to write.

"Buncha losers!"

The loud, angry shout came from the crowd. Standing in front, a red faced older man wore an outraged, disgusted look.

***

It was Memorial Day, around 1990, although I am no longer sure of the year. I am not a veteran. I could never have dreamed of marching with those who had served. But that year, I did.

I arrived in downtown Santa Barbara and walked the parade route past the various military units as they were forming up. I found the Vietnam veterans grouped on a side street, milling around, talking and smoking. Some wore fatigues, some jeans, others a combination of military and civilian attire. As was their custom, they had not dressed in their parade uniforms. As I watched, a veteran beckoned me. After some hesitation, I crossed the street.

"Are you a Vietnam vet?" he asked.

"No, but my brother was. He died in combat there."

He looked at me for a long moment. "Then, you have to march for him."

Stunned, I shook my head. "Oh no, I couldn't do that, I wasn't there."

He looked me in the eye. "Your brother was there, and he can't march—you have to march for him."

For a moment, we stood silent, then putting his arms around me, he began to quietly sob. Soon, we were both crying. The others came close and they too began urging me to march. I hesitated, and then, I saw in their faces, *if you were my brother, I'd want you to march for me*. I agreed to march.

The parade began. Marching by in formal uniform, WW1, WW2, Korean War, then our turn. With my fellow marchers in their jeans and fatigues, we began.

"Buncha losers!"

A red-faced man in the crowd stood out. The veteran marching next to me, muttered, "Just ignore 'em."

I did so for a moment and then furious, I broke out of the march and ran back to the man. "My brother died in combat in Vietnam." I screamed at him, getting in his face. "He was not a loser!"

Startled, he leaned back. "Well, uh … I landed at Iwo Jima," he said in a weak voice.

Incredulous, I stared at him for a moment, and then shook my head in disbelief. I left him, caught up with the Vietnam vets, and we completed the march.

That evening, I wrote the editor of the *Santa Barbara News Press*:

Fellow citizens:

Yesterday, I had the privilege and high honor of marching with the Vietnam veterans in the Memorial Day Parade. As we marched, a man shouted from among the bystanders, "Buncha losers."

This letter is for that man and all others like him. I don't know your name and it doesn't matter. What does matter is that my brother, Butch, was drafted, went to war in Vietnam and performed his duties as required by his country. Doing so, he died there.

He left behind a devastated young wife, now a widow and single mother to be, an unborn daughter he will never know and who will never know him; a grandmother, mother and father; six siblings, countless relatives, and friends.

You, one of the lucky ones – a survivor of Iwo Jima – you, of all people, should appreciate his sacrifice.

Butch was not a loser. He was a warm, loving young man of twenty-one. His comrades-in-arms were just like him: someone's husband, someone's dad, someone's son, someone's grandson, someone's brother.

Not losers. Heroes.

You are no doubt a patriotic man. You served your country as you also were required to do, just like my kid brother, Butch. I can understand your frustration when you see the military pride you respect demeaned. But, to our country's great shame, it did not honor the Vietnam veterans upon their return, as it did you and your comrades. The Vietnam veterans deserve no less. Thank you for your service in WW2.

The newspaper published it the next day. For days and even weeks thereafter, acquaintances would stop and thank me for defending the Vietnam veterans.

***

Oftentimes over the years, my mind would drift back to that cold, snowy Christmas Day in Kokomo, Indiana. Family and friends gathered in front of Mom and Dad's house to see Butch off to Vietnam. As we surrounded the flagpole, Dad asked Butch to pull the halyard that slowly raised the Stars and Stripes. As the flag neared the shiny brass eagle at the top, it began whipping in the chilly morning breeze. I looked at Dad. Tears streamed down his cheeks. I had never seen our dad cry until that moment. In a voice choked with emotion, he vowed, "We will not lower this flag until Butch is safely home."

The years passed, and the flag slowly disintegrated. Each time I visited, it was a sad reminder of those happy days, so filled with hope and joy. In my final visit there, as I came over the hill, the flag pole slowly came into view. The shiny brass eagle was now a dull green. And the flag, the consecrated flag, was shreds. Until his own death, Dad steadfastly refused to allow it lowered.

***

On July 10, 1970, the helicopter in which he and his squad were being extracted from a combat operation, was hit by a rocket-propelled grenade. It crashed and burned. Seven young men lost their lives. Burned over 85% of his body, Butch put up a valiant fight, but succumbed to his injuries two days later.

Butch did come home, just as had more than 58,000 of his comrades. Relatives and friends filled the chapel in Kokomo, Indiana, his hometown, to overflowing for his funeral. The mayor decreed that all flags be flown at half-mast that day in his honor. Strangers from nearby cities who had also lost a loved one in Vietnam came to pay their respects.

Butch was buried in a tiny cemetery in the countryside near Point Isabelle, Indiana among his family and ancestors. He received a military burial with honor guard. The mournful, end of day "Taps" echoed across the rolling, nearby cornfields. Rifle volleys cracked into the blue afternoon sky as his wife was presented the triangular folded, memorial flag. This highly-decorated son of factory workers was an honored hometown and American hero.

***

Now in my eightieth year, forty-five years have passed. But still, when I think of him, I see that jovial, chubby cheeked teenager. He smiles, he laughs ... he is forever young. Among my many tributes to him over the years was a visit to the Vietnam Veterans Memorial Wall in Washington, DC. There on Panel 08W Line 013, *Carey J. Pratt* is engraved for the ages.

I ran my fingers over the shiny black surface until I felt the indented letters of his name. Head bowed, I remembered anew my anger at his unnecessary loss. So angered I had been unable to cry. Then, as so often in my life, I sought solace in writing. Alone in the quiet of my office, I would write a paragraph, and sob uncontrollably. I wrote of his life, how he was loved by family and friends, how he was a wonderful person. I wrote of how proud we were of him, and that he truly was our hero. I read it at his funeral, and the local newspaper published it the same day.

It was the highest honor of my life to march for my brother.

Poetry: Downsizing (Photographs and Memories) by Judith Ayn

Judith Ayn (a pen name to protect both the innocent and guilty) is originally from the East Coast. She has been happily settled in California for three decades and is working on a series of pieces to exorcise her Yankee demons.

Photographs in albums
Are stacked against a wall
They'll be the last to go
Most precious of them all

She's peered at her possessions
Weighed each in shaking hands
What to keep, what can go
No one understands

Ninety years of life are here
In boxes, bags and piles
Things once bought or given
Cause laughter, tears, some smiles

Memories escape the room
Life is growing short
She is moving once again
The photographs are not

Short Story: Ringo Starr and Grampy by Judith Ayn

July 7 is former Beatle Ringo Starr's birthday. He was born in 1940, making him seventy-seven this year (2017). Hard to believe he's a three-quarter century-old mop top. I owe him and his fellow bandmates most of the happiness I experienced growing up with their music. However, another special man, not a famous one, was also born on that day in 1904. Without him, I would not even exist.

My grandfather, "Grampy" George, should have lived to be a hundred. Instead, he died much too early, in his mid-seventies. My grandmother outlived him by decades until she finally retracted her claws from life and let go well into her nineties.

I think of my grandfather every day and believe he would have been proud of the person I've become. He was never a critical, judgmental man. Unlike his cold, cruel wife, full of ill will towards all, he chose to be loving, warm and supportive to his adult children and grandchildren. He shared Ringo's sad blue eyes, and like the former Beatle, he was known for being nice to just about everyone he met, despite his own problems in life.

Grampy performed manual labor for two companies over the years, neither of which offered him a pension. His work ethic was impeccable. He was the type of guy who could fix anything and rarely stopped moving. At home, he toiled in a small backyard garden. In the summer after watering his plants, he allowed himself time to watch baseball on television, or listen to games on the radio, if he still had chores to finish. He was one of many New Englanders who believed the Red Sox would definitely be champs next year, or perhaps the one after.

His cars, always pre-owned older models, were a big part of his life. He spent lots of time lovingly tinkering with, washing or polishing each one. Although he often dreamt of one day owning a brand-new vehicle, there never seemed to be money for that in the family budget my grandmother managed.

He lived to drive and his short Sunday trips were memorable, legendary. Once behind the wheel, Grampy would make up names for people he saw outside the houses we passed. He'd call out the moniker he'd invented, wave wildly and usually honk a greeting to confused strangers just walking along, minding their business on old Maine back roads. Then he'd tease my grandmother, cackling as he drove past yard sales she wanted to stop and investigate. If she insisted, he'd turn around for her, still chuckling and in good spirits. I found his behavior absolutely hilarious.

Grampy also loved cats and was affectionate as a parade of them joined the family and passed on through the years. Often, he'd be puttering around his workbench, listening to an old song by his beloved Elvis, while the current cat slept on the freshly waxed hood of his car. I can't remember one single time that man showed any temper. Later in life, I'd catch him crying, but he wouldn't say a word, just dab at his eyes and continue his work.

There was never a discussion of his past, or politics, or anything too serious. Instead, we'd talk about the Beatles, my favorites, and he'd shake his bald head when their music played, as if he were in the group and sported a shaggy hairdo, too.

He lived in the present. Obviously, Grampy wasn't perfect. He allowed my grandmother free reign to rule over the family like a nasty queen, a disservice to his children. He even gave up spending time with his own mother for my grandmother's sake, breaking two hearts with that choice in order to keep peace at home.

Recovering from a stroke shortly before his death, Grampy wanted nothing more than to take short naps during the day and just relax. My grandmother, though, continued to nag and badger him mercilessly. He soldiered on with her, marking their fiftieth wedding anniversary. Soon after, on a suffocating hot and humid August night, Grampy died in his sleep in the upstairs bedroom where my grandmother allowed no fan.

I'm left with photos of my grandfather and a couple of his paint-by-number scenes I was given. Luckily, my cousin and I reconnected after a rift caused by my grandmother, and we've been able to pool our memories of Grampy. He lives in our hearts and we've shared him with our children. July 7 is a very important day in history. Two good men were born then: one was part of a revolution in music; the other was my hero and with me for a very short time. Rest in peace, Grampy.

2015 Short Story Youth First Place Winner: The New Generation by Noah Sletten

Noah is sixteen-years-old now. He enjoys reading, writing, jogging, and playing video games. He has been writing for several years and has won first- and second-place awards in the teen division in two of the VCWC's short story contests. His favorite authors are James Dashner, James Patterson, Philip Reeve, and Garth Nix. His favorite genre is science fiction.

I've seen old videos of the old human planet. So large and vast, so pure and natural, so full of hope. And so diverse! There were forests of tall trees, plains of grass, and deserts of sand. You could find dozens of species of thousands of genera of millions of phyla. The sky was the limit, and we kept pushing that limit. And all that pushing finally broke it.

The effects of pollution hit us like a truck. Millions around the world were sick, clean water and fossil fuels were depleted, and fallout was everywhere. Finally, ol' Mr. Sun was heating up with his increasing solar flares. So, all the best and brightest minds got together and decided that it is time that we leave the cradle of Earth and reach out into the galactic neighborhood—in other words, we got the hell out of there.

So, we built an armada of giant ships and scattered ourselves across the universe in hopes of finding a new, better planet to screw up. And that is where my story picks up.

Oh, I'm sorry, did I not tell you who I am yet? I tend to get wrapped up in myself sometimes. Old habits die hard.

My name is Hexter Pierpont. My friends call me the Hex. It's supposed to be an old English word for a curse, but to be honest, my life is actually pretty cushy. I live in the *S.S. Hyperion*, one of the escape ships for the human race. In the old days, humans had the vision that starships would be epic, sleek vessels with eye-catching designs. But in reality, the *Hyperion* is really just a huge cylinder with a slightly larger solar sail in front. At least, that's what I've been told. Only trained professionals get to look outside the ship. That's always been my lifelong dream—to become one of those astronauts. But until then, I'm stuck in the "temporary" home of the humans.

The *Hyperion* has almost all the same features of Earth — it has rivers, lakes, trees, and snow — and yet it all feels *fake*. That's because we live on the inside of the cylinder, so the ground curves *up* instead of down. It has to do with centrifugal forces and magnets and whatnot — I dozed off during that lecture. Really, I'm just waiting until I can get out of this 'hood so I can get out into the wild black yonder, as they call it.

Anyway, to recap — everyone's on a ship, looking for a new home, and I'm itching to get out of here. That's the end of the exposition. Really. I know I tend to go off on tangents, but I promise to stay on track. Are we cool? Good. On with the story!

This adventure begins on an ordinary day in Neighborhood 7. I'm walking home from lacrosse practice, feeling pretty good about myself; so good that I take the transit home instead of my self-driving Magne-car. I've always thought the people on the transit are much more fun and interesting than the Magne-cars, which have big screens that play the trendiest songs or videos. Bor-ing. I'm sort of weird like that; I never got into all the hoopla over Smart-eyes or Magne-cars. I prefer face-to-face interaction instead of video-chatting.

So I'm taking the transit, and all is right with the world, when suddenly this shaggy guy staggers in, a glass bottle in hand, and stands right next to me. We're the only two on the transit. I can smell something on him, but I can't quite make it out. He glances down at my clothes – custom fit LeanJeans, a t-shirt, and a vintage baseball cap – and puts together that I must be in the high middle class. So, he gets right in my face and says with a slur, "Y-you think yer soo cool in yer fancy outfits. You think yer better than all of us. Well, sonny, yer not–ya hear me pal? Yer NOT!" He's shouting right at me, and I can identify the smell. *Alcohol*, I think, *he's drunk.*

I decide to stay quiet. Unfortunately, this just makes him angrier. "Whassa matter, hotshot? Too soft to fight me, eh? Y-you wanna fight me?" He says, fists clenched. I turn slowly toward him and calmly say "I don't want a fight."

Suddenly, the man swings his fist at my face. I dodge, his fist grazing my ear. I feel a sharp pain and stumble towards the other end of the transit, heart racing. The man staggers towards me, clutching his bottle like a club. "Let this be a lessin to ya," he says, the rage boiling in his voice, "an' all the Richies in this $@&%*!# town!"

In the second before I was about to get brained by a beer bottle, I remembered Policy 34 of the *Conflict Resolution* pamphlet: "If all else fails, use physical contact." Thus, as the man is about to bring down the bottle, I punch him in the jaw.

He cries in pain, staggers back to the door, and falls out onto the street with a startled cry. *He'll be fine*, I tell myself, *Services will find him and he'll get medical attention.* Still, it's unsettling to think that I may have killed someone.

My ear stings. I gingerly bring my hand to my ear. Blood. Mom will not be happy about this.

The transit stops at my street and I eagerly get off. I'm ready to clean up and put this whole afternoon behind me. Hopefully my ear isn't hurt that bad.

I walk into my house, where mom greets me. "Hi sweetie, how was – OHMYGOODNESS WHAT HAPPENED TO YOU?"

It's that bad?

Mom rushes over to check out my ear, her face pale as a ghost. I respond, "Oh, uh, it's nothing. I was taking the Transit, and–" I'm interrupted when Mom bursts out again. "You took the TRANSIT? WHY?" Yeah, I forgot to mention, my Mom *hates* the Transit. She thinks it's "a breeding ground for low-lifers and thugs." As you can tell, we don't get along too well.

"Mom, this was just a bad day. It'll never happen again."

"Well, you're darn right it's not going to happen again! From now on, you're riding home with Javen." Javen is my younger brother. We don't get along well either.

"Oh, come on Mom, with *Javen?* He's a total spaz!"

"You're riding with Javen and that's final. I will NOT have any son of mine becoming a hooligan like–" Mom never gets to finish because she is interrupted by a special bulletin by the captain.

"Greetings, fellow astronauts!" in his typical, overly cheery voice. "I hope you're having a wonderful afternoon!" *Fat chance*, I thought. "Right now we are passing over the planet Heylin-42D." We rush to the living room, to put on the nearest set of Holo-goggles to see outside. Instantly, the room falls away and in front of me I see a giant sphere of indigo and green blotches. A chorus of "Oooh"s and "Aaah"s rise up from the neighborhood.

The captain continues, "Heylin-42D was named after the famous Dr. Rotair Heylin, when he discovered the element Heylinium in the planet's atmosphere. Heylinium has a powerful photosynthetic potential, giving it an unmistakable green hue…" I zone out on the speech as I take in the beauty of the planet. The indigo terrain looks gleaming, almost alive. *Someday,* I tell myself, *someday I'm gonna go down there and explore that place, and I'll be the greatest astronaut ever to live!*

"…And that's why you have Smart-eyes, taking your internet life with you! Thank you all for tuning in, and have a good night." I hear Mom and Javen taking off their Holo-goggles but I keep watching. "Well, that was nice," Mom says, "Hexter, go wash that blood off your ear. We'll talk later."

I don't get up immediately to wash off. I'm too caught up in the spectacle. The raw beauty of planet is breathtaking. I want to reach out and touch the surface…

Then I notice a dot moving on the planet, and it seems to be growing. I'm starting to panic, because I realize that the dot is *approaching*! I'm paralyzed with fear as it lands on the ship. It looks like an elongated turtle shell with insect legs, a tail with a grasper on it, and a single, glowing violet eyepiece. Suddenly, it starts squirting a syrupy orange liquid onto the hull.

Before I can call the authorities, the creature looks directly at the camera, almost as if it knows I'm watching. It gives me a look like, *I'm not going to hurt anyone. Just trust me.*

I stop panicking and just watch the tiny craft do its thing. It waits a few seconds as the liquid dissolves the hull without actually destroying it, allowing it to crawl into the spaceship. After the craft is all the way through, the liquid seeps out, leaving the hull good as new.

I take off the Holo-goggles, blinking and shaking my head, trying to readjust to the real world. I decide that a little fresh air would do me good. I wash the blood from my ear and go outside. I ponder what I just witnessed. What *was* that thing? Why did it come into the ship? Where is it now? And why is the ground under my feet so squishy?

I leap back, looking at the ground in surprise. All the grass and soil on the *Hyperion* is regulated so you never have an uneven patch on your lawn. So why is that one patch squishy? I get even more concerned when the ground turns bright orange. I know what's coming, and I know what I'm going to do. As soon as I see the violet eyepiece come through, I grab on to the craft and yank it through. It puts up surprisingly little resistance, considering that it has a tail that shoots dematerializing orange goop. It's immobilized after a good slam in the back.

I lug it back inside and I take it up to my room, being careful to avoid Mom in the kitchen. I plunk it onto the table, digging out my old home medicine kit from fourth grade. I also get some pliers from the cabinet. Finding a chink in its armor, I pry the contraption open.

Inside is a small creature with wrinkly skin, a pincer-like mouth, six tentacle-esque appendages with what looked like leaves on the end, and two– no, four bulbous black eyes. It was truly an intriguing sight. I couldn't tell if it was breathing or not, so I poked it with the pliers. Instantly, the four bulbous eyes opened, and the tail of the craft lashed out and attached itself to my forehead. At this point I started to really freak out, trying to rip the appendage from my head. But it does no good. I'm about to yell for help, but then I hear a voice in my head. *Do not be afraid,* says the voice, *I am not wanting to be hurting you.*

I calm down a little bit and say to the creature, "Is that you talking to me? How do you —" *Do not be talking. Only think what you are wanting to say.* Slightly startled, I think, *Why are you here? What do you want?*

I am a resident of the planet #*#*#, the one that you are now passing.

Could you say that again? I didn't quite pick that up.

Oh, I have forgotten, some of the words in our language are not able to be translated into your human language. How rude I am.

No biggie. So what were you saying?

I am called #*#*#*#*, but you may be calling me Poot. I have come to study your human race, so we may be one species together.

Ew.

Not like that. Anyway, we —

Wait, so they just sent you to investigate us? Why not a team? And why not do it more directly?

That is classified.

Really.

Oh all right, you have gotten me. My species has no intention of inter-mingling with yours. Many did not even notice when you were passing by our planet. But I am different. I wanted to see the outer-places and meet different beings. But our species do not condone that. They want us all to stay here where it is safe.

I could see a hint of anger and sadness in his bulbous, black eyes.

I know how you feel.

But I built this spacecraft in my dwelling, in secret. And when you came in your big cylinder, I shot up into the air and hitched a ride. And we are here now.

I can't help respecting Poot, following his (or hers, or whatever) dream and living on the edge. I reminisce back to earlier in the afternoon, when Mom got mad at me for taking the Transit home.

I see you are feeling the same way, Poot suddenly chimes in.

Oh yeah. I forgot that he was reading my mind. Yeah, I guess our species have more in common than you might think, eh?

I am supposing so.

Hey, sorry about your spaceship there. I'll help you fix it.

It is no big E.

We laugh together for a bit. Poot's laugh kind of sounds like a kitten meowing at its loudest, with a sawmill running in the background. Suddenly, I have an idea. *I can help you see the stars, you know.*

Really? You are able to do that?

Sure. Wait there. Can I take this off for a second?

The tail loosens its grip on my forehead, and I pull it off. I run downstairs, grab a pair of Holo-goggles, and run back upstairs with them. I place Poot's mind-reading tail thing on my forehead once again. Instantly Poot is asking questions. *What is the meaning of this?* He inquires.

These can project images from outside the ship into your eyes.

Those only have two of the eye-holders. How will I be seeing through them?

You can see things through my eyes, right?

That is correct.

Well, I'm going to put these on, and you can see it through my eyes.

That could work.

I put on the glasses, and once again I see the indigo and green planet, farther away now. You can see the night side as well as the day side, and an array of lights dance across the dark surface, much like Earth was hundreds of years ago. Thousands of stars dance and twinkle across the sky, and the red sun looks like a big red marble in the distance.

I take off the goggles and look at Poot. Even with his alien face, he is overcome with emotion. His four eyes are getting watery. He thinks to me, with a sincerity that I can feel, *Thank you.*

2016 Poetry Youth Second Place Winner: The Salvation Story, Part I by Noah Sletten

We've come so far as beings
With a sentience that's all our own
From hydrogen-powered airships
To a wheel chipped out of stone.

We thought we were unstoppable
When we learned how the atom behaved
But somehow we still must obey the force
That summons a man to his grave

All the people in the world
Aware of their imminent demise
Studied and theorized the cause of this plague
While the answer was before their eyes

It all began in a garden
Where joy and good health ruled all
But then a young couple broke their dear Father's heart
And our proud species… began to fall

That father had overseen all of creation
He put all of the stars in their place
He adorned the whole wide world
With the image of His glorious face

When the young couple sinned the first sin
That image fell out of balance
The whole of creation became thorny and cruel
And our souls became an abhorrence

Now, that father wouldn't leave us to rot
He wouldn't be much of one then
So He devised a grand master plan
To rejoin us into His kin

2015 Short Story Adult First Place Winner: Coming Clean by Lee Wade

Lee has won awards for short story, poetry and playwriting. Published by Lillenas Publishing House, VCWC Press, and others, she is editor and Chief of Encouragement at DreamLight Press, assisting authors in multiple genres since 2010. (writersdesk.126@gmail.com) The USC graduate lives in Newbury Park with cheerleader/critic/college sweetheart, hubby, Keith.

"You're lucky Nick knew how to swim," Larry said, looking at the mess in their yard. Paper plates dotted their pool like lily pads. "He could have drowned."

"Not lucky. I knew. He used to ·be a lifeguard." Sandy consigned a "Congratulations, Nick and Kayla" banner to the rubbish bag. "In a previous life."

"A previous life?" Larry fished a string of paper Chinese lanterns from the hot tub. "I thought Kayla introduced the two of you at George's birthday party last month."

"She did. He didn't recognize me, or he put on a very convincing act, so I went along. I didn't expect him to stick around. The next thing I knew, Kayla was in love." Sandy rolled her eyes. "And Aunt Barbara and Uncle George were begging to use our place for this engagement party."

She waved her arm over the detritus like Vanna White. "This," she said, "probably saved a life."

"I don't see how starting an argument with your cousin's fiancé and tripping him into the pool counts as an act of salvation."

"I had to do something. Kayla needed to see what he's really capable of. You saw how nasty he got."

"Most guys don't like being made a fool of in front of their friends and soon-to-be relatives. I'd be pretty pissed, too."

"Even so, you'd probably treat it like some kind of bad joke. You might have thrown whoever you thought pushed you in the pool, but not the furniture and the food. You wouldn't have cussed out everybody and everything in sight and destroyed the place." She stopped harvesting finger sandwiches and crudités from the lawn. "Would you?"

He met her stare dead-on.

"You most certainly would not have left without me."

He ended the stare-down with a sideways look. "Not a chance."

That he was here at midnight cleaning up the disaster she'd created was proof that he loved her. Or that he was as wacky as she was. Whatever. He'd never leave her.

"Nick didn't even *look* at her, Larry. He *left* her. You'd never do that."

"I might sell you to the highest bidder, however."

She didn't take the bait. "Larry, she cannot marry that man!"

"Why not?"

"He's a good looking con man – a phony."

"Sandy – he's a nice guy! I like him better than the loser she was into last time. The guy had green teeth."

"Larry. I'm not joking."

"Okay, maybe his teeth weren't green, but Nick adores her. So, he got a little intense…"

"He. Is. Scum."

Larry stopped righting overturned chairs. "And you know this how?"

"I told you. From a previous life – before I met you. Believe me. He is not to be trusted."

"Sandy? Are you jealous?"

"No!"

"The guy is loaded."

"Yeah, with his ex-wives' money." She waggled her hand.

"So, the guy inherited a few bucks. That's not a crime," Larry said. "Better for Kayla."

"Not really," Sandy said.

Nick's tragic rags-to-riches story wasn't a secret. "Heiress Lost in Jungle" was news for months. Nick's wife, Shelbourne Industries heiress, Ophelia, vanished on a humanitarian relief trip. Circumstances indicated her survival was extremely unlikely. Her husband was her sole heir. The ex-personal trainer was not only tall, dark, and GQ handsome, he was rich.

"Honey, this isn't like you. Why can't you just be happy for Kayla?

Sandy crammed in more debris.

"You ruined her party."

"Better her party than her life. I did it *for* her, Larry." She snatched up the trash bag and stomped away.

"Don't expect a thank-you note." he called after her.

She tromped across the lawn, the overstuffed bag bouncing behind her. Her blonde hair, still damp from the pool, glistened, a halo in the moonlight. "I did it for her!"

Had he not heard her voice break, he would have laughed.

Inside, he found her sitting on the sofa in the dark, her face wet with tears.

"Come with me, sweetheart," he said. "Please."

She stood, and leaning against him, let him lead her to their bedroom. She wouldn't let him turn on the lights. They undressed in silence. In their bed, he held her. She told him stories.

"His name was Carlo when I met him. Giancarlo Vitelli. I was fifteen. He was nineteen. He was the lifeguard. He was polite, deferential and cute, super cute. I was in love with him. Me and every other teenage girl in town. And he knew it. Even our mothers loved him. They went on and on about his good manners. They thought he was safe – like a big brother. He had a car and because he was over eighteen, he could legally carry teenage passengers. Our moms sometimes asked Carlo to drive us places when they couldn't. Among my friends, getting to ride with Carlo got you points. A gold star if it was just you and him. My first time was a lot of fun.

"He played the radio really loud. We sang along. When Mom got a part-time job, he picked me up after piano lessons for a few weeks. He made me laugh."

She was a kid again, ponytail flying, racking up points. The happy memory passed, and Larry must have felt her stiffen.

"On the day after my sixteenth birthday, he told me he had a gift for me. He drove into the foothills, parked his car and made me make love to him. He told me I was a woman now. I didn't know how to feel. I wasn't ready. I had been afraid, but he was gentle, and I thought I was in love. I thought I was special. I thought he loved me. He told me I had to keep it all a secret. I had sex with him whenever he wanted for the rest of the

107

summer. By September, the secret couldn't be kept any longer. I was pregnant.

"He was furious. He said I was a stupid bitch, but he'd fix everything. A few days later he asked my mother if he could take me to listen to a band playing about forty-five minutes away. It was a big deal because she only let him take me places close to home. I begged to go. I was excited that he wasn't mad at me anymore. He took me instead to an apartment building in the poorest part of town."

Larry must have felt her tremble then.

"A woman in a white doctor's coat let us into an apartment. In the living room was a table with stacks of towels on it, a TV, and a couch. Carlo handed the woman an envelope. She opened it, counted the money inside and put the envelope in her coat pocket. She looked at me but spoke to Carlo. 'Kinda young, Carlo. You should be more careful, take precautions.' Carlo said it felt better without. He flopped on the tired leather couch and picked up the remote.

"The woman motioned me toward a bedroom. 'You ready, honey?' I started crying. She told me not to worry. She'd done this many times. She pointed to a bathroom at the end of the hall."

Sandy quoted the woman in a tender tone. "'You probably want to pee first. Take off everything on the bottom. Wash-up down there, then come on back'."

She paused, then went on reciting history.

"She gave me a towel from the table in the living room. I headed down the hall, sobbing. Carlo was yelling that he couldn't hear the TV."

"Bastard!" Larry drew her closer. She lay still, her back pressed to him. He lifted damp strands of hair from her cheek.

After a deep, deep breath she spoke. "When Dinah — that was the woman's name — was through, a red mass of tissue about the size of an orange — our baby — lay in a plastic basin to be taken out to the garbage. She gave me a shot that hurt like hell — vitamin K to ease the bleeding. After about an hour, Dinah said I could go. She gave me some iron tablets to take at home to keep up my strength. I thanked her.

"Carlo laughed as we got in his car. 'Told you I'd take care of everything.' He sang to the radio all the way home. All I could think about was how to keep this secret from my mother. Carlo dropped me off. I went straight to my room. Told Mom I had a headache. I faked being sick for almost a week until she threatened to take me to the doctor."

"So, when did you tell her?" Larry asked.

"Never. Everybody thought I was a good girl. Especially Mom. She trusted me. I couldn't do that to her. About six weeks later, my best friend, Lori, died in her sleep. Internal bleeding. Carlo used to give her rides, too. I always wondered — what if...? I should have said something then, how could I? Everybody would know....

"After graduation, as soon as I could, I left. With Mom's blessing which I didn't deserve. She tried to keep me up-to-date. Whenever one of my friends, including 'that nice boy, Carlo' made our paper, she sent me clippings. I missed her yet dreaded her phone calls because I'd have to talk about him.

"Then Carlo left town and dropped from Mom's reports. I drank an entire bottle of wine to celebrate. The hangover was worth it. So was the four-hour drive home. I'd been gone two years.

"Mom's last Carlo report was a newspaper photo with the caption, "Hometown boy spotted at L.A. premiere." I prayed I'd never see or hear of him again. Petition denied.

"I was working in an upscale boutique near the college the next time I saw him. I recognized him at once. Tanned and toned, he was even better looking than he was at nineteen. I was ashamed, then angry that I even thought so. Despite our history, I determined to be civil. Maybe he had changed. Anyway, I needed the job.

"Before I could say anything, he introduced himself as Tony Quinn. He was on his honeymoon and looking for a trinket for his beloved. The woman on his arm reminded me of myself. She fluttered her eyelashes, pushing her hair behind her ear when he looked in her direction. She looked at his mouth when he spoke as though jewels fell from his lips. She giggled at every *double entendre*. I'd laughed like that. She seemed as naïve as I had been at barely sixteen. I felt sick.

"Three years later, I'm watching the news. 'Actress Irene Dunne found dead in hotel pool three days after her third wedding anniversary. It was the woman from the boutique. They said she was pregnant. They said her husband, Tony Quinn, was too distraught to speak on camera. I had nightmares for days.

"Whatever he's calling himself these days, this man is scary. Bad things happen to women close to him. This time, Larry. It's Kayla." Fresh tears traced the tracks of old ones.

***

Sandy's stories came to Larry in waves. He absorbed them until she fell asleep in his arms, physically and emotionally spent.

He rose early, careful not to wake her. He'd hardly slept. The dots were arranging themselves in ugly pictures. He made himself coffee and toast and checked his computer.

Thirty minutes later, he called George. He did his best to apologize for the wrecked party and got an earful. He endured the harangue. When George agreed to rendezvous, Larry was relieved. He left a note for Sandy on the kitchen counter, grabbed his keys and his phone. He dialed as he rushed out.

***

Paul Brewster trapped the phone between his shoulder and ear. "Detective Brewster."

"Hi, PB. It's Larry. Can you meet me at Heritage Square in about twenty minutes? By the fountain?"

"Maybe. Should I wear a flower in my lapel so you'll recognize me? Good morning to you, too. Long time no see. How's the wife and kids? Still got the dog? Oh, wait. Those are your lines, right?"

"Hey, man, sorry to be so abrupt but it's serious. I don't have time to explain it right now. Can you get away?"

***

At the fountain, Larry and Paul slapped each other on the back in greeting.

"Alone together at last," Paul said, grinning. "Why all the drama?"

Larry gave him a condensed version of the wrecked party and Sandy's revelations about Nick.

Paul Brewster asked questions, jotted some notes then made a couple of phone calls. "We'll get this guy, Larry," he said.

An older man with a slight limp walked briskly toward them.

"Uncle George?" Paul said.

Larry nodded.

"Want me to disappear?" Paul asked.

"No. He's pretty upset and…."

Paul grinned. "You need a bodyguard?"

"Nope. Just help me convince him."

"You called this meeting, Larry, so let's get on with it," George said as he arrived. He nodded at Paul. "Who's he?"

Paul extended his hand. "Detective Paul Brewster."

George kept his hands in his jacket pockets, looking hard at Larry. "You called the cops?"

"We're old friends," Paul said.

"Watch your back," George said. "You wanted to talk, Larry. So, talk."

Paul interrupted. "Mr. Winston, you asked why Larry called me. Based on what he's told me and shown me, I believe your daughter's fiancé may be a very dangerous individual. Until I can satisfy myself that I'm mistaken, I'd advise you to keep Kayla away from him."

Concern replaced anger on George's face. "What do you mean — dangerous? How did you find out?"

"You can thank Sandy later. Kayla's at your house, right?

"Yes."

"We're sending a unit over just in case Nick shows up. Would you call Mrs. Winston and ask her to call me if they hear from Nick?"

George's hand shook as he accepted the business card Paul offered. He phoned Barbara. Assured that Nick hadn't called, George left at once.

Larry dialed Sandy again. Still no answer.

"Ride with me," Brewster said.

***

Sandy smiled as she read Larry's note. *Meeting George at Heritage Park. Back soon.* "Thank God," she said. Her phone rang. She reached across the kitchen counter for it.

"You always did have great legs."

She shrieked turning toward the voice. The ringing stopped.

"Carlo," she said in a thin whisper, tugging at the tail of her nightshirt.

He ogled her. "Your door was open, so I let myself in.

"Get out!" She laid the phone on the counter.

"That's no way to treat an old friend."

"You were never my friend!"

"Friends, lovers." He shrugged and walked toward her. "I can't have you messing up my gig. You know that, don't you?"

She didn't flinch. "Why marry Kayla? She's got nothing."

"Not yet. But she's a Daddy's girl, like the others. She's a very sexy woman and I'm a very patient man."

"I'm not," Paul Brewster said. "Show me your hands!"

Sandy handed Larry her phone. "I recorded every word."

"Party's over, Nick," Larry said.

2015 Short Story Adult Third Place Winner: Slaying Dragons
by Barbara Piszczek

Barbara is a transplant from Michigan who came to California in 1999. She works at UC Santa Barbara as a Development Analyst. Previously, she worked as a grant writer, specializing in health and education grants for schools and non-profits. Barbara was featured in Quintessence, *the Ventura County Writers Club (VCWC) anthology as both a writer and an assistant editor. Barbara was the editor of the* Windows *and* Serendipity *anthologies published by VCWC. She writes articles for the newsletter. She is fond of late-night walks, movie marathons, and people appreciating her critiques.*

I hear the buzz of my cell phone before the caller's name appears. My hand, already reaching for the device, freezes. It hovers there as the phone rings two more times. By the time I force myself to grab the phone, it has gone silent. I stare at the screen and, after a few moments, the tiny voice mail symbol appears at its corner. I don't listen to the message. I don't want to think about it.

"You haven't forgotten what courage is," whispers the doubt inside me, "you never knew what it was."

But I did. Once.

***

"You're ruining it." Cousin Kyle's face was blotchy red with fury, fists clenched hard at his sides, crushing the cardboard tube that served as his sword. "You're supposed to be the captured princess."

I held a matching weapon in my hand, one of Grandma's afghans tied at my neck as a cloak. "I can be a knight, too." Three sets of eyes stared at me, but I refused to budge.

"But we need a damsel in distress," said John, Kyle's brother. Confusion had etched a line between his brows. "Who else can play her?"

"What about Queenie?"

At her name, Queenie, Grandma's miniature collie, yipped in excitement. She ran between the four of us, panting and eager to be let in on the fun.

"See, she likes the idea!" I picked her up, and she wiggled in my arms, straining to lick my face. Her tongue scraped against my cheek.

"Queenie won't stay still. We can't use her." My brother, Mark, squinted at the sky before tugging down the brim of his baseball cap. "We need the princess to stay in the tower until we rescue her."

I glanced at the tower, a heap of rocks. Grandpa and Grandma had acres of farmland, and when the soil was tilled in early spring, larger rocks were hauled away to the join the pile. The damp stones would dry in the sun, the rich earth became smears of brown and grey that made me think of bird poop. "I don't want to." Queenie whined as I tightened my hold on her, nuzzling my face to encourage me to pet her. I set her back on the lawn and she rested her furry body against my leg.

"Are you going to play the right way or not?" Kyle stood in front of me, arms crossed now, his cardboard tube limp in his grasp from his manhandling.

"Why can't we slay a dragon instead? The rock heap could be a dangerous beast threatening the castle." I looked back toward our grandparents' house, white with its jaunty green trim and red brick chimney.

Every summer, this was our playground for two carefree weeks. My two cousins, my brother, and I chased each other in games of tag, ate apples fresh from the tree, and swam in the lake near a bonfire pit. There, every night, we toasted marshmallows and made s'mores that we devoured while the hot white fluff oozed from between the graham crackers. Grandpa taught us about the constellations and let us peer through his telescope. It was magical.

But this summer was different. Kyle, the eldest at twelve, was sullen and prone to picking fights with the rest of us if we didn't do what he commanded. Grandma said he was getting a case of the growing-ups; I thought he was just being a jerk.

"Why can't I be a knight like the rest of you?"

John's cheeks had reddened in the bright sunlight. "Come on, Kyle. Let's quest to slay a dragon. It'll be fun."

"I don't want to play anymore." Kyle grumbled and whacked his sword against a tree. The abrupt sound roused a group of ravens perched there, and the birds cawed their irritation as they took flight. Queenie barked and chased after them before returning to watch us.

John's shoulders slumped. "Well, what do you want to play, then?" He sounded tired, and I had a feeling that John said that phrase to his brother a lot.

Mark plopped onto the ground, stretching out his legs and scratching at a mosquito bite in a thoughtful manner. "Let's ride our bikes to town to get ice cream."

"It's too hot." Kyle twisted his cardboard tube into a pretzel.

"Go swimming." I took off the afghan, hugging it in my arms. I chose a lush patch of grass to use as my mat. I could feel a trickle of sweat slide down the back of my neck and was grateful for the shade of the tree.

Kyle ignored me, looking at his brother. "What do you want to do?"

"How about we ask Grandma and Grandpa if they'll take us to see a movie?"

Mark shook his head. "Grandpa already left to pick up something from the hardware store. We could play with the remote control helicopter that I got for my birthday."

"Yeah, let's do that." John nodded, a grin splitting his face.

"I get to go first." Kyle rose to his feet.

Mark started to frown, then sighed. "Fine."

We started back toward the house, tall weedy grass whipping our legs as we ran. Mark went straight to the garage, looking around the shelves where Grandpa stocked his tools and spare parts. Kyle, John, and I followed and the four of us examined the shelves.

"There it is." Mark pointed at one of the storage cubbies that Grandma had given to us for our toys.

Kyle yanked it out of John's hands after he freed it from the crate. "I'm first."

John nodded. "Yeah, yeah. Here's the remote."

I watched as the three ran back outside, then crept inside the house to place the afghan in the laundry room. I could smell rich aroma of gravy as Grandma prepared dinner. Beneath the meaty scent was a hint of vanilla from baking; Grandma never let the heat get in the way of making good food, even during the hottest summer. Grandpa said she served in the Navy during World War II, and that a stuffy kitchen was nothing to her.

I ran outside to trail after the boys, braids beating a tattoo against my back.

Kyle had already gotten the helicopter in the air, flying the toy in crazy loops.

"Careful, Kyle. Don't break it." Mark kept reaching for the control, but Kyle elbowed him away.

"Relax, I won't." Kyle smirked and sent the copter higher into the air. A sudden gust sent the toy tumbling in the wind before it crashed into the tall boughs of a maple tree.

"You broke it!" Mark swung a clumsy fist at Kyle's arm.

Kyle grabbed his wrist. "Don't."

"Maybe it's okay. It looks like it just got caught in the branches." John tried to separate the two.

"So climb up and get it." Kyle gave his brother a push.

"You should get it. You're the one who flew it into the tree." Mark stood at the trunk of the tree, gazing up into the leafy tangle of branches.

"It's your helicopter."

Mark bit his lip, cheeks paling despite his faint sunburn. "But...."

That's it. "I'll get it." I marched over to the trio.

Kyle sneered. "You wouldn't even climb onto a pile of rocks."

I ignored him and tugged off my sneakers and socks, my toes digging into the soil. "Give me a boost, John."

John held out a hand for me to step onto, then pushed up as I reached for the lowest branch. With his help, I swung myself onto the sturdy limb and began to scale the branches. The bark was smooth under my bare feet and the green leaves brushed against my hair. Bright sunlight speckled through little gaps among the leaves, but it was cooler within the tree's arms.

The boys watched as I made my way higher. A chipmunk chattered at me as it scurried away to track my progress from a safe distance. I had never climbed this high before, but the memory of Kyle's scornful eyes and Mark's fearful ones urged me on and I weaved my way through the maze of limbs, my grip sure despite my sweaty palms.

When I reached the copter, I settled in a crook, inspecting the way the toy was snarled in the twigs. The plastic blades of the copter had pierced a leaf and the rear rotor was trapped inside a cluster of twigs.

"What's the matter? Are you stuck?" Kyle's voice taunted me.

I didn't answer him. I wrapped my legs about the branch, lying on my belly to keep my balance. With steady fingers, I worked the toy free and smiled in quiet triumph. Tucking the copter under my arm, I descended, watching each step to keep from slipping.

"She got it!" Mark cheered.

John beamed and held out his hands to take the toy from me so I could lower myself to the ground.

Mark examined his helicopter. "Hey, it's not broken."

"Kids, it's almost supper time. Come on back to the house." Grandma's voice carried to us from the house. We walked back, my shoes slung over my shoulder.

"Did you have fun today?" Grandma smiled as we entered the kitchen, Kyle pushing his way in first. The screen door banged behind us.

"Alexis messed up our game. She wouldn't be the princess for us knights to save."

"Is that so?" Grandma smiled at me, then tsked. "Well, you all need to wash for supper."

The boys raced to the bathroom, but I lingered behind, resting against the comfortable form of my grandmother.

"Perhaps tomorrow you could call Heather down the street to ask if she wants to play?" She stroked my hair while she held me in an embrace.

"I would have been a good knight. I could have defeated a dragon."

Grandma crouched to bring us eye to eye, a twinkle in her own. "Of course, Sweetie. You were meant to slay any dragon you face."

***

The only monster I defeat now is mountains of paperwork. I have reports to complete and data to compile, a never-ending cycle that once made me feel accomplished. Now, it just gives me a throb in my head like my skull is splintering open. Aspirin and strong coffee will turn the pain into a hollow emptiness, and I swallow both in quick succession. Afterwards, I rub my temples and start reviewing my lastest project; a few minutes pass before the black squiggles on the page resolve into words. I work, letting the tedium turn my face back into a blank mask. I work, because I'm good at it. Or at least that's what my performance reviews say.

I glance at the clock. Noon. Six hours until. The panic, buried deep in my consciousness, bubbles up and bursts like a grade-school volcano. My breath quickens as my fingers twitch on the keyboard. My phone interrupts, ringing again, and this time I don't pay attention to the name or the number on the screen before answering.

"Hi, honey. Sorry for calling you at work."

"Hi, Mom. It's fine, I was about to take lunch."

"Are you okay? You sound out of breath."

"I had to run to reach my phone." The lie comes easier than the truth.

"Mark wanted to make dinner for the family tonight. You know, that cooking class the two of you were going to do? Will you come? Mark, Lisa, and the kids will be here by five."

I can hear the tap of her fingernails against something, which peppers our talks like a metronome keeping time. If I had to guess, I'd say that she's sitting at the kitchen nook, reviewing her calendar for the week. Monday, noon. Make Alexis feel guilty.

"I can't."

She exhales, and I can picture the press of her lips, the narrowing of her eyes, and the furrowing of her brows, but only for the briefest of moments. "Oh? A date on a Monday? Bring him along." The nails are still now, expectant.

"No, nothing like that." Her disappointment is a tangible thing though the phone line. "Just a work thing. It starts at five."

"I thought you hated those things. Surely you could skip it just this once." Her tone is vague, uncertain. Or she could be distracted by ticking off an item on her to-do list. Make Alexis feel guilty.

"It's mandatory. I don't think I can get out of it unless either you or Dad were admitted into the hospital. And even then, I'd need a note from the attending physician." My own voice sounds overly bright, like the forced cheer you hear in retail clerks' voices during the holidays.

"You needn't be so dramatic." If I use formal speech when I'm nervous, Mom uses it when she feels her maternal instincts are being questioned.

"Sorry, too much coffee."

"It's not good for you, you know."

"I didn't get enough sleep last night." The truth feels appropriate this time.

"And coffee will help? You should drink chamomile tea at night."

"I'll try that."

"Well, you're missing a treat. Your brother is making beef Wellington. Didn't you say you always wanted to learn how to make that?" The tap tap is back, and weirdly, it comforts me.

"Some other time. Maybe you could save me some?"

"Of course."

"I need to get lunch, Mom. I'll talk to you later."

"All right, honey. Kisses."

"Kisses."

***

The sky is already darkening as I leave work at half past five. I huddle into my winter coat, pace quick as I walk to my car. The reminder alarm I set on my cell phone yesterday chirps happily at me, and I dismiss it with a jab of a finger.

Driving takes my mind off the nature of my destination for a short time as I navigate through rush hour traffic. Cars were inching along the freeway, but even with traffic, I reach the office five minutes before my appointment. I sit in my parked car, wringing my hands against the steering wheel. I watch the minutes tick by on the clock, then finally trudge into the building.

Every movie and television show hasn't prepared me for how normal the waiting room is. I don't even have a chance to sit before a door opens and a smiling, dark-haired woman greets me. "You must be Alexis Whitaker. I'm Dr. Anna Mendez. Come in, please." She steps aside to let me pass.

The room is decorated in earthy tones, soothing, with touches of dark red and green plants to give the eye something to process. I sink a bit into the cushion of the couch, hands clenched in my lap.

"Why don't you start by telling me why you came here today?"

"My grandmother told me that I could slay dragons. That I could be brave."

"Alexis, what you're doing right now is brave. You're facing your dragon."

2015 Short Story Adult Honorable Mention: Mother Load by David Panaro

David is a Hydrologist on weekdays, and Winery Tasting Room Manager on weekends, David has written many technical reports, grant applications, letters and memos - however this is his first attempt at being a Short Story author. Mr. Panaro has a completed but unpublished fiction novel languishing on his computer and aspires to be a published writer/author after retiring from his current careers.

Stories of Geology

Chill morning air woke the man from his sleeping bag. Pulling a deerskin pouch from his jacket pocket, he removed a topographic map. The secret destination should not be much further. Gear soon secured on the back of his gentle burro, Jake, they set off to find the fortune. An old miner had described a gold seam atop a steep slope in "pure white overhanging rock" just before dying. A newcomer in this land, the man had taken care of the old geezer in return for room and board, but had himself fallen victim to the condition called "Gold Fever".

Around midday, the man stopped to look back, wondering if he'd made a wrong turn somewhere along the way. Was he was being followed? His rifle loaded, a large Bowie knife on his belt, the only animal he feared was the most dangerous of all – man. It was eerily quiet as he turned to go on, but the air was suddenly shattered by a sharp crackle. He quickly turned, but saw nothing. His ears strained to detect the slightest rustle, his eyes squinted to probe the brush, grass, and trees for any hint of movement. The world seemed to freeze for a few moments until the swift beating of his heart made him realize he was over-reacting. Jake's ears fluttered away a couple of flies while his stance and posture remained unchanged. Must have been a pine cone falling onto a dry branch, the man reasoned as he turned to continue.

They held to the path, man leading burro in silence until they dropped down a bank to cross a small stream of crystal clear water where the man paused to pull the map out for another look. This was surely Bear Creek. They were less than a mile from the white outcrop he believed to be quartzite, the host rock for almost all lode deposits. He glanced up at the sun. One o'clock by his reckoning. "We're making good time," he announced out loud to Jake as a gesture to spur the animal onward. As if a burro could understand. Although obsessed with finding gold, he was also keenly aware people would kill him to take it, so he was careful to stay on hard ground and not leave any footprints that might reveal their route to the secret mother lode.

"Just west of a small bubbling creek," the old miner had described the find. The man studied the hillside ahead, straining to see a hint of gold color in the midday sun. He reflected for a few moments, rubbing his chin, wondering if he was on a fool's errand. He tugged the rope to proceed, but Jake did not budge. The four-hundred-pound beast was firmly planted. He tugged again, somewhat harder, then jerked the rope first up then down until the animal bellowed at being so inconvenienced. Not until the man threw his entire weight against the unruly animal did it again resume their slow walk.

His struggles with the staunchly stubborn burro had deflected his concentration, but a flash off to the right suddenly caught his eye. Like the brim of a woman's gaudy Sunday hat some 60 feet above his head loomed an overhanging outcrop of white quartzite. Hurriedly, tying his beast to the nearest tree, he fumbled to retrieve his small shovel and hand pick before scrambling up the steep slope. Was this his "Eureka Moment"? He clawed his way upslope over sharp-edged loose rocks. Every foot of progress seemed to result in two feet of backsliding until just above his head – but out-of-reach – he spied the glistening and unmistakable color of gold, a few thin stringers of metallic wealth in parallel horizontal layers, each about the thickness of his little finger.

The rock overhang was a good 12 feet out from the top of the slope and at least 6 feet thick. A couple sticks of dynamite would blow the slab down – if he had any – which he did not. He would have to lower himself over the outcrop and try to chip off as much gold as he could before pulling himself back up. However, he had only 20 feet of rope. He looked down at his partner for another solution. Despite what the man believed, Jake was not his partner. Just a man and his burro. One the beast-of-burden to the other, simple as that. Still, it bothered him that Jake was not excited about their new find. The little critter would pay for this unwillingness to help by having to carry all the heavy gold back to the assay office. The man thus chastised and swore at the burro as if it were a human partner that had reneged on a sacred pact. However, the burro simply whipped its tail back and forth while slowly chewing grass as if there were no care in the world.

It took the remainder of the day to work around the mountain to reach the top and make camp. Evening light was fading as the man took a can of beans off the fire using his coat sleeve as an oven mitt before dipping a dry biscuit into the still bubbling juice. There they were, two lonely souls chewing away, face to face but not making eye contact. The miner looked up at his companion with a look of disdain, still perturbed that the animal was not being any help. Was Jake sufficiently trained to lower him over the precipice and still pull him back up with a verbal command? Probably not, but the man was running out of ideas and had to consider every option, no matter how stupid.

Within an hour of sunrise, the man had examined every inch of rope for flaws, frays, or weak spots. He had enough confidence that it would bear his weight. Faced with a sixty-foot fall onto sharp rocks there would be no allowance for error. Using the four-foot long laces removed from his boots, he'd rigged up a sailor's bosun's chair using Jake's canvas pack cover to fashion a diaper-like swing. He used the leather tie-downs from Jake's pack to extend a loop through a crack in the quartzite slab to serve as his anchor point. Tugging the rope a few times, then jerking a few more, gave him confidence it would hold. "This is probably the most stupid thing I have ever done," he said aloud dropping over the edge with sledge hammer and chisel in his jacket side pockets.

He was not directly above the gold exposure and pushed off with bare feet to swing over to reach it. Unseen, the sharp rock lip cut into the hemp rope fibers. If he died today, it would be his own fault, or rather his biggest and last mistake. The initial drop over the lip was the hardest. His palms and feet were sweating. His fingers strained from gripping the rope with thin leather gloves. Purposely not looking up or down but only at the white rock close in front of his face, the man could feel tension throughout his body.

He repeated the maneuver once again to reach the vein. There at his left shoulder was pure gold not two feet from his face. He so wanted to pull off a glove to touch it with his fingers but knew he could not. The rope had carried his weight as hoped. With great trepidation he loosened his grip on the rope to retrieve the hammer and chisel from his pockets. Placing the 10-inch steel chisel against hard white rock, he struck the first blow with his sledge hammer. It suddenly felt heavier than ever before. A slight breeze ruffled his hair as beads of sweat formed on his brow. It was not hot, he was sweating from nerves and pure fear.

The first blow was followed by a second – dislodging only a small chunk of the white rock with some gold attached – which immediately fell away. He instinctively glanced down to follow the shard only to see it disappear amongst the tens of thousands of similar-looking chunks far below. His ears heard it hit so he knew it was down there somewhere, yet he just realized this plan had not been thoroughly considered. He'd completely forgotten to think about how he was going to catch or collect the gold. Putting rock chunks in his pockets would only add weight to the already strained rope, but letting them fall away could add days as he searched for each precious piece.

Feeling weak after chiseling away for what seemed like hours, he stopped, then dropped the hammer and chisel to mark the spot where all his hard-won gold would be waiting down below. Sharp pains ran throughout his body as he pulled himself up. Reaching the upper lip of the rock slab, he pulled up and over to safety. The rock lip had eaten halfway through his already way-too-thin lifeline. His toes were badly cut from trying to grip the hard, sharp rock, so he crawled over to retrieve his lifeline from the anchor location. The loop had slipped up the crack with only a few millimeters being the difference between success and death. Crawling over to Jake on hands and knees, he managed to fall across its back to get back to camp. Gathering the chunks of gold ore could wait until he bandaged his feet.

Back and forth on hands and knees across the slope before inching upwards, he searched for his precious pieces of gold, careful not to miss any that might be covered by loose gravel. Several pieces were collected before reaching his hammer and nearby chisel. Each chunk was placed into Jake's gallon-sized canvas feed bag. All the while the burro just stood and watched him, not helping as usual. At least that's what the man thought whenever he glanced back down at the animal. The fear of someone, even a burro that could not speak, claiming any portion of his wealth, his gold, started to create paranoia. All that day and the next, the novice miner continued to search the rocky slope for any piece of hard-fought gold. The thought that he might leave even one piece after he had worked so hard, created a mood of panic. The thin leather gloves soon wore through from painstakingly sifting through so many sharp rock shards. The man's anger toward his lazy, uninjured partner increased every hour as he scrambled over and across the steep incline.

After gathering all the gold ore he could, his food supply exhausted, it was time to leave. The canvas bag weighed perhaps 40 pounds. Minus the white quartz, he would be lucky to end up with several ounces of yellow gold. The faint tingling in his toes had evolved into a stinging excruciating pain. To take even one step took supreme effort, but the man knew he had to get back for medical care. Large holes in his tattered pant legs revealed his seriously scraped and cut knees—a result of crawling on sharp gravel. Scary thoughts of infection distracted his mind while pain flooded his body. He needed to concentrate on getting out of this desperate situation he alone had created. Dumping all non-essential items, his sleeping bag would serve as a saddle, and a short strap over the burro's shoulders would balance the canteen and gold bag.

Though he had never ridden Jake, the little burro could handle his weight. Reaching Bear Creek, the man stopped to wash and soak his aching toes and cut knees. A large mat of green moss floated by and he lunged forward to snatch it from the creek. Native Americans had used moss as a mild antiseptic and cushion to bandage wounds, so the man inserted moss pieces into the boots and tied some of the spongy material to each knee.

Weakness, pain, and hunger interrupted their slow progress back toward civilization when the man dozed off and fell hard onto the ground. The shock of hitting hard dirt barely woke him from the haze and fog his brain had slipped into. Some 30 minutes later, the man regained his senses and called to his partner who had wandered some distance away looking for better grass to eat. His request was totally ignored, so he raised the volume of his voice, and shouting, repeated his order. All this elicited from the animal was a strange note of fear in its glance. The little beast had never known the man to speak in such a way. Something was different, and it sensed danger—it knew not what danger, but in its brain arose a cautious apprehension of the man. The burro flattened its ears down at the sound of the man's voice, and its posture froze, but it would not come.

The man struggled to his feet before motioning his companion to approach, yet despite the man's attempt at quiet calmness, the beast stood its ground. The painful sensation in the man's feet left him biting his lip to endure this erect posture. A sense of suspicion and survival had been planted into the burro's mind. The sound of the man's voice, although familiar, now seemed predatory, rendering the little animal's customary allegiance questionable. On hands and knees the man crawled slowly toward the burro. This unusual posture triggered more than excited suspicion, causing the little animal bolt and gallop away.

The man now realized his partner and traveling companion was actually afraid of him for the first time. He could not catch the little beast. There was no way he could run with these feet. The burro would have to come to him. It was a matter of life and death for the man. His ride gone, the man pondered his inevitable fate, and fell to the ground in despair. His water, gold, and sleeping bag had just run off. His knife, rifle, and five rounds of ammo would do nothing to postpone a slow death as his only fate. Crawling to the nearest small pine tree, the man reclined onto the soft, warm sand beneath it. The sand felt good on his back and he soon dozed off hoping to die in his sleep.

But sleep did not bring death, only the faint scent of burro as he awoke. He rolled over and there was his old friend, partner, and travelling companion. The one he had so maligned many times over the last week or more had returned and was munching on the very tree where the man had laid down ready to die. If this was Heaven, it was a cruel joke. If not, the two partners would make it back and live to tell the tale of the Mother Lode.

2015 Short Story Adult Honorable Mention: Going Home by Glenn Rowe

Glenn has two degrees, and a lot of experience, in the field of psychology (both in clinical and real-world settings). He also has an undergraduate minor in English with a concentration in Creative Writing. He is one who understands (and longs for) the elemental connection with Mother Earth that modern Mankind seems to have forgotten. He has been a member of three Writers' Groups – two in Alabama and one here in Southern California. He is currently affiliated with the Writers Group sponsored by the Goebel Adult Community Center in Thousand Oaks CA.

Dawn breaks over the eastern horizon. I pause to greet Sun, then climb into my pickup and begin my commute. Like a canoeist on the bank of a wild and turbulent river, I gauge my timing carefully before plunging into the streaming traffic. Cars, trucks, semis and buses, closely packed and five abreast, surge along the freeway. I am caught up in the current, working my way gradually, carefully, into the center of the flow.

My eyes watch the swirls and eddies ahead, my hands make gentle corrections to my course, but my mind is free. Through the week I toil and sweat to earn my pay to buy my bread. But not today. Today is different. Today I'm going home.

My pulse quickens and my anticipation grows. I think of the items beside me on the seat:

Knife, very sharp and riding comfortably in its sheath.

Flint, dark and cold but holding the secret of fire.

Blanket, frayed and tattered, but warm.

Poncho, to shelter from wind and rain.

Food and Cord, so that Nature will not be diminished by my passage.

Aspirin, a concession to my aging bones and joints.

Coffee, a concession to my remaining addiction.

Hiking Boots, a concession to my soft City feet.

Emergency Kit, a concession to Murphy's Law.

Water Filter and Canteen: sorrowful concessions that some joys are gone forever.

From freeway to highway to county road, from concrete to blacktop to gravel, and finally to dirt. The roadway narrows to a rutted wagon-track before it disappears altogether. As far as the eye can see, there is nothing but wilderness. My commute is over. I've come home.

Hawk soars on widespread wings as I lace my boots – wheels and stoops as I take my last sip of fast-food coffee – climbs skyward again, prey in talons, as I shoulder my pack. Sun is halfway up the morning sky. I place him at my right shoulder and begin walking.

At first my feet are clumsy and uncertain, my breathing fast and ragged. The land ahead seems too wild, too rugged. An inner voice expresses doubt: You cannot do this... it has been too long... you have grown old and weak... turn back. But I do not listen, and soon the voice is still. My steps regain their old sureness, and my breathing evens out.

I walk the contours of the land, occasionally angling up and over a ridge. I am in no hurry and there is much to see. There you are, Rabbit, peering out from beneath the sagebrush. You think you are hidden, but your inquisitive, twitching nose gives you away. Be glad I am not Coyote.

I pause in the shade of a wind-sculpted juniper, drink from my canteen and read the messages in the dirt. Rabbit has been here, too, as has Coyote. Many birds have feasted on seeds and insects. Mouse's tracks lead to her burrow, and Rattlesnake shed his skin on that rock over there. Bear shambled through, stomach empty and temper short, just after the snow melted off.

It is good to be home! For the first time in years I am free from schedules and deadlines. In this place, time is measured by Sun and Moon and Season, and not by the relentless ticking of the clock. Gone from my ears are the sounds of telephones, traffic and sirens. Gone too is the crow-like clamor of insistent but heedless people. Gone from my nose is the stink of diesel-smoke, smog, and urine-drenched alleys. My eyes are no longer assaulted by neon scribblings or bit-mapped warnings.

There! In the distance, Deer stands poised, eyes darting, ears swiveling, nose testing the wind. Motionless, I watch as he lowers his head, then count silently until he looks up. He resumes grazing, and I begin circling downwind. Before he looks again, I assume the stillness of a lightning-struck snag. Move, count, freeze, make no sound, feel the wind. Eagle screams high above, her voice almost lost in the vastness of the sky.

I am so close I can smell him, can hear his breathing, the ripping of the grass as he fills his mouth. He is weary and hungry for he has run very far, but still he is uneasy. He senses my nearness, and his head stays up much longer. His beauty so fills me with joy that I cannot help but laugh, the sound very loud in the momentary stillness of the wind. Deer bounds away, his curving leaps long and graceful, until he is out of sight.

In other days and other times, Deer, you would have fed me. Your hide and sinews would have protected me and kept me warm; your bones and antlers would have provided my tools. But not today. Today your wildness and beauty satisfy another hunger; they meet other needs. Be at peace. I will remember you.

Sun is high overhead. I eat and rest among trees in the bottom of a draw. A trickle of water flows here. Mindful of the pollution of Man, I filter it into my canteen. It is cold, and tastes pretty good, but it is not the same. Stretching out on a bed of fallen needles and leaves, I listen to the whispering counsel of the mountain breeze.

I awaken to the rattling croak of Raven as he eyes me from the safety of a high branch. Sun is well along his afternoon journey. It is time to move on.

Crossing a ridge, I gaze down into a broad valley. A stream twinkles as it makes its tumbling, weaving way through massive boulders, their shoulders rounded and smoothed by the ages. Cottonwoods crowd the banks, sipping life through their roots. Sage and Juniper crown a low knoll. Glancing at Sun once again, I decide. Yes, I will go there, gather wood, and settle down for the night.

I move more swiftly now. My way is blocked by a sheer drop, and I scout along its edge to find a way down. There. A narrow, steep-walled rift angles down like a time-worn ramp. Its floor, deep in shadow, is strewn with rocks. The layered bedrock on either side, fractured long ago as Mother Earth heaved and trembled in mountain-birth, resembles the walls of a forgotten city. Niches and caves appear as windows and doors, while hardy plants cling to the crevices. This is a spirit-place, and my backbone tingles uncomfortably. My nose wrinkles in recognition that Skunk was frightened here, too.

The stream chuckles and calls out to me as I reach the valley floor. I enter the grove just as Sun hides his face behind the western mountains. Dove and Whippoorwill mourn the end of the day. I must work quickly.

I use my knife to coax sparks from the flint, blowing gently on them until the tinder catches. Soon the small fire crackles, lighting and warming my camp. The food is filling, and the coffee tastes good. The night air is cool, and so clear that I can see almost back to The Beginning. Stars are everywhere. Moon begins peeking over the horizon.

Owl glides silently overhead, her breast and wings briefly shimmering in the light of the fire. She is a big one. Beware, Rabbit. Take heed, Mouse.

I make my bed on the moon-dappled ground, pulling the blanket snugly around me. Coyote calls and, far away, another answers.

It is good to be home.

2015 Short Story Adult Honorable Mention: Sounds and Motion, Motion and Sounds by William Stermer

William has been a full-time writer in the street motorcycle field for thirty-seven years writing road tests, product tests and features for magazines, along with seven books. However, fiction is his love. Now that he is semi-retired, he would like to devote more time to fiction.

Every Friday she worried. She worried about how he would be this weekend. She worried about keeping out of his way.

"Got any more coffee over there?"

Carol turned from the sink where she had been staring at the snow, out the slatted window of the mobile home, and hurriedly grabbed the coffee pot. "Anything else, Ricky?" He went on eating and took a slurp of the coffee. There was nothing else.

Her husband was big, and he hunched his shoulders while he ate. She once told him he looked like he was worried somebody was going to try to steal his food. He didn't like that. Nobody kidded Ricky for long. He would hunch further, and his little eyes would scowl menacingly.

Always it was sausage, eggs, and toast. And coffee. He'd sit staring off, or maybe he was looking at the latest issue of *Hot Rod* magazine. In the heavy plaid shirt, dirty quilted red vest, black knitted hat, and the scraggly hog-bristle beard he was a picture.

Carol went on staring out the window. Her head hurt. Then something thumped against the wall in the front bedroom and the crying began. It was two-year-old Melissa. Carol hurried down the hall. Melissa stood in her crib, clutching the wooden railing with her tiny hands. Her face was screwed out of shape and she was crying hard, like somebody was squeezing it out of her.

"What's the matter?" Carol looked down and regarded her four-year-old running his toy car along the floor. "Larry, why is your sister crying?"

Without looking up, Larry answered blankly, "I doe know."

Melissa's wailing pierced Carol's head. Then came the, "Hey! Hey!" from the kitchen. She picked up Melissa, cradled her and carried her into the living room where they slumped onto the couch.

"Hey," Ricky snapped, "keep them kids quiet."

"I think she dropped something out of her crib."

"Ain't no reason to be screamin' her fool head off. Hey, got any more toast over there?"

"I think there's some bread in the toaster."

"Well, push it down. I gotta get to work."

She sighed and slowly got up from the couch, carrying Melissa. At least the crying had stopped. Carol pushed the lever down on the toaster. "You know, Ricky, it'd be real simple to get an extension cord and put the toaster on the table. That way you could—"

"On the table? What, now I gotta make my own breakfast?" He turned back to his magazine. "Sure, you don't do nothin' around here all day anyway. I may as well get my own breakfast."

"But then you could have your toast—"

"An' I told you don't bother me when I'm studyin'. Can't you see I'm studyin' here?"

He had the *Hot Rod* magazine spread out in front of him, the page littered with bread crumbs. He was studying. She watched him reading, his mouth laboriously forming the words. Ricky had wanted to be an automotive designer ever since tenth grade, but he had dropped out of school the next year to work at the body shop. They got married when she became pregnant, and he now made his living sanding and painting car bodies. He faithfully read *Hot Rod* every month and told anyone who would listen that he was going to be an automotive designer.

Ricky shook the crumbs from the magazine onto the floor and the ritual began again. She had told him a hundred times to shake them onto the plate, but he just grunted and did as he wished. He closed the magazine and stuck it under his arm, then stalked to the CD player and took several discs from the rack below.

"You ain't gonna take that Elvis one, are you?" Carol moaned.

"Yeah." He held it up to her.

"I was gonna listen to that today."

"You lose."

"Why don't you take that Ronnie Millsap one instead? You like that one."

"I'll take 'em both."

"Ricky. No." The faint hardness came into her eyes.

"Don't you never tell me no, woman." He glared, and her eyes snapped open wider, betraying her vulnerability. Her lower lip drooped.

He picked up his sack lunch and turned to the children. "You two be good today, ya hear?" Ricky started for the door and Carol called, "Hey, ain't ya gonna give me no kiss?"

He stopped, turned, and came as close as he ever did to smiling. "What'd you do this mornin' to deserve a kiss?"

"Aw stop it."

He gave her a thick, raw, tobacco-smelly, hard kiss on the mouth.

The pickup started in a gush of blue smoke, and through the window she saw him ram a CD into the player and turn the volume way up. He gunned the motor, spun the tires in the snow and backed out hard, nearly clipping the mailbox. Then in a roar of whirling tires he spun around in the street of Harmony Village Trailer Court and headed for work. The sound and motion still rang in her head.

He was like that. Long periods of silent brooding, occasional softness, then when something angered him he exploded. That was Ricky. Never subtle. He wouldn't know subtlety if it came up and smashed him in the face.

She sat at the table and lit a cigarette, then poured herself a cup of coffee. Oh God, it was Friday. The weekend was coming. A weekend when Ricky would be home, and it would start all over again. She had to plan again how to keep away from him this weekend.

***

Her mother called at noon. Could Ricky come over tomorrow and thaw her pipes? The blizzard had blown snow under her mobile home and the water pipes were beginning to freeze. Carol sighed. "I'll ask him." Well, at least she could be inside talking with her mom while he was outside. But asking him would be worse than actually going there.

Ricky came home from work just after 4:30. The weekend was beginning. He took off his work clothes and left them on the bathroom floor. Then, in old blue jeans and a sweatshirt he sat on the couch and scratched his head.

"Get me a beer," he said to no one in particular.

Moments later she silently handed him a can. Then she heard, suck, suck, suck, and he gave a soft belch.

Larry and Melissa came in and ran a toy truck around the carpet until Ricky barked, "Hold it down!" They moved to the corner opposite him. Ricky scratched his head. "Kids got to respeck their parents," he said. But to him respect was cringing, when he came around, and keeping out of his way.

"You kids been good today?" he barked.

They looked up hesitantly, then went on playing self-consciously.

"Whatsa matter, can't ya hear? I asked you sumpin'."

They looked up wide-eyed, so full of respect they couldn't speak. Larry nodded faintly, then he took the truck and ran off down the hall.

"What's for supper? Hey, what's for supper?"

"I'm makin' spaghetti."

"Cook the meat this time, willya?" He turned on the TV and found a game show. He stared at the picture, the shadows playing across his face, mouth gaping, beer idly cradled in his lap. The sound blasted out of the set during the commercials, roared when the contestants picked their numbers, shrieked when someone won.

They ate in shifts. He didn't like the mess the kids made at the table, so she fed him first. He chewed with his mouth open, talking – when he did – with his mouth open, laughing at the cartoons with his mouth open, spraying food on the table. He had another beer, then departed the table with a melodious belch. Ricky sprawled on the couch and lit a cigarette.

After supper, while he was still amiable and a little drowsy from the beer, she told him, "Mama called."

"What'd the old bat want this time?"

"Some snow blowed up under her trailer and she needs her pipes unfroze."

"Get your brother to do it; she ain't my mother."

"You know Frank ain't good with tools. Come on, Ricky."

He grunted and stared sullenly at the TV. It had worked. He hadn't argued further. They were going! Friday night had been a breeze.

***

The next morning, Ricky had sausage and eggs and toast. And coffee. Carol fed the kids afterwards while he sat on the couch and smoked, watching talking ducks and vicious dragons and a rather hapless coyote.

Ricky hated going to her mother's. He sullenly smoked another cigarette while the kids fought over a toy on the floor. Melissa picked it up, Larry grabbed her hand, but she pulled it away too hard and hit herself in the forehead. Ricky heard the thump and turned to see her face go into a soundless grimace, the mouth twisting terribly, then she exploded in tears. Ricky lit another cigarette. "Oh, Christ," he said, shaking his head.

Carol rushed in. "What happened? Oh no!"

"She hit herself in the head. Let's go."

"She's crying."

"Let's go!"

Ricky threw on his coat, then scooped up Larry and the diaper pail. He burst out the door and trudged through the snow to the Pontiac. Carol was soothing Melissa when he stomped back in. "You ready yet?"

"Just a minute."

"Ain't no more minutes." The sound and motion was starting. He reached down and yanked Melissa away, then grabbed Carol by the arm, pulling her out the door across the snow and into the Pontiac. He jerked it into reverse and bashed out of the driveway.

Carol's mother lived ten miles away in a faded white trailer that sagged against a bare hillside. Ricky pulled into the driveway and strode onto the rickety add-on porch. He pushed through the door and made his way to the kitchen. It was smoky and noisy, smelling of coffee, cigarettes and body odor. They were all there: her mom, the neighbor lady, and Frank's wife. Around the table, the women were talking and flicking their cigarettes for emphasis, licking their fingers from the sticky buns on their plates. Fat, white arms puffed from their Kmart blouses, their hair pulled back, chins wagging.

"Hi Ricky. Hi Carol. How's little Larry? How come Melissa's crying?" Carol's mother rose from the table, pushed it away and maneuvered around it.

Frank came in from the living room saying, "Hi. Gimme your coat, Ricky. Want some coffee?"

Carol noticed that Frank had on a nice, new sweater. At least Ricky wasn't scowling much, and he did accept a cup of coffee. Carol joined the women at the table.

Ricky wandered into the living room in his dirty red vest. "How ya doin'," Frank asked.

Ricky regarded Frank coolly. His brother-in-law worked in the office of the can company in town, and he acted like he didn't like to get his hands dirty. "Your ma needs her pipes unfroze."

"Yeah," Frank said uncertainly. "Thanks for coming over to do that for her."

Ricky shifted position on the couch and glared at him over one shoulder. "She's your ma...ain't you gonna do nothin' for her?"

"You know I'm not much with tools, Ricky. But sure, I'll help you."

Ricky lit a cigarette slowly and deliberately, feeling a little smug. "Kin you use a screwdriver? Kin you use a snow shovel?"

"Sure. That's no problem."

"Good. Then you go out and get that skirting off the trailer and shovel the snow out. When you get the pipes clear, you come and get me, ya hear?"

"Uh, well sure, Ricky. I guess I can do that."

Once Frank had gone outside Ricky chuckled, poured himself another cup of coffee and lit another cigarette. Carol came over to him immediately.

"Why ain't you goin' out with him?"

He looked at her like she was very stupid. "'Cause he's gotta get the skirting off and shovel it out first. Then I'll take the torch and thaw out the pipes."

She kept her voice urgent, but down. "Frank don't even know how to open a can. How's he gonna get that skirting off?"

"Look, I'm sittin' here tryin' to drink my coffee. Git back where you belong and don't bother me."

She clenched her fists and her shoulders rose, but when he looked at her hard she skulked back to the table. The talk there grew very quiet, and even the kids moved out of the living room and into the kitchen. It was just the way he liked it.

Ricky could hear Frank working on the skirting for the longest time. He was having trouble. But finally, Ricky heard the sound of scraping and shoveling underneath, and Frank eventually stomped in, kicking snow from his boots. "It's cleared out. You may as well go out, Ricky."

But first he smoked the rest of his cigarette way down, and leisurely finished his coffee. Finally, he carefully donned his orange hunting cap, slipped into his jacket, fiddled with the propane torch and stepped out.

***

They were finally able to leave. Lunch was over and the water was flowing in the taps. Ricky stood around while Carol said goodbye to her mother. Finally, he scooped up the diaper pail and Larry, and headed for the car. Carol joined him with Melissa a minute later. He knew it was coming but didn't care. She knew it was coming but couldn't help it.

"Why'd you do that to Frank?"

"I didn't do nothin' to Frank."

"You said *you* was gonna work on Momma's water pipes."

"I *did* work on Momma's water pipes."

"You said *you* was gonna do it, not Frank."

"All Frank did was get the skirting off and shovel; I thawed the damn pipes."

"You think you're real smart, don't you? Getting' Frank to do what you said you'd do."

"I did what I said I'd do! An' she's his momma, not mine!"

"You didn't even say goodbye to Momma. You just walked right out and little Larry didn't even get a chance to say goodbye, and…"

There was no escaping her now that they were in the car, so he did the next best thing. He floored the gas, slewing the Pontiac sideways, then he straightened it out and floored it again, roaring between the high banks of snow, the road rough and jabbing, the car rocking and swaying. Carol screamed at him and Melissa awoke and began to cry. But he kept it nailed, the roaring going on and on, the sound and motion filling his head until the stop sign on Route 42.

Ricky smiled because she had finally shut up. He squealed the car out onto the highway as Carol slumped back into the seat with a shuddering cry. And it was only Saturday afternoon…

Short Story: Mr. Mangy Calls the Moon by Natasha Buran

Natasha is a writer, director, and actress from Thousand Oaks, CA. She is a librarian-in-training, studying at the University of North Texas. As an aspiring children's author, Natasha likes to write stories about inanimate objects with big personalities. She blames the moon for just about everything. Visit her online at natashaburan.com.

Mr. Mangy worked for the Department of Phenomena in the Celestial Forces Unit. For precisely 39 years and 364 days, he climbed the mountain every evening and called the moon to rise above the horizon. He'd be lying if he said it was an easy task.

Most of the time the moon was depressed. Sometimes it was full, but other times it was just a sliver. Not very grand in comparison with the almighty sun.

"What's the point?" the moon cried that evening. "People like the sun more. Don't they remember sunburns or heatstroke? There's no such thing as moon-stroke! Even Shakespeare had it out for me. 'O, swear not by the moon, the inconstant moon.' Didn't Juliet die in that one? Remind me."

"A tragic death of star-crossed lovers."

"Good," the moon said. "I hate happy endings."

Crickets chirped, and a coyote howled somewhere in the distance. Sometimes, the silent moments between Mr. Mangy and the moon would make him uncomfortable, but the moon usually decided to rise when it ran out of things to complain about.

"Well, I think I'll go up now."

"See you tomorrow," Mr. Mangy said, clapping his hands together. "It's an important day for us, remember?"

"What's tomorrow?"

The words rippled through Mr. Mangy, stinging his old and fragile heart. "Oh, nothing. Forget about it. Enjoy your rise."

"I'll try."

Mr. Mangy walked down the mountain, knowing very well that tomorrow marked his 40th work anniversary. How could the moon forget that? Didn't it care?

Of course, it had never once bothered to ask Mr. Mangy about his personal life, his love life (or lack thereof), his parents who had passed away, or the terrible people in his department, like the secretary who kept stealing his staplers.

How could you spend your life with someone and not care to really know them? Mr. Mangy knew everything about the moon.

It hated when coyotes and wolves howled at it. "I'm right here, you ugly mutts. Stop yelling at me!" It didn't appreciate stories about the man in the moon. "The man? The rabbit? Who makes up these things?" The moon especially disliked astronauts. "They weren't even invited."

The moon would never rise without me, Mr. Mangy thought bitterly.

As he watched the moon shine over the forest and a cool wind caressed his face, Mr. Mangy had a sudden tingly urge to be… irresponsible. Perhaps, he would forget to show up tomorrow evening. Let it slip his mind. Be wickedly preoccupied. Yes, that would show the moon a thing or two. Only the trees could hear Mr. Mangy's naughty chuckles as he continued down the mountain.

The next evening, Mr. Mangy returned from work utterly disappointed that no one in the department acknowledged his anniversary. Instead of cake, Mr. Mangy came home with two staplers in his briefcase, thanks to Jennifer and her sticky fingers. So Mr. Mangy decided to throw his own party. He browsed his cookbook collection for something spectacular to celebrate his forty years of service. He owned the cookbooks of every celebrity chef on television, but his absolute favorite was Ina Garten, Barefoot Contessa.

Mr. Mangy wasn't a decent chef, but he found comfort in looking at pictures of food or watching cooking videos. If he turned the volume higher, it was almost like someone was in the kitchen cooking with him. The sizzling, the pots and pans clanking, and the knives chopping were music to his lonely ears. He flipped through Ina's cookbook and his mouth watered. He couldn't possibly make something so delicious. Maybe another time when he had the proper ingredients. Tonight, his usual bowl of pho would have to do.

Around this time, after supper, Mr. Mangy would slip on his sneakers for his nightly hike up the mountain, but tonight he forced himself to stay put. He went to the window and snapped shut every curtain in his home.

If the moon doesn't appreciate me, I won't appreciate the moon!

There was only one thing left to do: watch *Barefoot Contessa* reruns. Ina was having a dinner party in the show. As Mr. Mangy thought about who he'd invite to his own party, he drifted into a deep sleep on the couch. Hours later, still in his work clothes, and in an uncomfortable position, he awoke from his nap.

Mr. Mangy checked his watch and read it was two minutes until midnight.

I wonder if the moon rose without me? he thought stubbornly.

Dragging his feet to the window, Mr. Mangy pulled back the curtains. Brilliant warm sunshine poured inside the cabin. He stumbled backwards, shielding his eyes.

BANG-BANG-BANG!

The sound came from the front door. Squinting, Mr. Mangy opened it to see a woman in sunglasses on the other side.

"Are you Mr. Mangy, the employee assigned to the moon?" she asked.

This was it. This was what *Barefoot Contessa* and rebellion got you.

Mr. Mangy burped in his mouth, reliving the taste of pho. "I think I'm going to be sick."

"There's never been an incident like this before. The sun can't set unless the moon rises. That's how it works. Is there a reason you've neglected your duty?"

Mr. Mangy frowned. *His duty.* The word stuck in his unbrushed mouth. He had climbed a mountain every day for forty years just to coax a stupid piece of rock. How many nights were wasted convincing the moon that "Walking on Sunshine" wasn't a catchy song? What did the moon ever do for him? It didn't even remember their anniversary. It was so simple. They would never be friends.

"I don't doubt the department will be looking for your resignation," the woman said. "Do you have anything to say for yourself?"

Mr. Mangy listened to birds chirp outside the cabin. He took a breath of the midnight air.

"I don't care if the moon is entirely made out of cheese, it will never be invited to my dinner party."

Then Mr. Mangy slammed the door on her. Next, he opened every curtain in his house and let the sunshine in. Dust motes floated about and made him sneeze, but he didn't care one bit.

"Now," he said, rubbing his hands together. "Who's up for a midnight tan?"

A month later with more sunlight in the day and no job, Mr. Mangy was able to do all the activities he had ever wanted. Except throw a fancy dinner party. Dinner parties needed friends, and after disgracing the department, Mr. Mangy's only source of conversation was with his garden. However, one evening (or was it morning?) as he was tending his herbs, Mr. Mangy noticed his beautiful plants were turning brown.

"How odd," he said, touching the shriveled mint leaves. "You can't die on me now. Not before I host a dinner party."

"Oh, dear. I think it's me," a jolly voice said.

Mr. Mangy would know that voice anywhere. "Hello, sun." He sighed.

Mr. Mangy had never met anything so cheerful. He put down the watering can and picked up his purple polka-dotted umbrella. He popped it open, hoping the sun would get the message and leave him alone.

"You need to talk to the moon! You know this isn't right. Think about the other side of the world, for goodness sake. Everyone needs the sun!"

"What I *need* is for you to get out of my face!" Mr. Mangy stomped off with his umbrella and went inside his home. He closed all the curtains, not allowing one drop of sunshine to enter his cabin.

Mr. Mangy thought as he sat in the dark. *Be it the sun or the moon, both are cosmic twits.*

As most sensible people know, one does not mess with the big, bright star in the sky that gives us life and light. So over the next few days, the sun unleashed its wrath: the temperature rose well past the 100s, the air conditioner busted, and Mr. Mangy was forced to cut his favorite trousers into short shorts.

"You don't have the legs for those shorts," teased the sun when Mr. Mangy went out for the newspaper.

"Shut it."

But Mr. Mangy couldn't keep it up. He was getting letters in the mail, knocks at the door, phone calls all telling him to talk to the moon.

Can no one else talk to the darn thing?

While Mr. Mangy fanned himself with the newspaper, the telephone rang throughout the cabin. "Oh, for goodness sake," he shouted, picking up the receiver. "What?"

"Hello, Mr. Mangy," said a woman's voice. "This is Cathleen from the department. We met last month after the incident."

Mr. Mangy folded his old legs, trying to ignore the sweat building up behind his knees. "Well, well. Cathleen is it?" He couldn't help but smirk. "Have you found a replacement yet?"

There was silence on the other side of the line.

"I didn't catch that?" Mr. Mangy said.

"No, we haven't."

"That's a shame," he said, still smirking.

"Please," Cathleen said, "the moon refuses to talk to anyone else."

"And what's in it for me? I don't work for the Department of Phenomena anymore."

"We can negotiate something," she said, her voice changing as if she had a special treat for a puppy. "I have someone who wants to speak with you."

"If it's the moon on the line—" Mr. Mangy began.

He heard shuffling on the other end.

"Hello, Mr. Mangy," a sweet calming voice said.

Mr. Mangy dropped the newspaper and unfolded his legs. His heart beat rapidly and he pressed the receiver hard against his ear. It wasn't possible. How could it be?

"Ina?" he whispered. Just saying her name out loud sent shivers down his back.

"It's me," the voice said. "Barefoot Contessa. I heard you and the moon are having some problems."

"Well, not really. I—I'm not having any problems."

"You know what's the best recipe for reconciliation?" Ina's honey voice asked.

"Tell me," he said, holding the phone with both hands.

"A dinner party."

This was a dream. Barefoot Contessa had said the words dinner and party in the same sentence. Was this really happening to him?

"If you bring the moon back, how about I invite you over?"

"You mean I can be on the show?" He took a deep breath. He could have his own spinoff if he played his cards right. He could be signing his own cookbook by next year.

"Of course," Ina laughed. "We'll call it 'Moonlit Dinner'."

"The moon has to be there?" Mr. Mangy asked, his hopes dropping.

"I don't think I can host a moonlit dinner without it."

It was like Barefoot Contessa had smushed his heart for one of her famous Peach & Blueberry crumbles. Mr. Mangy hung up the phone, his entire body shaking.

This couldn't be happening. He had never hated so many things at once! The sun for killing all his mint, Ina Garten for betraying him, the moon for...everything! The stupid, stupid moon! He'd go right now and tell the moon what he really thought of it, holding nothing back. Mr. Mangy slipped on his sneakers. He climbed the mountain, his breath tightening from a whole month without exercise.

"HEY!" Mr. Mangy screamed when he reached the top.

The moon rose slightly above the horizon to see who was shouting and by doing so the temperature dropped a few degrees.

"Mr. Mangy?" the moon said. "Is that you?"

"You ruined everything, you stupid jerk," Mr. Mangy said, his eyes prickling suddenly. "Barefoot Contessa called and I hung up on her because of you!"

"*The* Barefoot Contessa?" the moon said.

"YES! We were going to have a lovely dinner party, I was going to be on the show, and start my own spinoff. It's all ruined thanks to you." Mr. Mangy's voice cracked. "Why can't you do anything on your own? I hate this job and I hate you!" Mr. Mangy began to sob fat, ugly tears.

"Do you really mean that?" the moon said.

"Y-Y-Yes. I h-h-hate you." Snot dripped down his nose. He wanted to throw up, he wanted to stop, but he couldn't.

The moon was silent and let Mr. Mangy cry for a bit longer before it said, "I missed you."

The moon was well above the horizon now, stars twinkling around it.

Mr. Mangy wiped his nose on his arm. "But why?"

"I dunno," the moon said sheepishly. "I thought we were friends or something."

"Or-some-thing," Mr. Mangy said in between sobs.

"We're not friends?"

"Of course, we're not friends," Mr. Mangy snapped. "Friends have conversations. You've never ever once asked me anything about my life. I know this is a professional job and all that, but a little chitchat ... would ... be ... nice." Mr. Mangy wailed harder into the night.

"Chit chat?" the moon said through Mr. Mangy's sobs, "Ummm. Okay. If you were to host a dinner party like Barefoot Contessa, what would you serve?"

Mr. Mangy wiped his nose again. "I-I'd start with a goat cheese herb log and crackers."

"That sounds nice."

"And-and my first course would be split pea soup.

"Tasty."

"The main course would be a lamb roulade with mint pesto."

"Mint pesto?" the moon exclaimed.

"It's really nice," Mr. Mangy said, thinking about the mint in his garden and forcing himself not to cry again. "And I'd make roasted potatoes."

"What's for dessert?"

"Chocolate mousse, of course," he said, turning his back to the moon.

The moon was quiet again. There it was. The uncomfortable silence that plagued Mr. Mangy. What was the point in coming here and crying? He didn't feel any better. The moon couldn't possibly miss him. It only missed rising and being the center of the night. Mr. Mangy expected the moon to take off now and leave him to his uncontrollable emotions, but instead, it asked a question.

"So, do you think, I could come to your dinner party?"

Mr. Mangy looked back at the moon, completely full, and shining on him. "My party?"

"I've never been to one before. I can't eat anything, but I can watch you eat, I guess, and we can talk. Or you can talk and I can listen. Or something."

Mr. Mangy watched the moon rise higher. Wind blew, cooling down the sweat on his exposed arms and legs. He shivered and rubbed his arms. It sounded as though something had sighed in the west.

"Or something," Mr. Mangy said, wiping away his tears. Could he hear the pan sizzling already?

"But if you don't want me to..."

"No, I want you to come," Mr. Mangy responded before slowly adding, "You can be my guest." *A guest. At my dinner party! I better go buy the ingredients.* "I guess, I'll see you tomorrow," Mr. Mangy said, turning to leave.

"Goodnight, Mr. Mangy. Don't be late!" the moon called.

Mr. Mangy descended the mountain, his heart thumping happily with each step.

"Goodnight, moon." *You cosmic twit*, he thought fondly.

2016 Poetry Youth First Place Winner: Sonnet with Kitchen Sink by Lindsay Kim

Lindsay was eighteen years old. She attended Viewpoint School. She has been recognized by the National Young Arts Foundation, Sierra Nevada College, and the National Council of Teachers of English, among other organizations. Her work has been published or is forthcoming in Sierra Nevada Review, Winter Tangerine Review, National Poetry Quarterly, and elsewhere. When not writing, she enjoys playing piano and studying classics.

My brothers and I pick fishbones from between our teeth,
begin the slow act of drowning in mother's kitchen sink.

Among the dishes I find her collections of sharp things:
paring knife, wishbone, library of salts. I know this

brief story—at this sink she'd once discarded a goldfish,
soft dead slip, mine. In the breath before the moment

I saw her, I'd tacked my knees to the tile, unhinging
my jaw to play every animal I knew. Me: kitchen girl,

this time sterile-limbed, peeling apart, delicate as flour
on the cutting room floor—all open and pretend

and gutted. Lately my brothers tell me I am falling
again, into scraps and winter bones. Always

this time of year. I wait out days for light. Let them
teach me another new animal, and then another.

2016 Poetry Adult First Place Winner: World Dance by Bijaya Eaton

These days Bijaya wears the hat of being a mother to two brilliant elementary school girls who are growing up way too fast. Hats she's previously worn include a waitress at a cheap diner, a check-out-clerk at a cheap bookstore, and a Silicon Valley engineer. Bijaya's looking forward to wearing many more hats in the future. One she'd especially like to see fit is that of an acclaimed writer.

I read about the sun today
In Spanish.
Same letters arranged in different jumbles
Stumbled off the tongue
Confusing the eyes, ears, the neurons
From familiar fire.
Then there arose
Different rhythms, la
Órbita del mundo
Changed la baila
mundial.
But the sun stayed the same.

2016 Poetry Adult Second Place Winner: Except to Say by Anita McLaughlin

Anita has been writing poetry since high school. After graduating from Otis Art Institute in Los Angeles, California, Anita and her husband actor Lee McLaughlin raised race horses. Anita started a business designing and manufacturing jockey's silks, taught 3D animation and has spent the last twenty years creating and art directing video game art. She has been a member of the Julie Williams Cottage Workshop Poets since 1999.

I agree the steak was bad
the cafe with its tilted sign
a poor choice
you were right

except to say the pie was good
the waitress kind

you can say it's all my fault
the rain fell
the truck got stuck

except to say sun split clouds
dried our socks

yes, we were snake-bit
horses went lame
hay got wet

except to say miracles
born with wobbly legs, flicky tails
filled the barn
warmed the nights

2017 Poetry Adult Second Place Winner: The Rat by Anita McLaughlin

"Rat!" mutters Martin the pest guy
His mouth sidewise in a crooked grin
He puts out traps, leaves me
Alone, in my house, with a rat
Bam!
The rat, the trap, under the sink, 2:00 AM
I pull on boots, tap the cupboard door
Rat sounds erupt, fill the kitchen

I scream, push a chair against the door
I call, Martin laughs
I beg, he says he will be there
In the morning

The rat and I wait for three days
I can't eat or look at food
The rat rattles behind the door
I dream about rats, Google rats, Draw rats

I kick the cupboard door
The rat kicks back, I imagine
He grinds his ratty teeth on the other side
Lusts for the chance to rip my face

I imagine him fierce with rage
Focused on revenge, claws sharpened
His head the size of a cocker spaniel
Eyes blood red

In the morning on the third day
Martin opens the cupboard door
I see the rat is dead
His soft gray body
Is
Beautiful

2017 Poetry Adult Honorable Mention: Grandfather's Photograph by Anita McLaughlin

Why can't I remember this dark man, old man, who stands under a tree
Stands with scarred fingers touching a rough wooden chair
Why can't I remember his words; simple words like toast and tea

What song does he hear, what long journey does he see?
Man wearing a crusty black hat on his dusty gray hair
Why can't I remember this dark man, old man, who stands under a tree

Why can't I remember the scent of ash, wet wool, old whiskey
Did he arrive wearing this grey suit, a suit of patches and tears
Why can't I remember his words; simple words like toast and tea

Why can't I see his blue marble eyes; eyes that snatched at me
Eyes that whispered secrets of copper mines and hunting bear
Why can't I remember this dark man, old man, who stands under a tree

How do I guess his secrets; secrets of a young man dancing at sea
Secrets of hunting in Austria; loving women with ribbons in their hair
Why can't I remember his words; simple words like toast and tea

Why can't I remember the man who came to visit my mother and me
Who stayed one day; left chocolates and paper wrapped pears
Why can't I remember this dark man, old man, who stands under a tree
Why can't I remember his words; simple words like toast and tea

Short Story: Misplaced Bride by Theresa Schultz

Theresa's passion since childhood has been writing. She was a real estate agent for thirty-one years. One of her first articles was for RAW Real Authentic Women magazine called "This I've Learned." It was a beautiful magazine; however, because the editor lost several strong advertisers, it folded before she had a chance to become famous. But it did inspire her to put the three books she wrote under one umbrella called This I've Learned, *a collection of self-help books. Her books are:* Dear God, I'm Divorced, It's Like…, Getting twenty-five Years of Experience as a Real Estate Agent, *and* It's a Happy Day. *Two of her stories have appeared in previous VCWC Anthologies.*

Carol stared out the hotel window and watched the rain pour over Chicago. She didn't expect rain on the morning of her wedding. She was alone, but that was what she'd wanted. The knot in her stomach wouldn't go away. She couldn't forget about the argument with her fiancé, Tony.

When it was time to put on her wedding dress, she wished her mother was there to help her. Yesterday, when they took a stroll together in the park, they found a bench to savor their time together. They were oblivious to the people around them. Carol hesitated until they were ready to leave before she told her mother about the argument with Tony. Her mother tried to assure her they were both nervous and it would be okay.

Carol blurted, "I want to spend the night at the hotel. I need to be alone."

Neither one looked at the other during a long silence. Her mother stood. When she turned, she noticed a man hovering too close.

Let's leave," she whispered.

Their stride was almost a run.

"Did you see the tattoo on that man's bald head?" her mother asked.

"Yeah, but I couldn't figure it out."

"I think it was a snake."

That conversation was only yesterday, but to Carol it seemed much longer. She felt sad because she knew her mother was hurt when she told her she wanted to be alone. They once giggled about the fun they would have putting on her wedding gown.

The wedding was at eleven. Carol had arranged for a taxi to pick her up at ten-thirty. People cheered and clapped when she walked through the lobby in her wedding dress. She loved the way people stared at her when she waited just inside the door, so she could see the taxi without getting wet. A limousine drove up. The driver, dressed in a black suit, got out and stood looking around. He came inside and walked toward Carol.

"I figure you must be Carol," he said. "I have a surprise for you. Your mother hired Fredericks Limousine Service to drive you to the church."

Carol was delighted. She hoped this meant her mother was no longer upset. The driver held an umbrella for her as they hurried to the limo. Carol loved the way her dress took up most of the seat.

"Your mother was concerned you were by yourself. She wanted you to be safe," the driver said.

Carol smiled. "I didn't think it would take us this long. Are we almost there?" Carol asked. "The church is only four blocks away."

The driver nodded.

"Could you go a little faster? I don't want to be late for my own wedding."

He looked over his shoulder and smirked. "Don't worry, Miss. Isn't the bride supposed to be a little late?"

"No. No, that's not what I want. Hurry, it's almost eleven. Do you know where it is? We've gone more than four blocks." Carol raised her voice. "Where are you going? We're already late."

He looked at her in the rear-view mirror. "Well, well, looks like the bride is getting the jitters. Why don't you just relax? I'm sure we can find other things to do than go to a wedding."

Her whole body felt numb. "Who are you? Why are you doing this?" Carol yelled. "I want out right now!"

"What do you want me to do, drop you off on the side the road? I can see the headlines now... 'Bride stranded on the side of the road in her wedding dress'."

"Please, what do you want? Just take me to the church. I'll pay you whatever you want. I need to get to my wedding."

"Oh, you'll pay, all right. Do you have money?"

"Not with me. Please just drive to the church. We can talk about it after the wedding."

"No, we need to talk about it now. Aren't you worth ten grand to your man?"

"Ten grand? Ten thousand dollars? Tony doesn't have that kind of money. Don't do this to us. This is our wedding day. Please! Please!"

"It's business, strictly business. I need money and your man needs you."

When he turned to look at her again she saw his mustache wasn't real and neither was his hair. She couldn't hold back the tears. "Please, don't hurt me."

"No one's going to hurt you if I get the money. All I want is the money."

"Does Tony know?

"Of course, he doesn't know. You need to give me his cell phone number."

Carol rattled off the number.

"Don't talk so fast," he said moving toward the curb. He pulled a pen from his front jacket pocket.

She repeated his number. "His phone might not be on. He would turn it off during the wedding."

"Well, maybe that's a good thing. We need to let him worry a bit first. Everyone needs to worry about you."

Carol wanted to jump from the car. The door and windows were locked. The rain made it impossible for anyone to see her frantic waves. He drove into a commercial area and stopped at a storage building. He leaped out and opened her door. "This is where you get out," he said.

Carol pushed away when he reached for her arm.

"Relax. You won't get hurt if you just do what I say." He fumbled with a key, and then lifted what looked like a garage door. He shoved her inside.

"Don't leave me. Let me out of here." she screamed.

The door slammed down. She was left alone. A dim light seeped in under the door. It was enough for her to find the light switch. The storage space was empty. Her screams were in vain. There was no one to hear. She wondered about the people who were waiting at the church. What were they thinking? What would Tony do? Would this cause her dad to have another heart attack? She held her stomach. She sat down. The floor was cold, so she curled up, and wrapped the train of her dress around her. The soft satin felt good. She didn't move.

She was startled and jumped when the door finally flew up. There was a man in jeans and a t-shirt.

"Who are you?"

"Let's just say I've had a make-over."

Carol realized he was the limo driver without the mustache and toupee. The snake tattoo on the top of his head told her he was the man who was listening when she was with her mother.

"Well, well, it seems like your groom doesn't think you're worth ten grand."

"You talked to him? Tony doesn't have that kind of money," Carol said holding her dress as she struggled to stand.

"He wouldn't talk. He hung up on me. But hey, I'm fair," he said spreading his arms. "I don't want to hurt you, so I called him again. I told your man where to leave the money before two o'clock today. You'd better start praying that it's there."

He slammed the door. Once again she was isolated. Tears smeared her make-up. Her satin dress was her only comfort as she curled on the floor.

She jumped up when the door finally opened. The driver motioned for her to go with him.

"Let's get out of here," he said. "Lucky for you, I have the money."

"Where are we going?"

"I'm going to drop you off where you can hail a cab. But I'm warning you, if you call the police, you'll be sorry. So don't try anything dumb."

Instead of the limousine, he led her to an old beat-up Ford. She glanced to see the license plate, but it was covered with mud so thick the rain didn't remove it. Carol crowded into the back seat. The car was as dirty on the inside as the outside. She scrambled to get out the second it stopped. She clutched the train to her dress as she hurried to the curb. She was glad there was no one to see her before a cab came.

The cab driver chuckled and said, "I've never picked up a bride before. I'm not going to ask any questions. Just tell me where you're headed."

"Capital Hotel," she yelled. "It's on the corner of Willow and Main Street. You'll have to wait for me until I can get some money to pay you. I have a room there."

"This one's on me," he said. "I don't know what's going on, but by the looks of you, I think you need to get to that room as soon as you can."

Carol clutched the key stashed in the tiny pocket of her dress as she hurried through the lobby of the hotel. She stopped when she heard her name.

"Carol. Are you all right?" She turned and saw George, their best man, running toward her. She dropped into his arms and for the first time sobbed.

"It was awful. Really awful. I was so scared," she said. "Where's Tony? How's my mom? What happened at the church?"

George took her hand and walked with her to a nearby couch. They sat down. "I was with Tony when he got the ransom call."

"What did he say?"

"He hung up on the man. Tony thought you planned it as an excuse not to marry him."

"He really said that?"

"He told me you'd argued and both of you realized you didn't really love each other, but it was too late to cancel the wedding."

"Tony. Maybe Tony plotted the kidnapping."

"No, Carol," George said taking her hand. "He didn't plan it. The kidnapping was for real. When the man called back, I insisted on talking to him."

"What happened? What did he say?"

"He thought he was talking to Tony. He said I had until two o'clock to put the money in an old wooden box on the corner of First and Hickory Streets. He threatened if I called the police, I wouldn't like what might happen. Tony said to count him out and then stormed away in his car."

"He didn't care. He didn't even care what might happen to me."

"I'm really sorry, Carol. I'm just thankful I was with him when he got the call."

"What about the ransom money? How did you get it?"

"I called my dad. He works at First Savings Bank. I don't know what he did, but he was able to get a loan for the money. Luckily, the bank was able to mark the bills."

George walked Carol to her room. "Change your clothes and rest for a few minutes," he said. "I'll be back to take you home. I need to make some phone calls. There are lots of people who are very worried about you."

"You know George, you're a hero. I might have died if it weren't for you. I'll be indebted to you for the rest of my life."

"I think I might like that," he said brushing his hand on her cheek.

***

Two years have passed since that terrifying day. But Carol was grateful when George raised his glass for a toast on their first wedding anniversary.

"Thanks to a groom who drove away. And the bald man, in prison today."

Carol chimed in, as she clinked his glass, "Cheers to the 'best-man' yet."

2016 Poetry Adult Third Place Winner: Girl in Blue by Karen Kinrose

Karen grew up in Haddonfield, New Jersey. She became a social worker in England after graduating from Georgetown University in 1975. From England she moved to Santa Barbara where she met her husband through a musical theatre production. Their union resulted in two daughters and a move to Ventura to raise their family. Karen became a Financial Advisor in 1994 and has recently begun exploring other avenues of interest including poetry writing and painting.

Her place of pride above my parents' fireplace
Purchased years ago for that special spot
The young woman's gaze intrigued Mom and Dad
Reminded them of me they said in my turbulent hippie days.

Wedged in the corner of a blue velvet couch
Long dark hair pulled snug behind her head
Hip-hugging jeans and rust colored turtleneck
Coal black eyes look outward see only inward.

Lives with us now an unwelcome guest
Attacked and defended again and again
Unhappy and depressed says my husband
Quietly daydreaming I reply.

Truth is I see this girl's inner sadness
The unsure sense of something amiss
Alone and lost in that tightly framed space
Not knowing where it all will lead.

I'd like to release her from her plight
Reveal her questions will be answered
What is buried deep unearthed released
Won't be easy but she will do it.

Perhaps it's time to find another painting
A pleasant one with hills and trees and cloud-bearing skies
Discard this prickly reminder of my past
Replace her with something we can both enjoy.

Yet I hold back.
If I take her down where would she go?
Who would take care of her?
What would I lose of myself if she's no longer there?

2016 Poetry Adult Honorable Mention: Never Gone by Sharon Sinczewski

Sharon has a master's degree in Clinical Psychology and would love to work with children or senior citizens someday. She would also like to get a degree in creative writing to further her love for writing. She is currently planning a self-help novel on the death of her younger brother and would also love to publish a book of poetry someday. Sharon is also an avid reader who loves to spend time with family.

I can't count how many times I've wondered about you
It's been too many years since I've been able to see your face
I never thought I'd have to memorize it

The questions that run through my head sometimes paralyze me
I'm worried I will forget what you look like; your laughter
withering away like a dead flower
I once knew every feature of you; they all seem to fade with time

When I see a little boy with blonde hair and blue eyes, I think of
you
I wonder if you would have been a husband or a father by now
I can't help but see that same young man who had the whole world
in front of him

You were in every piece of my past
I always assumed you'd be in my future
When I lost you, I lost a piece of my childhood; A part of my soul

Sometimes I think I will always be looking for you
Searching through strangers to find that boy I once knew
You are there in every sunny day
You are the gentle breeze on my skin on a cloudy day
I know you aren't gone

2016 Poetry Adult Honorable Mention: Meditation Frustration by Kim Reed

Kim left the snow of Buffalo, NY in 2005 to pursue a new life in sunny California. She quickly found like-minded souls who shared her interests, including spirituality and writing. She is a former newsletter editor of the VCWC. A non-fiction writer, this is Kim's first foray into poetry.

Inspired by how the Buddha sits

I sit, too. And wait.

Judgments tap dance in my busy brain

Gnats of

anxiety

angst

longing

regrets

fear

sadness

Waltz to their incessant tune.

Breathing in

Breathing out

My own sweet brand of insect repellant

Turns my brain

"OFF"

Gnats slowly slip away.

I polish the silence.

2016 Poetry Adult Honorable Mention: Toad Ode by Ron Loewe

Ron is a retired high-school English teacher. He was a charter member of both Thousand Oaks and Westlake High Schools. Concurrent with his teaching he became a teacher/writing consultant for UCLA and U.C. Irvine as part of the State's writing project. Ron co-authored a teacher's textbook, Participating in the Poem *and also published professional education articles and poems in the English Journal. Now retired, He continues to write and publish and most recently taught Memoir Writing at the Senior Center in Merced, C.A. and Simi Valley Adult Ed.*

Bofus Americanas—the boggy Socrates, truly believes;
Sitting upon his throne of clotted mud and rotted leaves,
    That authentic beauty lies within,
    And reflects his wisdom with his grin.
Reigning regally, he watches the insects on parade,
While enraptured by the cricket chorus serenade.
    Though critics use his oily, pebbled, toxic cloak,
    And his thunderous echoing croak
    To call him nature's amphibious joke,
That philosopher absorbs the insults with stoic aplomb
Then blends them into a unique kind of laudanum.
    Posing—with snowy belly, round, and smooth, and plump,
    He sculpts himself into an invisible, camouflaged lump,
Then watches the waltz of the damsel flies
With his sharply-focused, bulging eyes.
    Here, in his home among the marshy reeds,
    He's content in knowing he has all he needs,
        And sits immobile, with his happy grin,
        Relishing the real beauty that lies within.

2016 Memoir Honorable Mention: Apple Daises by Ron Loewe

Mother's Day was fast approaching. Last year, when I was six, I had picked her violets from the banks along the railroad tracks near my house. She cried when I gave them to her. I didn't want to make her cry again.

This year, I decided that the perfect gift for her was the apron I had seen in Woolworth's Five and Dime store. But I didn't have any money.

Mother's Day was only four days away. Then I saw Grandpa Fritz sitting in his big Adirondack chair. I would ask him for some money.

I was disappointed, but not surprised by his answer. "I don't just give you my money," he said in his heavy German accent. "You pick the potato bugs, then I give you two dimes."

This was one chore I always tried to avoid. But time was running out.

When I finished knocking the ugly pests into the empty tobacco tin, Grandpa Fritz reached into his pocket and selected two shiny dimes from the coins in his hand.

"Vat you want the money for," Grandpa Fritz asked. "Candy no good for you."

"I want to buy Mom an apron for Mother's Day," I said.

"I give you another quarter if you clean up the workbench."

Now I had forty-five cents. The apron cost $1.50. I knew Grandpa Fritz would not give me any more money. We sat quietly in the shade. Then Grandpa Fritz spoke. "Mrs. Schieder has weeds in her garden. You do a good job, like I teach you. Maybe she pay you."

I politely rang Mrs. Schieder's doorbell and offered to help her. She was happy. I wanted to do a job Grandpa Fritz would approve of. Mrs. Schieder called to me from her swing on the front porch when I closed the gate as I was leaving.

"Come sit. I have some Kool Aid for you."

I thanked her. She reached into her apron pocket and handed me two quarters. I refused at first, like Grandpa Fritz expected me to do. Her persistence overcame my reluctance.

My father would be home from work soon. I would ask him for the rest of the money I needed. Like Grandpa, he refused.

"That's a great idea," he said, "but you would be prouder if you earned all the money, wouldn't you?"

"I've got an idea," my father said. "Tomorrow morning walk along the alleys and see if you can find some pop bottles. Mr. Nesimier, at the grocery store, will give you two cents for each one."

"How many will I need to find," I asked.

"I tell you what," my father replied. "If you find at least ten, I'll give you the rest of the money."

The next morning, I ate breakfast quickly, took a gunnysack from the garage and searched the alleys for pop bottles. I had walked nearly the whole length of our alley before I found two bottles. I needed eight more.

One house on the next alley had five of them. Just as I was leaving that alley to go to the next one, Mrs. Weigel saw me. She was working in her flower garden.

"You're a Loewe, aren't you?" she asked.

"Yes, Ma'am," I replied.

"What are you doing? What's in that gunny sack?"

'I'm collecting pop bottles," I stammered.

"Check over by my back door. Take them all. They're too heavy for me to carry."

The bottles were lined up on her back stoop. There were more than I could carry. I counted out thirty of them. My dad was right. I did feel proud of myself.

When my father came home from work, I showed him the money. We counted it out together. I had earned $1.59.

"You tell me what apron you want," he said, "and I'll get it for you after work. I'll leave it in the car so your mother won't see it."

I tried my best to describe the apron. It was pink with tiny red roses. It had two pockets, like my mother always wore. One for clothespins, and the other for my handicapped brother, Del's bottle.

It was trimmed in soft pink trim with jagged edges she called "rick rack."

When my dad brought it home I proudly showed it to Grandpa Fritz. "We wrap it for your mama tomorrow," he said.

"But I don't have enough money for wrapping paper," I said.

"You go back to the grocery store. Ask Mr. Nesimier for some butcher paper. The paper he wrap the meat in for your mama."

"But that won't look nice," I said. "White isn't very pretty."

"We make it pretty. You go in the house and get an apple."

How could an apple make paper pretty? I gave Grandpa Fritz the apple and ran up the alley to the grocery store. When I returned with the paper, neatly rolled up, Grandpa Fritz had already selected a small can of red paint that had been used for painting my bike.

"We close the door so your mama don't see," he said. "Lay the paper out on the workbench. Put something on the corners." He stirred the paint. "Now I show you something special," he said. He opened his pocketknife and set the apple on the workbench with the stem pointing up. He sliced down on four sides, leaving a square white core.

"We eat the apple first," Grandpa said, "then we decorate the paper."

I ate my slices quickly because I wanted to see the surprise. When Grandpa finished his slices, he laid the apple core down. He sliced through the center of it with the stem pointing one way, and the bottom the other way. Then he picked up the two pieces.

"Close your eyes," he told me. "Okay, now open them." Inside the apple core were two perfect daisies.

"Now we paint this piece of scrap wood. Make it thick. Touch this piece of apple in the paint. Watch. Not too hard! See!" Then he placed the paint covered piece of apple on the paper. When he lifted it, it printed a perfect outline of a white daisy bordered in red. It was like a rubber stamp.

"Now you help me. Not too many flowers. Not too much paint. Bare spots okay."

I was happy, even under Grandpa's vigilant supervision.

"Enough," Grandpa said. "Now we let it dry. You help me clean up."

"I'm proud of you," my father said when he saw the paper. "You earned your own money." He squeezed my shoulder. "Mama will like the paper as much as she will the apron."

Grandpa and I wrapped the apron the next day. We tied it with kite string. "We keep it here until Sunday morning. You cut a rose and put it under the string. You don't stay in bed. You get up early and give it to her."

On Mother's Day, I gave my Mother the present with the rose tucked in the string. She hugged me and said she loved me. But she was crying.

I didn't understand it then—but I do now.

2016 Short Story Adult Honorable Mention: Invasion by Rob Loewe

My door number is two-one-three. There are other doors to the sides. Above. Below. All around. Other people, faces really, live behind their numbered doors.

In the morning rush to our cars, we sometimes look up from our cell phones and say, "Hi. How are ya'?"

"Fine."

"See ya'."

"Have a nice day."

We take turns merging into the morning traffic, tailgate each other for a while, then split off to spend our day inside our cubicles. And it goes on. And on.

Until the weekends – when all the doors are open and it's, "See ya' at the pool."

"Don't forget the party tonight."

The weekends are so communal.

That Saturday, a sharp repetitive knock prompted me to shout, "I'm hurrying. Come in." It had to be my impatient friend eager for his first tailgate party.

The door opened. A gloved hand waved a knife near my face. A powerful arm pushed me against the wall.

Like phantoms, two more rushed quietly in from the sides.

The waving knife signaled me not to move. The second one turned the dead-bolt. The third one quickly roamed the other rooms. He closed all the shutters. Perspiration beaded on my forehead. This was not a rehearsal, it was a reenactment. They had done this before.

My audible gasp broke the silence.

"Ah, you're scared? Good. Where do you keep your money?" His was a modulated, deep, basso voice. An actor's voice full of calm menace. The deadness in his eyes told me he needed things to go his way. He dressed like a leader. Designer jeans, expensive sneakers, and a plaid, unwrinkled shirt. He smelled of cologne. A sharp contrast to his two minions.

"My wallet's in the bedroom, on the dresser." My choked reply was weak.

The roamer returned with the wallet. He gave it to the Knife.

"Sir, there's only thirty-four dollars in here." His condescending formality added another level to his aura of authority. This was going way too fast.

"I don't carry much cash," I replied. His steady unflinching stare told me he didn't believe me.

He moved closer and touched my chest with the knife. "Sir, you need to be honest and cooperative." He paused for dramatic effect, then continued. "We've been watching you. Your Mercedes convertible and all these designer clothes tell me you're lying. Where's your real money?"

"I go to the ATM, or I use my credit cards."

"You mean you're willing to die for thirty-four dollars?"

The low, slow, icy tone panicked me. I didn't think they would kill me. Now I was unsure. I saw a wide spot of blood on my shirt. When had he stuck me? He was an expert.

"What else do you have that's worth our bother?"

"My computers and my audio system," I stammered.

The second one, dressed in camouflage, lifted one of my laptops and showed it to Knife. He looked at it, turned it over and threw it down. Then he stepped on it.

"Sir, we can't fence this. Your name's etched in it. Maybe you think this is smart." He paused. "It isn't. It just makes people like me angrier. But I'm smarter than you. So are these guys." Another pause. "You'll see. You'll see."

Silence.

"Do you have your name on all this fancy audio equipment, too?"

"Yes," I squeaked.

"You are definitely beginning to aggravate me." The knife jiggled in his hand. He was struggling to stifle his rage.

His sudden shift in attitude prompted him to guide me into the living room. I fell backward over the ottoman.

There was a knock on the door. My heart raced. I would be rescued.

"Gary, you in there? We're ready to leave."

I was ready to shout out to save myself.

Knife instinctively knelt to put his lips next to my ear. "Don't make a sound. Not even a cough. If you do, I'll stick this knife in your ear all the way into your tiny brain." I knew he meant it. His fresh minty breath emphasized his threat.

The knock came again. More persistent and louder this time.

"Gary! Gary! Open up! We're leaving in five minutes."

The silence was punctuated by the rhythmic ticking of the clock.

"Okay, I gotta' go get my stuff. I'll see you down in the parking lot."

He walked away. I was left alone with the three of them.

"On your flabby stomach, rich boy!" His calmness was gone.

Why wasn't I protesting? This was not fair! I was splayed out like some sacrificial lamb, lying here without even a bleat. Why had they chosen me? Then I knew. I simply had more than they did. It didn't matter that I had worked hard for all of it. All that mattered to them was that they wanted it, too.

Because I did not roll on to my stomach a boot caught me in the ribs. The pain took my breath away. Camouflage and Roamer rolled me on to my belly.

"Bend your knees! Get some of his fancy ties! We'll tie him up," Knife quickly ordered.

The other two walked into my bedroom to fetch the ties. They threw them on the floor beside me.

"You tie his hands, and you tie his feet," Knife said. "Tie them well. I don't want him to get loose while I decide what to do with him." He sat on the ottoman and stared at me. Then his eyes took on a distant, vacant look. What was he remembering? What was he planning?

"How about we tie his hands to his feet," Roamer said. When he knelt beside me his baggy gang-banger shorts swallowed his tattered sneakers. He had not bathed recently. His breath smelled of convenience store jerky and old popcorn.

"Yeah, better yet, let's tie a noose around his neck and then to his feet. I saw this in a western movie. They called it hog tyin'," Camouflage added.

"Let's use this one for the noose," he said. "It's still got the price tag on it. Eighty-seven dollars! Eighty-seven dollars for a damn tie? Man, you got more money around your scrawny neck than you got in your wallet. You— really – are – stupid!"

I had to protest somehow. I couldn't just lie here like a bent spoon and slowly choke to death. But how?

"What do you guys really want?" My attempt at confrontation was too feeble.

"We want your money, you rich yuppy punk! Where is it?" Knife said. The outburst signaled his instability. I was afraid.

"I told you. All I've got is what's in my wallet." I immediately regretted my tone.

"And I told you, you're not as smart as I am. You and I both don't know what I'll do next. So just tell me where you're really hiding it."

I knew it was coming before I felt Camouflage's boot smash into my ribs again.

"Kick him! Kick him! Kick him!" Roamer crazily chanted and clapped his hands. "Then maybe he'll tell the truth"

The blows took my breath away. I was gasping for air. The noose tightened with each spasm. I began to cough.

"Ha! Ha! Ha! He's chokin' his dumb-ass self."

I felt Knife's finger between the noose and my neck. I was grateful. I had read somewhere that victims often felt gratitude toward their abductors. Was I doing that? Was I being grateful? I saw the blurred faces through my watery eyes. This can't be happening. I always thought that if you left people alone, they would leave you alone.

"Please. Please," I mumbled.

Knife knelt to hear my whimper. "Quiet, sir. Don't make another sound – ever. Get one of his socks. An athletic one. Stuff it in his mouth."

Roamer returned with a white sock.

"Open your mouth."

The noose tightened when I turned my head away. Roamer pulled on my jaw. I tried to tighten my lips. Camouflage knelt to help. He pinched my nose together. I struggled with them as best I could until I was forced to open my mouth in a desperate gasp for air. I tried to bite them. I had to do something.

"Hey, he's tryin' to bite me!"

The kick to my head stunned me. I tasted the cotton sock as it dried my tongue.

"Tie another tie around his mouth so he doesn't spit it out." Knife said. He seemed to have ready solutions to setbacks.

Now I was on my stomach like some mute rocking horse. All I could see were feet. I heard Roamer and Camouflage breaking the audio equipment. Knife sat calmly on the ottoman with his feet on my back. He pushed down intermittently to tighten the noose. When I choked, he slipped his finger under it to relieve the tightness. He was toying with me. He was enjoying his experiment. "I want you alive – for a while." I could hear him breathing deeply. Roamer went into the kitchen and began stomping on my dishes and souvenir mugs and glasses. He came back into the living room.

"He's got lots of expensive booze. You guys want any of this before I break it?"

He walked over to me and poured wine on my head.

"How much you pay for this? It tastes like bad beer."

At first, I was confused, then I realized that the knife was in my nose. There was a slight tug, and then I felt the salty taste of blood as it turned the sock red.

"If we only get thirty-four dollars from you," Knife whispered, "you're at least going to have to pay big money to replace everything we smash. Maybe you won't be so smug and pompous from now on. I'm trying to think of some way to get some payback for our inconvenience." His eyes were focused in a blank distant stare.

The stomping suddenly stopped. There was another sharp repetitive rap on the door. This time there were more voices. I was safe after all!

"Gary. Come on. It's time to go!"

Silence.

"O.K., we're leavin'. We'll see you there."

"Don't forget, it starts at two."

"Bring the ice chest – and the beer."

The boot pushed down on my head. I was choking. The finger relieved the tightness again. I flopped on to my side. This helped – if I didn't struggle.

I should have pushed him out at the beginning. But, what chance did I have against three of them? They were in before I could think. Why was I feeling sorry for myself? I should be angry. I knew long ago that life was not always fair, but I never thought I'd be the one that proved it was true.

"Should we dump out his fish?"

"They're the fancy kind. Maybe we should eat them like in that movie."

"No, just pour some booze in the tank. If they make it, good for them. If not, too bad."

He held the knife close to my eyes. I could see the fine milling marks in the blade. Was this the moment before death when everything comes into sharper focus, when all our senses are heightened and events flash with lightning speed through our minds?

"Since we aren't getting anything from you, I decided to give you something. A little present that will always remind you of us." He put the edge of the knife against my right cheek, near my eye. This time I felt it dig in. He took a deep breath then drew the knife slowly toward my ear. My neck was suddenly warm. My shirt collar was sticky wet. He put his face close to mine and smiled.

"We know where you live. You're always going to remember us."

The boot caught me across the nose. The next kick hit my left eye. I can't remember the rest of them.

The next morning when my friends convinced the landlord to open the door they found me in the walk-in closet.

"Did they take anything valuable?" the policeman asked.

How can I tell anyone what Knife and Camouflage and Roamer really stole from me?

No one knows that I am now another unwilling member of a secret club. We have a ritualistic code. When we sense each other in crowds, we look away when our eyes meet.

Another quick glance, an imperceptible nod, then we try desperately to smother the memories that flood back. "Knife" was right. We always remember. We strive to survive on anonymity and an unrealistic hope that someday, somehow, we will be able to forget.

But it goes on. And on.

2016 Short Story Youth First Place Winner: Completely Perfect by Sydney Edgecomb

Sydney (in 2016) was a junior at Laguna Blanca High School in Santa Barbara, California. She enjoys writing, reading, and riding horses in her free time.

I check myself over in the mirror. The powder and foundation cover the dark circles that hang from my eyes. The blush colors my hollow cheekbones. The mascara brings life to my dying eyes. I run a hand over my face, slowly, letting my fingers drift over my features, features that I used to admire, used to love.

"Can't forget the lip gloss," I scold, searching the counter for the little round tube. The lip gloss hides the quivering of the chin, the trembling of the body. I pull the sleeves of the hoodie over my frail arms, ones that used to be so strong, so unyielding. The hoodie is soft to the touch; it's warm, giving me a comforting presence. I never forget the hoodie, no, not like the lip gloss. I let my fingers pull the hood over my head, covering the missing chunks of hair.

I don't cry often, I'm not like that, but I had cried when I felt the hair fall from my head to my fingers. It was like losing an old friend. I don't know why I did, I never even liked my hair, a blond mess that sat atop my head like a mop, little curls always escaping my fingers as I tried to put it into a ponytail. But when little gold patches of hair fell into my lap, I clearly remember tears falling with them.

Sometimes I wonder why I do this, why I put myself through this every morning, spending so much time to make myself look like someone I'm not anymore. These people's opinions don't matter. I'll never see them again after high school. But then I realize I don't do it for them. I do it for me. You can't very well be in denial that you're dying if you look like you're dying, it's the first rule of dying… I think. How would I know, I don't know anyone else like me? My mom tried to get me into one of those groups once, you know, the ones where people like you sit in a circle and talk about your feelings and your fears? I had to put my foot down and refuse. Why? Simple. I don't want to get attached to anyone. The more attached to someone I get, the more people I hurt when I finally . . . well, never mind. And if those people are like me, which they are, there is no point. I won't like them anyway. They'll remind me too much of myself.

I try to stay active; a busy mind is the best distraction. It's hard. I can't very well do the things I used to. To put it simply, I'm weak. I can't run, I can't swim, I can't play on the volleyball team, hell, I can't even walk up the stairs. And it's almost impossible to stay in denial when you can't walk up the stairs. It is a simple, but sensitive balance. One must stay busy without exhausting themselves, especially when one is dying. It is pointless to pretend that this balance does not exist. Everything in the world is a balance, essentially, two things, two equalizers. Up and down, happiness and sorrow, abominations and delights, destruction and creation, living and dying. One must uphold that balance, for it will not uphold itself.

Checking myself over in the mirror one last time, I decide that I look good enough and head to the kitchen. I breathe in deeply. Pancakes.

Pancakes. The signal that another morning routine is about to start. I take the final steps into the kitchen and sit down at the table.

"Hey Mom," I say over to her. Her back is turned away from me as she pours a glass of orange juice. She turns to say hello as some orange juice spills over from the top of the glass. She reaches for a paper towel.

"Good morning," she replies happily, giving me a smile that doesn't quite reach her eyes. "How are you this morning?"

"Fine," I reply, trying to sound happy while taking a slow sip of the orange juice she placed before me.

She sees through my facade, like she does every morning. She's my mother, I don't know what I expect. Sometimes, times like this, she looks so old. I'm not insulting my mom, I just mean she looks like she has the weight of the world on her shoulders. She does this thing where she pinches her forehead with her thumb and forefinger. It's a dead giveaway if she is sad, or frustrated, or both … and she's doing it now. "Any improvement is good," she says half-heartedly.

"Of course."

"I made pancakes." Her offering.

"Thanks, Mom. Smells delicious." My offering.

"Hon, have you thought about what I said the other day?"

I shrug, my face blank of emotion. I had thought about what she had said. It's what she had been saying for the last three months.

"Honey, you can't do this forever. People will ask questions. Eventually things will come up and you'll have to miss school. Wouldn't it be better just to tell your classmates?"

Things. I think taking a small bite out of a pancake. *Things will come up, she says. I hate things.* She looks like she is going to say something else, but I cut her off. "Mom, I have two months left of high school, then it's done, then it's over. I can make it 'til then. I'm the valedictorian! I was voted 'Most likely to succeed!' I'm supposed to be the girl who's got it all together. People don't want to know that the girl who's got it all together, doesn't have it all together. People don't want to know that girl is dying!"

She flinched. I might have raised my voice.

"Okay," she says resting her hand on mine. "I understand. Just know, that it's okay if you don't. Somethings we just can't help."

I don't think we were just talking about going to school anymore, so I started to leave. "Thanks, Mom." I kiss her on the cheek. "I love you."

"I love you too," my mom replies. This exchange, once taken for granted, is now a vital part of every morning, every afternoon, every night. Three little words, followed by four more, have come to mean more than an entire conversation. They are a part of our small grasp on normality. They hold everything together in our shaky relationship. They balance.

I never used to doubt myself. I used to make a decision and loyally follow it through. I would stand up to my teachers in class, debate facts and state my argument. It was one of the reasons I was so popular I think, I got the reputation of the advocate. I was actually rather good at it as well. I had all the factors one needs to start and finish an argument: confidence, intelligence, and courage. Looking back, I know how stupid I was to argue with my betters. I don't fully understand why I would do it in the first place. Once I started there was no way I could back down, even if I was wrong, it is the principle of the thing. It is one thing to lose because you are defeated, and another to give up.

I do not like giving up.

I suppose that's why I'm still here today, still breathing, still thinking, still being. My refusal to give up. Doctor Rosenthal says people like me, people who can beat it, are a rarity and that I should be very thankful, that I should thank God for my health. But I know it isn't any God who is to thank for my health. Simply put, I know that the thing that is keeping me alive is the same thing that is trying to kill me,

Me.

I am the thing that is keeping me alive. I refuse to give in, refuse to give up, and refuse to stop trying. I will be normal and be in denial till it kills me, and trust I know, one day, it will.

Keys in hand, I open the door and blink in the early morning sun. My silver car waits in the driveway and as I walk toward it, I check my reflection in the tinted window. I see the valedictorian, the Miss Perfect, the volleyball super star, looking back at me. You can't doubt that. You can't doubt Perfect.

2017 Poetry Youth First Place Thirteen Plus Winner: Code Blue by Sydney Edgecomb

Then suddenly I am next,
to the metallic machines
beeping steadily, supporting his life
supporting mine.
The line jumps,
the music stops.

     Like a dam that breaks,
     they come forth like a tide
     an unheard cry, calling to action.

Electric paddles reply
to a pale complexion.
Chest compressions pass,
in rapid succession.
I stand there stilled,
remain unaffected.
A sallow sack of skin, a rancid rotting corpse,
I take it in and scream, until my throat is hoarse.

     They thought they could save him,
     they went corrected.
     You cannot save,
     what does not want to be resurrected.

2016 Poetry Adult Honorable Mention: Girlfriend Days by Channa Carter

Channa – 2016 was her last semester at Ventura College. She transferred and is living on campus at California Lutheran University. She is elated for the changes occurring in her life and now she has added VCWC poetry awardee to her resume.

I call you bitch and you say Ima hoe
We laugh at our elevator pose

You take my glasses and I take your scarves
But stealing flannels was only the start

Taking my hand in yours cause we figure we're counterparts.
Gazing at your moving frame, style, and lips just to miss the gentle words.

You laugh again at realization that I'm in space and you're my planet.

2016 Poetry Adult Division Honorable Mention: The Postlude by Robert Banfill

Robert Banfill is a retired software professional who has thirty-years' experience dabbling as an amateur poet. Never published and only competing in a few cowboy poetry contests he has decide to share some of his work in contests and grow his skills and understanding of poetry. His writing palette includes a wide range of western, romantic, nature and humorous subjects.

She waits each day, within her chair
the music slowly playing there
within her frail and withered frame

The chorus and the next refrain
of notes and rests all measured out
in quiet cadence by her soul
for none to hear the melodies

The whole unwritten works
that summed her being and her worth
in never ending symphony

Poetry: Shallow by Rhonda Noda

Rhonda grew up in the small town of Galva, KS. She lived in McPherson and Wichita, KS. Her husband stole her away May 2004 and she has never looked back. Since she has lived in California, she has met many amazing people. She joined the Ventura County Writers Club to keep writing and improve her skills. She enjoyed being the President of the VCWC from September 2014 to August 2016. Her poetry reflects the many aspects of the ups and downs of life and loves. These poems offer a glimpse into what life is and can become. Enjoy.

You wrote to say you found the love of your dreams
That you hoped to make her your wife it seems
Your excitement was overwhelming and unsubdued
I could feel the vibrations streaming through
The air was thick with disgraced emotions

As I read your letter filled with delight
I stared at the screen in total fright
My jaw dropped in disgust at the acrylic words
A diesis shoved into my soul, ripping it open
Emotions caught in a crime of timing

In my reply I tried to be open minded and kind
Met with more of your joyous descriptive words
A callous reply of "I thought you would be happy for me"
A calculated judgment of not being completely free
My shock was substantiated not at all light

Distaste still remains unresolved echoing in my mind
Cacophony of words seeping through my veins, arctic air
My face flush red hot as I read more – the hurt swells
Disbelief of the callous insignificant words filled with happy joy
The cost unseen still to be discovered in future episodes

A good friendship stained with invisible blood – scarred forever
The dissonance of your attitude slays me to my knees
Completed haunting of a friendship turned sour and cold
A shallow representation of this friendship unfolds
Time spent of hours on end disappears into darkness…

Poetry: Thunder Roars by Rhonda Noda

The thunder woke me this morning
I thought of you, wishing sleepily
Grabbing a pillow knowing…
A daydream will only bring me, you

That perfect someone unflawed
Fitting together like a tight fitted glove
Soft leather, smooth, flexible, with a soft scent
Easily molding and bending to the other's needs

Soft smooth silk like cloth seducing our skin
Light streaming through the shades
Soft touches ease our soul's desires
Melting a long-standing desire to touch the other

The thunder roared, waking me this morning…
Sleepily I send you a message to draw near
Come to me to play in the soft morning light
While the lightning flashes and the thunder roars

Poetry: The Player by Rhonda Noda

A plea of loneliness draws within
Lonely hearts begin to blend
With soft seductive words
Emotions intoxicate the air
The lust unfolds before them

One heart plants a seed to grow
One playing a game as pleasures unfold
Hiding intentions with bedeviled words
Vows of intent of loving thee only
While others wait behind the scene

A hurtful game of Love begins
Intent on securing hearts for thy self
A list begins to build
For pleasures unseen
Playing with no rules, thus ripping apart

A lonely heart in love with thee
Screams in pain and agony
As the player teases and taunts
Unwilling to acknowledge their wants
Needing only to be close, feeling desired

The played heart cries in distressed pain
Pleading for relief from the disdain
Hoping to hang on and win the game
Watching as they feel a fool by being played
Seeing the player find another to please

Boldly and freely without emotions
Holding close another only to be played
As they begin to gather their own collection
Not caring who is hurt or taunted
Only knowing what they want

With no care of others' feelings
These players roam freely
Throughout the world
Lonely hearts have to beware
These players really don't care.

2016 Memoir Third Place Winner: The Catch by Wesley J. Ginther

Wesley, from Charles, MO is a retired newspaper-advertising executive of The Santa Barbara-News Press, Santa Barbara, California. He retired in 2004 as National Advertising Director and moved to Cottleville, Missouri in 2010 with his wife, a former newsletter editor of this club. He is also a freelance journalist, graphic artist, landscape artist, accomplished photographer, and avid golfer. He writes short stories and essays and is compiling a collection of his short stories including a prizewinning story from a past VCWC Short Story contest that appeared in our anthology Windows.

I was asleep when my wife screamed my name, "Wes-leeeee!" with an emphasis on the ending.

I sat up in bed – startled, confused and desperate to comprehend. Samantha our dog, who had been asleep on my legs, also jolted awake and was barking from the middle of the bed.

My wife screamed, "Wes... it's alive!"

She knelt on her side of the bed, yanked the bedding from all sides and pulled it up and around her. Her face was ashen, her eyes filled with horror, her voice quivered as she gasped, "He ... he had a ... a mouse. It went under the bed."

I slid out of bed, my arthritic feet registered pain upon hitting the floor in spite of landing on soft carpet. I got on my knees and peered under the bed but saw nothing. It was too dark to see anything. Mary Beth yelled something about our cat Smokey, playing. She repeated, "I thought Smokey was playing with his toy mouse until the mouse jumped out of my slipper and ran under the bed!"

I couldn't see anything, and my glasses kept slipping off my nose. To be heard above Samantha, I shouted, "I need a flashlight."

"It's in the bathroom, next to the Jacuzzi."

I pushed myself wearily to my feet, went and retrieved it. I peered under the bed again. No cat. No mouse. I stood up and saw Smokey at the end of the bed, strutting toward the door, a small grey blob of fur held gently in his mouth. I moved toward him, but he scampered down the hallway like a burglar escaping police.

I stumbled after him and into the living room, flipping each light switch I passed. Samantha and Mary Beth followed right behind me. In the center of the room, Smokey stopped and dropped the mouse. The mouse darted. Smokey was quicker with a pounce. The mouse stopped and changed direction. Mary Beth yelled something about the mouse. I couldn't understand.

I ran to the laundry room and grabbed a broom. *I'll knock him senseless or dead ... and get rid of him.*

Mary Beth grabbed a paper bag from the kitchen counter, Samantha close at her side. We converged in the living room where Samantha barked and Smokey played with his prey. I swung the broom downward as the mouse darted toward our couch. Smokey jumped back, startled as the broom hit the floor and the mouse escaped. Samantha moved around us trying to stay out of the way but still in the mix.

Mary Beth yelled, "Don't you dare kill that mouse! I don't want blood on my rug."

The space under our sectional is only three inches of clearance...so small that Smokey couldn't crawl to the mouse. I stuck the broom handle under and swept it back and forth. The mouse shot out a short distance but upon seeing us darted back to safety. After about fifteen minutes of swinging the broom around the floor, of lifting ends of the sectional up and down, and of opening and closing the recliner sections, I realized the mouse wasn't coming out. It was a standoff. I couldn't do anything more and I was dead tired. I announced, "I'm going back to bed."

Mary Beth said, "I'm definitely not sleeping in our bed – he'll bring that damn mouse up onto the bed." She retreated to the guest bedroom and shut the door.

I closed our bedroom door, realizing her intuition was right. I turned the lights off and crawled under the sheets. Moments later, I heard a soft meow. I knew that sound. It was Smokey. He wanted back in the bedroom. I opened the door. He strutted in and dropped the mouse at my feet. It was lifeless. I reached down and grabbed the tail. Mouse in hand, I walked into the bathroom and flushed him down the toilet. *Good riddance.*

Loudly, so Mary Beth could hear, I yelled, "It's safe to come to bed. The mouse is gone."

I heard her open the guest bedroom door. "Are you sure he's gone?" She peaked around the doorframe.

"Yes, really. I gave him a burial at sea."

As she snuggled next to me, I asked, "What were you doing with the paper bag?"

"I thought Smokey would drop the mouse on the floor and we could hustle it into the bag...take it outside and turn it loose."

I laughed. "Just how were we going to 'hustle' a mouse?"

"Oh...you'd figure out how do it ... somehow. You always do."

Yeah. Big deal! I'm the hero ... no, not really. It wasn't me. Smokey caught it. I rolled onto my side, my back touching hers. I felt her shallow breaths. *Should I tell her what I think I saw just before she came into our bedroom? Do I tell that I thought I saw another blob of fur dashing along the baseboard? It seemed just ... a quick flash. Do I dare tell?* I shuddered.

No. No way! Don't even go there.

2016 Memoir Honorable Mention: Momma Didn't Raise No Hero by Christian Spangenberg

Christian: This little tale tells the story of one scary afternoon in the twenty-first year of his life. One must understand that these memories have been filtered by the passage of more than fifty years of an ongoing adventure. He is a novice poet and writer working on his craft in Camarillo, CA, his home for the last thirty-five years.

We were in a dusty rice paddy with our disabled helicopter and the bad guys were shooting at us. The door gunner in another Huey, our company maintenance ship, had just taken a round in his neck and was flopping like a decapitated chicken in the dust alongside his idling helicopter. The pilot of that machine was running at full speed toward his wounded crewman while the earth just behind him exploded in little dust storms as gunfire tore into the dry soil.

While this was playing out, I was prone in the dirt under the nose of my aircraft, attempting to become invisible, or at least, very small. Prior to all this excitement I had been reading in the shade afforded by our damaged helicopter while the crew from the maintenance ship repaired the handiwork done earlier by our little friends with their machine gun. While reading, I kept my "chicken plate" (chest armor made of steel and ceramic) with me. Now, I held that armor shield propped vertically between outstretched arms while attempting my invisibility trick.

From what little cover that chicken plate provided, I could see muzzle flashes in the tree line and our M-60 with its belt of ammo, ready and available only a few feet from where I was hiding. In a moment of incredible stupidity, I imagined myself standing "John Wayne style" with that "60" at my hip, sending a stream of tracers into that tree line. A short second after regaining my sanity and discarding that plan, I realized my fingers holding the chicken plate were now exposed to incoming fire.

This realization caused two things: The first was an attempt to hold the plate with fewer fingers. The second great idea involved yelling to my crew chief who was hunkered down a bit closer to our machine gun. "Grab that M-60 and take care of that guy in the trees!" In the chaos of the moment and in that crazy scene playing out like some Hollywood movie, his reply was perfect ... a raised middle finger.

Just then, the other Huey with its wounded crewman now on board, lifted off in a cloud of dust. That left us and our broken aircraft the only targets for our friend in the tree line, who for reasons unknown, took a little break from his target practice. In that moment of relative calm, I revisited my earlier question about how I came to be such in such an absurd situation.

Before this ill-fated flight, my year of war was nearly completed. I had recently celebrated my twenty-first birthday and was only a few days from going home. Several months earlier, some genius in our command had decided that no one should be assigned any combat flights in their last two weeks in country. This policy was intended to insure "no one will be killed on their last day in Vietnam." I wondered if the originator of this idea realized that everyone who lost his life in this war, did so on his last day in that land...

Only a few days into my enforced "retirement" and experiencing something like "withdrawal symptoms" I persuaded someone in authority to allow me one more flight with my old crew. With new perspective afforded by my current situation, I could see that was indeed, a very foolish request.

For the next hour, I remained hidden beneath my helicopter while the maintenance crew, the only real heroes in this story, worked their mechanical magic and our little friend in the trees occasionally fired his machine gun just to remind us that ... yes this is real and if you get out of here alive, you should abide by one of the oldest pieces of military advice. "Never volunteer for anything!"

With our helicopter repaired and once more receiving fire from the tree line, we scrambled into our Huey and with doors open and engine cowling flapping in the wind, managed to hover to safety behind another stand of trees. After a round of handshakes and exaggerated back slapping, we were back in the air, heading home, each one of us now quiet with our own thoughts of this crazy afternoon.

I'll never know what the others in that helicopter were thinking during that short flight, but I came to realize, in those few moments, that Momma didn't raise no hero.

2016 Memoir Honorable Mention: Three Short Mean Men by Saxon E. Sitka

Saxon is the son of Emil Sitka, an American film and television actor who worked in Hollywood, California, for decades beginning in 1946, most notably in The Three Stooges films. Saxon heard his father tell many stories of his experiences on and off the set with the Three Stooges, but it wasn't until his dad passed away that he became aware of his father's ongoing popularity with Three Stooges' fans. Saxon has been invited to Stooges' film festivals, conventions and fan club meetings to speak and make presentations about his father's experiences. He has decided to put his father's stories into book form and to include as many mementos and photographs as possible.

My father was a Hollywood movie actor during the forties and fifties. Although he worked with big stars such as Broderick Crawford, Lucille Ball, Tony Curtis, Joey Bishop, and many others, most of his own roles were small parts such as a waiter, a cab driver, or a butler. By the time I was born, my father had appeared in over a hundred different movies. As a child, I watched him in theaters and on television regularly.

Of course, being a young child, I didn't understand that it was all make-believe. When I saw my father on the screen playing a waiter serving a salad to Mickey Rooney, I thought he really was a waiter, at least for that day. When he drove a cab, I believed he really was driving Jack Lemmon around in a taxi, just like he drove his family around in real life. Likewise, when he appeared as a butler with The Three Stooges, I thought he really was a butler. Not knowing any better, it made sense to me.

When I was seven years old, I had a chance to visit my father while he was making a movie, although I still didn't completely understand the difference between movies and reality. My father had a big role in this film and was working from early morning until late at night for two weeks straight. After the first week, he asked his friend Lee to bring my brother and me to the studio one day to see him acting on the set of this movie. My brother, two years older and fully aware of the difference between acting and real life, liked the idea and was eager to go.

But I didn't understand. Why would we want to see Daddy at work? We'd visited him at his regular day job several times before and it was boring. Why would this be any different, I wondered. Still, it was a chance to miss a day at school, so I didn't mind.

My brother was enthusiastic, and by the time Lee picked us up to drive us to Hollywood I had begun to share my brother's excitement. We had never before seen the actual making of a movie. When we arrived at the studio, we were led into a drab-looking building and then ushered into a large darkened room. We were told we must be very quiet, say nothing, and just watch "the action" taking place under the bright spotlights at the other end of the room.

As our eyes adjusted to the dark we began to see "the action." Sure enough, there was my father, made up as an old professor, talking to three short men. He was telling them about an invention he was working on that could travel over land like a tank, go underwater like a submarine, fly like a helicopter, and even go into orbit like a rocket.

None of this made any sense to me. But with the fanciful props, heavy make-up, and elaborate costumes, all emblazoned by huge spotlights, it was fascinating to watch.

I noticed that, whenever my father stopped talking, the three short men argued and got mad at each other. They slapped one another across the face and were mean, especially the one with the dark hair hanging low across his eyebrows. One time he punched the fat one in the belly, causing him to howl in pain. How strange, I thought. But at least they weren't arguing with my father or slapping or punching him.

This went on until finally a different man stepped out of the darkness and said a few words we couldn't make out. Then the lights in the room came on. The spotlights were turned off and my father and the three short men all seemed to relax.

We didn't know what to do and stayed on the far side of the room as our eyes adjusted to the light. After several minutes, my father noticed us and came over.

"Hello, boys! Hello, Lee. Glad you came. Have you been here long? Did you get to see us shooting that scene?"

My brother and I said, "Hi Daddy!" and Lee said, "Yes, we saw quite a bit. Been here about an hour. Very interesting!"

Bending down to my brother and me, my father asked, "Did you like watching Daddy making a movie?"

I still didn't understand but nodded in agreement.

Suddenly, my father turned and straightened up.

"Hey, I've got an idea." He raised his voice and called out across the room, "Hey, Moe, Larry, come here! Can I get a picture of you with my boys?"

We followed his gaze across the room to the three short men who had been arguing, slapping, and hitting each other in the belly. Without hesitating, they said, "Sure!"

My eyes widened in fear. All I could think of is how mean they seemed just a few minutes ago, and now they were heading my way!

And the meanest one, the man with his hair combed down over his eyebrows, was looking and walking straight at me!

As they approached, they made funny faces and crossed their eyes. But I frowned and was worried about getting slapped or punched in the belly.

My father called out to another man, "Hey Ed, snap a picture of me and my boys, would you?"

"Glad to, no problem"

These mean short men walked up to us, but now they were smiling. Still, my heart was racing. I wanted to turn and run, but my father said, "Stand over here in front of me, boys, and Larry, can you go over here? Moe and Joe, can you stand over there?"

As the smallest one in the group, I was positioned front and center. Then the meanest short man, the one my father called Moe, moved right up behind me and pressed himself against my left shoulder.

Heart racing, barely breathing, I didn't know if he was going to slap me or punch me in the belly.

"Okay, everyone, smile!" said Ed the photographer. Frozen with fear, I couldn't even try to smile.

Poof went the flash bulb.

My father said, "Thanks, guys, that should be a great picture."

The group broke up and I thought to myself, "Whew, that was a close one."

But then Ed said, "Hey, let's take one more. And this time, you, the little guy in the middle, let's see a smile."

Gulp! We have to do it again?

My father huddled us all even closer this time and again I felt Moe pressing into my shoulder.

"Okay, come on, big smiles. Especially you in the middle."

My face turned red and I began to feel dizzy as I forced a smile to my lips.

Poof went the flash.

"Okay, guys, that was a good one," said Ed.

"Thanks, Moe, Larry. Thanks, Curly-Joe. My boys are going to love that picture," my father assured them as they said a friendly "Good-bye" and began making their way back across the room.

Watching them disappear, I whispered to my brother, "Hey, they weren't really so mean after all."

My brother, two years older and fully aware of the difference between movies and reality, smiled knowingly. "Of course not, silly. They're the Three Stooges. They were only acting mean, for the movie."

As his words sank in, I began to understand. So that's what they meant by acting. And now, many years later, I really do love that picture.

Short Story: A Weekend In The Country by Nathan Skyer

Nathan was born in Brooklyn, NY, and spent of his most formative years where the Bed-Sty, East New York, and Brownsville neighborhoods came together like tectonic plates grinding against one another violently. No, the family described here was not his, but not greatly different from some he knew as a youth. He managed to attend Brooklyn College and learned enough to make a career in newspaper reporting, writing for and editing company magazines, and freelance writing. How he wound up as an octogenarian in Camarillo, CA is something he still doesn't quite understand.

Danny pushed the diner door halfway open and spotted his Uncle Mike sitting in an end corner booth, his back to one wall, his left side against another.

A waitress was refilling the old man's coffee cup. In one fast pour, without ever appearing to look down, she refilled it to exactly one quarter inch below the rim then seemed to vanish instantly behind the counter. Danny saw his uncle smile briefly toward the counter. The old man knew and appreciated a professional of any kind when he met one and would undoubtedly leave her an outrageously generous tip.

But Danny also saw something else. Even before the waitress had finished pouring, his uncle's eyes had snapped up and fastened on Danny. The old guy's still got it, Danny couldn't help thinking, smiling mentally. Diner door only halfway open and he's already checked out who's coming in. He won't be blindsided or surprised by anybody. He does it instinctively ... can't help it.

"You're late," his uncle said as Danny sat down facing him. "I was beginning to think you weren't coming."

"You call, I come. You should know that by now," Danny said, watching his uncle stir three spoons of sugar into his coffee, taste it, then dump in and stir a fourth. Mike's sweet tooth when he was nervous was a family legend and joke. For a skinny little guy, he sure put away a lot of sugar. Maybe it was sugar and caffeine that kept him so alert – and alive. But what was he nervous about tonight?

"I do apologize for being late, though," Danny said. "Getting out of the Bronx was a real bitch tonight. The Yankees are playing a night game, some idiot kids are throwing a rock concert somewhere on City Island, and the president is landing at LaGuardia for some political crap in the city."

"He's not landing at LaGuardia. Upstate somewhere, at some military field," his uncle corrected. "I don't know why. Probably something to do with security. A marine helicopter is taking him to LaGuardia for a motorcade into Manhattan."

The old guy could be counted on to be up-to-date on everything that was going on, Danny thought to himself.

Uncle Mike made a tiny hand gesture and a cup of coffee seemed to appear magically in front of Danny. His uncle pointed a quick smile at where the waitress had been, but she was already gone.

"Well, anyway, that's why I'm late, and I apologize. But how about telling me why you wanted to meet all the way out here in Queens? We could have met somewhere in the civilized world, like the Bronx. There are diners in the Bronx. Or if you want to tell me something or ask me something, why not yesterday at dinner at Mamma's house? I could have heard you perfectly well, even over the noise of cousin Paulie chewing. I swear, if Mamma seats me next to him once more I'm gonna go deaf in that ear. So why are we out here talking in the middle of no-place?" His uncle didn't seem to hear him, although Danny knew he did. Mike heard everything.

"How's Janet?" Uncle Mike asked, looking past Danny, toward the door but focusing on nothing. "You see her much? How's she doing?"

Halfway to his lips Danny stopped lifting the coffee cup and his eyes narrowed, focusing on Mike's unfocused eyes. *Where the hell is Mike going with this?* "What the hell are you talking about, Uncle Mike?" Danny said, the cup still in mid-air. "We're divorced. I send her alimony checks regularly and the only time I see her or talk to her is a few minutes every other weekend when I take Tommy for our court sanctioned 'father/son alternate weekends'. You know all that."

"Tommy's a good kid," Mike said. "You know since your father, may he rest in peace, passed away, I think of you like a son and Thomas as a grandson. We're out here in the boonies now because I have to say some things to you I can't afford for anybody else to overhear – not even family." Mike paused and seemed to be arranging his thoughts.

"Your ex, Janet, has become a problem," he went on, "not just for our family, but for others. I don't know why, but she's been talking to people she shouldn't be talking to, people with badges, people from newspapers, people from television stations, saying she knows things she shouldn't know." Uncle Mike's eyes were focused now, locked on Danny's and they had a hard look to them.

Danny knew the look well, from when he once played an active part in the family's business. The look was unmistakable. It said, "this is going to happen."

"Janet has to go," Mike said softly, "and there's something you have to do."

Danny felt a chill. He knew his uncle was a nice guy. He also knew he was a dangerous guy. "So, you call me?" Danny said. "You want me to kill her?"

Slowly putting down the still untouched coffee cup, and leaning forward right into Mike's face, Danny said in the harshest whisper he had ever used, "Look, Janet is no bargain, nobody knows that now better than me. She's a bitch, and maybe a whore, and marrying her was the worst mistake I ever made. But she's my son's mother. And she's not all bad — she takes good care of Tommy, she's very good to him. Besides, I'm no killer and I never was. The worst I ever did was beat some people up, and I couldn't even do that very well. I would stop hitting them before they were absolutely convinced we meant business.

"I've been out of the family business for a long time now. You all agreed it just wasn't for me. I didn't quit the business, I was voted out. You yourself cast the deciding vote. And I think you and the family made the right decision. And besides all that, what makes you think Janet really knows anything? She was never the sharpest knife in the drawer. Even on a good day she needed help figuring out how to open a swinging door."

With the slightest of hand motions, Mike made another coffee appear in front of him, and he sugared it extra generously before speaking. "Look, I don't know what Janet knows or how she may have learned it. Maybe a little pillow talk one night when things were still good between you and her.

"Maybe an overheard conversation or two while you were still a couple and she was mixing with the family. No offense meant to you, but I think there are fire hydrants on Tremont Avenue brighter than she is and she knows nothing. But this time, what I think don't matter. There are others we do business with, outside our family, who don't intend to take any chances."

"I'm not going to kill her," Danny said in a voice so soft it was clear his words were non-negotiable.

His uncle looked at him with what seemed like pity ... or was it just disappointment?

"I never expected you to," Mike said. "Don't be an idiot or make me out to be one. I wouldn't want you to even try, because I know you'd screw it up. You said it yourself. This kind of business ain't for you. You stick to heating and air conditioning or whatever legit business you're into now."

"So why are you telling me all this?"

His Uncle Mike took a long time to answer, and even though they were alone in the back corner of an almost empty diner, he looked around furtively before speaking. "Because I know it's going to happen. And I know when. But I don't know how or who will be doing it. It will probably be one or more of our associates from out of town. I don't even know what town — and I really don't care — except for one thing."

"Yeah? What's that?" was all Danny could come up with.

His Uncle Mike suddenly looked as if he were in a life-or-death struggle with the devil to say what he had to say. Finally, a few words came, seemingly squeezed out with great difficulty. "I told you before, since your father passed away I think of you like a son, and Tommy as my own grandson."

"Yeah? Yeah?" Danny still didn't get the picture. He really wasn't equipped to be part of the family business.

Then, it seemed as if the devil gave up and the words spilled out of Uncle Mike in a quiet, flat, unemotional, businesslike monotone. "It's going down this Saturday. I don't know exactly what time or where or how. But I don't think it would be a good idea for Tommy to be holding his mother's hand this weekend while they cross the street or strapped in next to her when she starts her car, or sitting next to her in a restaurant near a window. You get me?"

Finally, Danny got it.

"So that's why we're here," his uncle continued. "I know this coming weekend is supposed to be one of yours with Tommy. I want to make sure you don't miss it for anything. And make it a full weekend. Pick him up straight from school as early as you can on Friday like I know you often do, and get right out of town. Take him up to the Catskills. Let him ride some horses. Take him canoeing – fishing – to an amusement park – explore a cave. Make sure a lot of people see you up there and can recognize and remember you later. Argue with people. Joke with people. Ask people stupid questions. Make sure people remember you. Leave a paper trail ... demand receipts for everything.

"I gotta go," Mike said suddenly. "If the out of town guys found out I told you all this, I could be killed for it. But family is family, and sometimes you just gotta do what you gotta do.

Never forget that – NEVER." He slid off the seat and started moving away, so eager to leave he could hardly control his feet, yet he remained the old Uncle Mike. He threw a fifty-dollar bill on the table. "That's for the waitress," he said. "You can pay for the coffees."

Through the window Danny watched his uncle's big old Cadillac pull out of the parking lot. He sat for a good while, thinking. He gave the waitress the fifty-dollar bill, explaining that it was from his rich friend who appreciated her skills but had to leave unexpectedly.

He ordered meatloaf and mashed potatoes but no coffee, although the waitress would have happily brought him buckets of it. Watching his uncle with the sugar had temporarily ruined his taste for coffee. He ate slowly, still thinking, then paid for everything and left a modest tip of his own.

Before leaving however, he stopped at the pay phone hanging just inside the door, pulled a pile of change from his pocket, dialed a number, and waited. "Hello Janet, it's Danny. Yeah, the check is in the mail. Yeah, you, too. I'm just calling to let you know I'm picking Tommy up straight from school on Friday, rather than from your place. I think we'll drive up to the Catskills, maybe ride some horses, take a canoe out on a lake, explore one of those tourist caves. Yeah, I agree, I think Tommy will like that a lot. Yeah, of course I'll be careful with him. And look, you enjoy whatever you do. Yeah. Okay. Bye now. See you Sunday. We'll probably be back pretty late though."

2016 Short Story Youth Second Place Winner: Morning Offering by Jack Stein

Bio. Jack (2016) was a fifteen-year-old sophomore at Laguna Blanca. He was the managing editor for the Fourth Estate Magazine and has been published in two newspapers and a poetry anthology. He has been writing for as long as he can remember, and he wrote a novel in seventh grade.

The man in black strikes a humorless profile against a sky of slate, and he casts no shadow upon the dying grass.

He is unshaven and doesn't wear it well. The lower half of his face looks greasy and sloppy. His hands are serpentine, fingers intertwining in a constant bouquet of motion. They are hands of apprehension, and it is an apprehension that he wears on his aging face. It is a face that does not stand out in a crowd.

He does not want to stand out in a crowd.

The man in black adjusts his collar, a blinding rectangle of white against shades of ebony. Rumpling the perfection over and over for no reason more than to recreate it. His eyes glint darkly, and the mottled light sparsely flashes in the bullets of sweat that dribble down his waxy forehead, down the bridge of his nose, between his eyes. These eyes, beady eyes, dart back-and forth. They don't know where to look, and, since they cannot look at nothing at all, are reluctantly content with their restive nature.

It is not a warm — nor even a mild — morning. What can be seen of the sun, flashing intermittently, low above the horizon, between threatening clouds, is not a warm sun; a frigid circle unhappily whiling away the moments before it can return to its blanketed isolation below the sea. The man sweats despite this. He mops his brow with his sleeve. Droplets trickle down his wrist; he does not notice. If he does notice, he does not care.

Far, far below, the sounds of the tides roar, waves crashing upon ashen rock. The edge is close, dangerously so, and the man's scuffed dress shoes— "work shoes," his daughter had called them — quivering mere inches away from the brink. The water is black and reflects only the deeds of the man who looks into it. Above the sounds of the raging seascape, barely audible beneath rasping gusts of wind, the man in black speaks. His words bear the sins of the countless men who have spoken them before.

"Dear Lord. . ."

It is a short prayer but one that he knows well. He used to say it every morning… not as much anymore. The creeping guilt begins to whisper in his ear, and he waves his hand, keeping the dark thoughts at bay. He clutches the silver cross that adorns his neck. Its corners have been worn down. What was once a bright metallic is now a dull murmur.

"I do not know what will happen to me today . . ."

Dullness permeates the man. It is riddled into his psyche, and he reeks of what could have been. There is no time now to dwell on such a distant past, however — not when the recent one holds such gravity. The past is a leech that hangs off the man, draining whatever remains of his youth drop-by-drop. A vampiric succubus driving out the faintest traces of morality that may have remained within this raven clad husk that now stands before the cliffs.

He tells himself many things: justifications, rationalizations, clarifications, ruminations. They bob and weave amongst the trenches of his conscience, ghosts of logical clarity that, when seen briefly, and through the warped lens of hindsight, appear worthy of consideration at the very least. The vague, velvety apparitions and figments of the mind's clockwork dance around the truth like shadowy puppets.

But when the puppets control the puppeteer, who holds the strings?

"I only know that nothing will happen that was not foreseen by You. . ."

Withdrawn from an inside pocket, close to the chest, his right hand holds a photograph. Stained with blotches of crimson, the figures that live within the crinkled paper gaze out with a lifeless melancholy. Soulless are the smiles that adorn pallid masks of skin and hair. The hand closes around the photograph, carefully folding along well-worn lines.

As the picture returns to the pocket, the wind picks up to a particularly forceful gale, one that rocks the alders but cannot seem to throw the man from his perch far above the mirthless Charybdis that waits hundreds of feet below. For a fleeting moment, he nearly thinks it will. And for one moment more he almost wishes it will.

But his footing holds.

His sweat is drying now. What began as apprehension has crawled its way to acceptance–an empty acceptance. Devoid of true feeling, it writhes in the spotlight of an eyeless gaze, pleadingly attempting a metamorphosis into something more. Heavy clothes stick to the man's ample frame, wrinkling and creasing across the many crevices that map the anarchist topography of his body. He pays no mind to the discomfort, he lets it nag him and creep across the surface of his mind. His thoughts are on the weight in his jacket pocket. It drags him towards the moist earth.

He can almost feel the reptilian hands that grope and grasp at his ankles.

His heartbeat is barely palpable, a smattering of variated spikes and valleys that pound in his ears as if a knock on a door .is muffled by a cotton sleeve. A cold weight against his chest, a leering reminder of the gravity of what he holds within the folds of his robes. The black metal has a frigidity that is even tangible through the layers of black cloth that feebly attempts to keep it at bay, and it is a bleak reminder of the ice that tickles the back of the man's neck.

The inching guilt slides slime-coated fingers up and down his neck and presses its bloated lips against his cheek, yet he cannot cry. To cry would be admitting the guilt is there, and to admit of the guilt would be admitting to the past. It was a past that he would give anything to forget and he knew then that it would not be so easily ignored. The battered cross still decorates his neck, and he wishes above all else that it could take him somewhere else. Why was he here, anyways? He remembers little of his arrival, even less of the events leading up to it, and wishes to look no further into the well.

But further he goes, and catches jarring glimpses of a murky, yet somehow immediate, past that he remembers as if it were years ago, not merely hours. It is hard to fathom the concept of time when yours has run out at last.

The glimpses follow him as he stumbles through the catacombs of memory. He hears a flash, sees a bang…there's so much noise. *Why is there so much noise?* A hand reaches for his, a man's hand, he pushes it away, instead reaching for what lies in his pocket…so much noise…he squeezes on the slim metal strip, no not the cross, but a different cross, something colder something pinched by demons…why is there so much noise…

chaos, pure raging chaos … *STOP THE NOISE* … the hand is no longer a man's but a child's, now a woman's, it is pleading, he sees its cries with a crippling sense of urgency … he can see the noise … two crosses, one around his neck and one in his pocket … *the noise the noise pleasepelasepleaaaseaPLEASEpleseaeSTOP.*

He is crying. The guilt has bubbled to the surface and is overflowing through the dark eyes of the man who bears the demon's cross. It sags in his robes and for a moment he fears it will sink right through. The tears are uncontrollable after only this brief time, he finally lets them go. Boiling drops crisscross his pale cheeks and splash upon the cracked and browning grass that lies crumpled underfoot. They melt into the dry stalks and disappear and yet he can almost see the dark, damp spots that mark the unholy water that spawned of his dark deeds, and he can almost see it staring back.

The man is a cripple, but only as of mere hours ago. His leg is a mangled slop of gristle and bone that limply slinks out of the bottom of his long coat, a carcass that drags itself along the ground as a wounded animal would. His teeth are gritted fiercely, his lips are dry and cracking, and he holds a dull wooden crutch under his arm; it helps some. Not with the pain, but with the manageability. He does not know why he ignores the pain, but that does not change the fact that he still does. Maybe he only ignores it for—

"I adore Your holy and unfathomable plans. . ."

the deeper pain that gnaws on the forefront of his thought and emotion, a pain that is merely a symptom of basic human transgression.

He has disregarded the plan. The plan, set, in stone, etched into the basic principle of the task, weighing slowly on his anti-prescience that lets him see with the 20/20 backwards foresight into the gravity of the path that he now staggers further and further away from. The plan was before his leg was shattered, before he felt that cold demon's cross clutched tenderly with exquisite force that bled power into his sweaty palm and gave his rage a voice and releasing his conscience. He knows now, he knows so much… he's lost his way, he can feel it. Something is not right, and he knows something is not right, and he's known longer than he lets himself remember.

Things were not supposed to go this way – that much is instinct alone. The air is heavy and imbalanced around his head, like a sack of sand that is unsteadily leaking. Warm wet blood oozes down his thigh and saturates his senses, and he reaches again into his pocket. He pulls out the picture and stares at it for an infinitely brief moment before raising it to his lips. He gently presses them against it, and his dusty, cold skin scrapes against the warm, wet scrap of paper that has been squeezed against his palpitating breast and caressed by the spray of the distant waves.

He does not fold the picture, does not return it to his pocket. He holds it in his left hand and grasps the silver cross with his right. The crutch falls and the man loses his footing, staggering toward the edge. His foot slips! He slides on the smooth, heartless grass and is dragged near to the beckoning blackness of the waves. Whatever resilience still remains within his crumpled spirit reaches out, he desperately sticks out a hand to catch himself. Fingers make purchase with dark, cracked earth and squeeze, squeeze for the love of God, and by some slight miracle he does not fall.

He pulls himself forward, back away from the abyss. He frantically searches with his eyes, sees the picture dangling on the rim of the precipice, curses his leg, curses his hands—

"And submit to them with all my heart for love of You," he watches the final memory of the family he forsook be swept by a particularly vengeful spat of breeze into oblivion. He is all at once lame and heavy, frail and bitter. He lies upon prickly blades that dig into his hands, wrists, and neck and spitefully cling to his clothing as he tries to push himself up. His hand once more creeps to the adornment strung in silver around his neck, and, with a newfound strength, tears it from his neck.

The chain snaps with a nearly inaudible plink that echoes in his ears with the impertinence of the act he has just committed before the eyes of the One he has sworn his life to, he One who has taken away all that made this life worth living, the … one …. who at some point decided who is worth salvation? The one, the one, the lord, the father, the one who took his heart, took his faith, took his soul, cast them upon the rocks that danced so close yet so distantly far only minutes before. The one who groped for his ankle and dragged him toward the sea below.

The greatest human fear is abandonment by—

"the Pope, and the Immaculate Heart of Mary…"

The ones that we trust and love, who we trust to guide us, the feeling that we get when we realize that they have led us off the path that they told us we should, no, we must walk upon, the line that we toed, desperate. The desperation of the knowledge that our ignorance has not been ignored. The bitter realization that we have lost the guiding force that makes us who we think we are, and who we think we are meant to be.

A silver chain with a dull, worn strip of metal dangling from the end cascades down into a sea of blue-black; the man who wore the chain for decades thinks of it no more. He pulls himself, weary, to his feet. His hand, shaking as it is yanked to and fro by the crushing winds, delves deep into the pocket of his black robes and retrieves the demon's cross that rests within this flap of cloth. It firmly grasps this that has taken so much away from the one who asked for so precious little, and sends it following closely behind the silver chain that has not yet even hit the water. Splash, the first. Splash, the second.

The man in black stands at the edge of the cliff and looks out. He thinks of a life spent reaching for a hand that wasn't there. The only comfort lies hundreds of miles below. Chapped lips flutter open, finishing the prayer that started an eternity ago.

"Amen."

The man in black looks down.

He fingers the white collar that snakes around his neck and relinquishes this final scrap of holy competence into the eager winds. He looks up and watches this last remnant drift up and up and up toward heaven.

Silence – the wind itself holds its breath as scuffed work shoes shuffle into line.

Splash.

2016 Short Story Youth Honorable Mention: Neverest by Ziv Carmi

Ziv (2016) was fifteen and a sophomore at Newbury Park High School. He recently published his first book, a twenty-six-chapter novel, Requiem For a Trade. *It is a humorous adventure about two kids who time travel in a world of their own creation in their comic books. He wishes to be a professional writer.*

Jane Doe was sick of carrying around a flamethrower. In fact, she was sick of the cold altogether. "Smith," she called into the swirling cloud of snow. "Did you find a place to camp yet?"

There was no reply. Jane shouted louder as a gust blew her voice off the sheer cliffs that were Mt. Neverest.

The temperature was dropping, and fast. Jane Doe looked at her thermometer: fifty degrees below zero. "How did I get in this mess?" she asked herself.

Jane Doe took out her flamethrower and used it to ignite a fire fifty feet away. Huddling beside it, she took out a satellite phone. "Meshugah," she said, her words unclear because of the chattering of her teeth. "All debts are paid if I die."

Higher up the mountain, Arkansas Smith was wandering through snow up to his waist. He looked at his thermometer: 74 degrees below zero. Smith laughed. It was the perfect place to test his strength. He soon arrived at a chasm that appeared bottomless.

Flexing his gigantic biceps, Smith pulled out a loop of rope – one hundred feet of it to be exact. With an expert flick of his wrist, the rope looped around a tree on the other side. "Doe! Hand me that…" his words trailed off as he realized that Jane Doe wasn't with him. *Guess I'd better find her. I need those supplies she's carrying.* Smith grimaced as he thought of the ten-mile slog back down to camp.

It took him exactly twenty-seven minutes and forty-six seconds to arrive at the clearing, where he found Jane Doe, semiconscious beside a dying fire. Her fingers were turning blue and her skin was clammy.

Smith first scooped up her backpack and flamethrower, then, dragging Jane behind him, he sprinted to a nearby cave, lighting a fire and putting Jane next to it. As color returned to Doe's face, Smith felt relief flooding through him. Marvelous though he was, he still would never be able to carry all those supplies by himself!

***

In another country, billionaire Winston Meshugah threw his phone across the room. "Reginald!"

Crash! A rocky semblance of Meshugah's head flew through the window, nearly hitting a passerby, who was scowling up at the penthouse the whole time.

Squeak! A head poked through the door just in time to see the last shards of glass tinkle to the ground. "Y-y-y-es boss? Do you want the window replaced?"

"Of course I do, you fool! Now, did you just hear that call?"

"Y-y-yes sir," Reginald's face was getting paler by the moment.

"Good, good. The Doe woman is cheating me. She's going to escape her debt by dying."

"How rude, boss-sir!"

"She promised me treasure, and I want it! The Chalice of the Snow Leopard is the key to unlimited power!"

"Of course, sir."

"Reginald, fly out to Tiugerhunda *immediately* and find me that chalice!"

Reginald looked like he was going to faint. "Yes, sir," he squeaked, removing his head from the doorway.

"Reginald!"

Reginald sighed and poked his head back in.

"I'm not paying for gear this time!"

***

Jane Doe's eyes fluttered open as warmth caressed her. Fire flickered in her peripheral vision as she saw Smith's shadow on the cave wall.

"So you're finally awake, Sleeping Beauty," Smith commented as he sharpened his knife. "That Chalice of the Snow Leopard isn't waiting for us."

Jane felt frustration surge through her. "Will it sprout legs and run off? I just survived hypothermia!" she snapped. "Give me a break!"

Smith looked at her. "I did give you a break. That's why you got your little two-day nap."

Jane Doe gritted her teeth. At least this way it would be easier to betray Smith and steal the chalice for Meshugah.

***

Reginald arrived in the city of Tiugerhunda, at the base of Mt. Neverest, immediately purchased as many parkas as he could, then hired a porter to carry his gear up the mountain. Thinking quickly, Reginald hired another porter to carry *him* up the mountain.

Thanks to fair weather by nightfall, they had reached the cave.

Peering at the cave mouth, Reginald noticed fresh footprints in the snow – footprints belonging to Jane's custom snowshoes. They couldn't have been more than a few hours old.

Taking several pictures, Reginald sent them to Meshugah. His satellite phone rang. "Sir!" Reginald said, holding the phone away from his ear.

"What is this?" Meshugah's voice could have rivaled a truck's horn. "Jane Doe is supposed to be dead!"

Reginald squeaked an inaudible reply, glad that he was halfway around the world from his boss.

"So, Jane Doe is cheating me, eh? Well, if she's alive, Reginald, make her excuses true."

"Y-y-y-you surely don't mean…"

"Find Jane Doe and make her pay. Do not let her walk off that mountain alive!"

***

Jane Doe stumbled and fell unconscious. It had been a day filled with raging rivers and giant chasms. She awoke once again in front of a blazing fire. Arkansas Smith was sitting next to her, sharpening his knife yet again. *Seriously, how sharp did he need that thing?* "Smith… How long was I out this time?"

"Too long for me to go on," Smith said.

"Why do you care all of a sudden? Earlier today, you were angry that I nearly died in that blizzard."

A flush spread across Arkansas Smith's face. "Uh…you're special?"

Jane laughed. "I think you're falling in love, aren't you? Kind of quick, isn't it? Guess somebody's sick of being in love with himself."

"Uh…" Arkansas was at a loss for words.

Jane smiled at him. "So you are falling in love?"

"Um…"

"Arkansas, you may be a macho man, but you really can't express your emotions, can you?"

***

In Reginald's pocket lay a pistol. The bullets inside had Jane Doe's name on them. He would be at the Temple of the Snow Leopard in no time. The question he kept asking himself was, could he really kill a person? He weighed the options in his mind. If he didn't, his whole family would be in Meshugah's reach. He had no choice…

***

Doe and Smith had finally reached their destination. They had survived booby traps of all kinds – pits, spikes, boulders, flying skulls, scorpions, crocodiles, and angry yaks – to get to the Chalice.

A loose tile suddenly caused Jane to trip and fall. She didn't get back up. There were no traps in sight, so Smith had no idea what was wrong. Why did she keep losing consciousness?

Concerned, Smith hoisted her over his shoulders and began to walk to the Chalice of the Snow Leopard. It was time to finish what they had started, together.

***

Smith picked up the Chalice of the Snow Leopard. He had checked its pedestal for traps and, to his surprise, found none.

As he began to walk out of the temple, Jane Doe stirred in his arms and said, "Meshugah. I'm sorry… don't kill me, please." She started thrashing. "I'll get it for you. Smith isn't a problem … You'll have your Chalice in no time."

Smith stopped cold in his tracks. Heartbroken, he realized the truth. The woman who had walked into his office and got him interested in this expedition had been manipulating him the whole time. Just as he had started to… what had he felt for her?

He set her down on the floor. Then he began trudging out of the temple, Chalice in hand.

***

Jane Doe awoke to find herself alone. She could feel that something was wrong. She got to her feet and ran after Smith. "Arkansas, what's wrong?" she asked, putting a hand on his shoulder. He roughly twisted away.

"You… you lied to me. You were planning to steal the Chalice all along!" His tone was shocked and sad at the same time.

"I had no choice, Arkansas. I have to pay off my debt."

"What debt? Don't lie to me. You're just as bad as all the others." He finally looked at her, anger flashing in his big green eyes.

Jane Doe took a deep breath. "Listen, Arkansas. Haven't you wondered why I keep fainting? I…" A red flush flew across her cheeks. "I have an unknown and incurable disease. I would already be dead, but this billionaire guy…well, he helped me a lot. I owe him so much and…" Tears swam in Jane Doe's eyes. "And he wanted the Chalice."

Arkansas wanted to believe her with all his heart. Could he?

176

Jane Doe fell against the wall. The sprint had sapped all her energy. It was then and there that Arkansas Smith realized his true feelings for her. Traitor or not, he had fallen head over heels in love.

He headed through the doorway, Jane in his arms and the Chalice balanced on his head.

***

As his eyes became accustomed to the light, Smith saw a figure pointing a gun at him. Then he saw the man put it down. The figure dropped the gun and shouted, "I'm unarmed! Don't hurt me! I was born in the 60s! I'm a vegan! I'm a pacifist!"

"Pacifist, my eye," Smith snarled, his rope ready to knock the man off the cliff.

Reginald stared at the ground. "I couldn't do it. Forgive me, my family. I'm so sorry. I couldn't have Jane's blood on my hands," he quietly said to himself.

Smith said, "You work for that billionaire, don't you? He sent you to kill us?"

Reginald quickly said, "I used to, but I just quit. He didn't want me to kill *you*," he pointed at Smith, "Just her. It's against my nature, you know. I was a flower child; make love not war, and all that!"

A steady rumbling suddenly began echoing through the cliffs. Apparently, the Chalice *had* been booby-trapped, after all. The ground was crumbling beneath their feet. With nothing to support them, Jane, Smith, and Reginald fell into the abyss, the latter two screaming all the way.

***

Jane Doe's first coherent thought was, *why is it so cold?* The thought quickly left her as she opened her eyes and saw the eight-foot-tall fuzzball beside her.

She screamed and pinched herself. This was no nightmare. The fuzzball smiled, showing three rows of sharp teeth, and growled, "Finally, hooman is awake! Hooman and hooman's friends tried to steal Yeti treasure four days ago."

It was then that Jane realized she was laying on a slab of ice in a cavern of ice. "Where am I?"

The fuzzball made a gargling laugh and said, "Stupid hoomans can't steal Yeti treasure. Yeti has. to protect treasure! Now hoomans in Yeti Village and await Yeti law."

"So that's what you are? Yetis?"

"I Yeti," the yeti pointed at himself. Then he pointed at another fuzzball and said, "She no Yeti. She Yeta." Pointing at another one, he said, "That over there is Yetu. I leader of Yeti Village, so I named Yeti. But we not Yeti, we no-men."

"Do you mean snowmen?"

"No, Yeti mean no-men. In Yeti language, we—" Then the Yeti spoke in Yeti language. "Argaheageheashgsehwejshsfhwquwe." Switching back to English, Yeti continued, "But hooman don't speak Yeti language, and Yeti don't speak hooman language very good. So Yeti just say we no-men, because we not."

"Can I just call you fuzzballs? This is too confusing for me to take in," Jane said.

177

Nodding, Yeti helped Jane up and out of the ice cavern, into a busy village filled with more fuzzballs. In the center of it were Smith and Reginald, surrounded by a crowd of fuzzballs, showing off their flamethrowing skills. "Yeti like hooman's flamethrower. Now Yeti have fun with Yeti kids."

Jane shuddered and said, "Won't your kids be hurt by the flamethrower?"

Yeti shrugged and said, "Yeti like steam baths. Flamethrower not hotter." Yeti put his hands to his mouth, growling a few words in Yeti language. "Ackackackackackacacchachachcahacaghahga!" Every fuzzball in the room turned and looked at Yeti. "All right, Yeti Village. Stupid hoomans now sit for trial for stealing Yeti treasure."

The fuzzballs stood up started talking excitedly among themselves. A roar spread throughout the crowd. "Xhsayugehuzehuizaiamahia!"

"Yeti and Yeti village think stupid hoomans be punished by moldy yak cheese," Yeti concluded. "After all, Yeti can't enjoy *all* of Yeti delicacy himself!"

A fuzzball, dragging a cart filled to the brim with reeking blue cheese wheels, set it in front of the three humans. Reginald said, shuddering, "With all due respect, I'm a vegan."

The fuzzballs made him do a thousand pull-ups instead. By the end, he wished he had eaten the yak cheese.

This is a fuzzball delicacy? Jane incredulously stared at her punishment. Multicolored fuzz covered the yak cheese, which smelled like the armpits of a dead skunk. She felt her heart begin to race. This was bad. She stared up as the whole world began to turn purple, then swayed. She felt goosebumps prickling her skin. She realized that she had entered the final stage of her malady. She saw herself sitting at the table, staring at the yak cheese. Then she saw nothing.

Yeti caught Jane as she fell, her skin turning a nasty shade of yellow and her breathing shallow. At most, she had half an hour. He took the Chalice of the Snow Leopard and spit in it. He explained to Smith and Reginald, "Yeti spit has mystical properties. Now just need to improve the flavor and have hooman drink from Yeti treasure and she healed."

Adding some rotten yak cheese, Yeti helped Jane drink from the Chalice of the Snow Leopard. Nothing happened. "This never happen before," Yeti said. "But then, Yeti never heal someone so sick."

Arkansas Smith felt his stomach churn. As he grabbed Jane's icy hand, he felt his whole world crumble around him. He could not lose her. He *would* not lose her. "Jane," he said softly, "You have to be okay."

***

Two police officers ran into Meshugah's office. "Winston Meshugah, you are under arrest for attempted murder, tax evasion, and blackmail. You have the right to remain silent," one said as he pulled out a pair of handcuffs.

Meshugah was shocked. He had made sure that the law would never catch him. Of course, he didn't know that Reginald had taped all of his illicit recordings and turned them in.

As Meshugah was led out of the building, Arkansas Smith and Jane Doe, brand new diamond rings on their fingers, stood by the police cars.

"Meshugah, you ignorant bully," Jane said, "it's not the Chalice that has power, it's the fuzzballs. *They're* the ones who can heal anything, even death."

Sweetness creeping into her tone, she added, "I want you to know my debt has been fulfilled. I have brought you the only treasure I brought back from Mt. Neverest."

Meshugah soon discovered that moldy yak cheese was an acquired taste.

2016 Short Story Second Place Adult Winner: Chirps by Wendell Lilijedahl

The youngest of three, Wendell lived the first eleven years of his life on the family farm near Modale, Iowa. His family moved to Pacific Grove, California. He emerged from high school in 1969 and left immediately for the East Coast. Wendell went to a marine engineering school, where he discovered a love for the sea. Wendell retired from the yacht racing circuit and returned to college. Drawn to finance and economics, he ultimately landed a career in the investment advisory business. He married well above his station to the intelligent and beautiful Elizabeth, and they have lived comfortably in Ventura for nearly thirty years. With a lot of spare time on his hands, he wrote his first novel. It was dreadful. But he is hopeful that the things learned in the process will lead to a much better outcome in the next one.

"You hear 'em now?"

"Hear who?"

Jack didn't look up from the campfire. "The Chirps, knucklehead."

Lester studied the hard lines etched into Jack's face by the gilded firelight. "All I hear are crickets."

"That's what you think you hear." Jack pulled at the bristle on his chin, disappointment evident on his face. "You just ain't listenin' right."

"I don't know how else I'm supposed to listen." Lester peered into the blackness around the camp. The trunks of massive redwood trees were the only shapes visible against the veil of the nightfall. "Sounds like forest noises to me. What am I supposed to hear?"

"The Chirps." Jack shot a harsh glare in his direction, his blue eyes piercing the firelight. "Jesus, Lester, you either hear 'em or you don't. It ain't that complicated." Jack took a pull from his beer and returned his gaze to the fire. Muscles flexed in his neck as he swallowed, the slump of his shoulders returned.

"Sorry…"

"Never mind." Jack seemed transfixed by the dancing flames. "It don't matter. And that ain't why we come out here anyway, is it?"

"I thought a change of scenery would be good for you," Lester said. A camping trip had seemed like a reasonable idea, maybe get Jack out of his funk. But now Lester was having his doubts. "You've got to let it go, man."

"You don't know nothin'," Jack said.

Lester took a long swig of his beer, then a deep breath. "She's gone. You've got to stop doing this to yourself—"

"You ain't gonna start in on me, are ya? Cause I've had about enough of that, and I ain't about to let up on it now."

"I was just thinking—"

"Yeah, you're right ... Mary ain't comin' back." Jack's jaw muscles flexed like he was trying to bite through the thought. "And if you dragged us out here thinkin' there's some magic in these woods that's gonna get me over her, we can pack up our crap and go home right now."

"Maybe you could start thinking about something else."

"Spare me the sermon. It ain't okay. It ain't *ever* gonna be okay without her."

"You can't just quit."

A puff of air came in from the south, pushing the campfire smoke in Jack's direction. He batted at the smoke with his free hand, rose to his feet and moved to the opposite side of the fire pit, facing Lester. Jack stood with his hands hanging at his side, the beer can tilted. The stark light of the fire against the blackness beyond made it seem like Jack was fading into it. His baggy jeans confirmed the recent loss of weight.

"So, what am I supposed to do? Go around pretendin' I got some reason to go on?" Jack took another drink from his beer. "That we ain't all doomed?"

"See, that's just it," Lester said. "You're freaking me out with this suicidal talk."

"I ain't gonna whack myself, if that's what you're worried about."

"Kind of." Lester felt only a slight relief. "You've got a lot to live for."

"Sure I do," Jack grumbled.

Lester shifted uncomfortably on his boulder perch, wishing he were sitting in his Lazy Boy chair at home. "Think about Jennifer."

"Jen hates my guts." Jack hung his head, choking on the mention of her name. "She blames me for Mary."

"She doesn't mean that, Jack."

"After the funeral, Jen said she don't ever want to see me again."

"She's just hurting from the loss of her mother."

"You don't know her, Lester. She don't say stuff like that without puttin' a whole lot of thinkin' into it. I'm dead to her."

"She'll come around." Lester hoped that she would. Although Jack had gotten pretty difficult to be around. "It'll take her some time to heal."

Jack shook his head. "They're in her mind now. Them Chirps, spreadin' their hate."

"Dammit Jack! You've got to stop that!" Even as Lester spoke, he reprimanded himself for engaging in it. He'd promised himself he wouldn't. "You have to stop all this talk about your alien nonsense."

"Somebody's gotta say it. Let 'em come after me. I got nothin' left to lose." Jack looked down at Lester with a fierceness Lester hadn't seen since they'd played football in high school. "Was it them Chirps that got you to bring me out here?"

For a moment Lester thought Jack was going to leap through the flames at him. He held up his hands. "What the hell has gotten into you?"

"Same thing that's gettin' into all of us! It's them Chirps. They're in our heads, Lester. Takin' control of our minds!"

"Stop," Lester said. "No more of this crap."

"It ain't crap. Those Chirps are brain-washin' us."

"What do you know about any of this?"

"Wasn't me. It was that professor, and Mary." Jack looked mournfully into the fire. "They both knew. They were tryin' to do something. But the Chirps took him down. Then they got her, too."

"Jack, nobody 'got her'. It was an accident. The driver admitted to losing control—"

"I was there, Lester. I saw it. That guy was possessed! Mary knew. She told me it was those Chirps that made him do it."

Lester looked down at the mocha-colored dust that covered his boots. "That's just crazy…"

"According to who?" Jack dropped his beer can and crushed it into the dirt with the heel of his boot. "Those people tellin' you what's goin' on, they have no idea." He swung his arm toward the darkness beyond the campfire. "Look around you Lester. The world is itchin' for a fight! Everybody hates everybody."

"That's just the media stirring people up, making a big deal about every little thing."

"You think what's goin' on in Syria and Iraq is a little thing?" Jack went to the cooler and grabbed another beer. "Look at all the hate there is right here in our own country. Those Chirps are everywhere, Lester. Fillin' us up with their hate. They got us goin' at each other's throats. And we're gonna do their dirty work for 'em."

Lester threw up his hands. "Can't you hear how ridiculous this sounds?"

"I don't care anymore," Jack said. "I ain't gonna stand by and watch without sayin' nothin'. The Chirps are gonna take over. They gotta get rid of us, and they know they can't do it on their own. But if they can get in our heads. Make us all hate each other—"

"Come on, Jack." Lester felt his attention drawn to the pulsating glow of the campfire. "You've been watching too much TV."

"It was that university professor. The one Mary worked for in Santa Fe. He's the one that cracked their code. He tried to tell the government. Tried to tell anybody who'd listen to him about it. But they all thought he'd lost his mind."

"Maybe he did."

"Not according to Mary. And I never knew a better judge of people. She knew all the research he'd done, and she believed him. The two of 'em had enough evidence to show us all what those Chirps are up to." Jack sipped his beer, looking deep into the campfire. "When his lab burnt down, cops said it was arson. Said it was him that did it. They put that ol' professor in the funny farm, and that was the end of him. Mary said it was rigged so they could shut him up. And when she found out about the fall, she knew it wasn't no accident."

"So, the professor's dead?"

"He didn't last two weeks in there. But nobody kicked up a fuss about it, not even his family. Mary tried. Got herself fired. The university said it was inappropriate, her makin' those allegations. Sons o' bitches. Damn near broke her spirit. But she didn't let up on tryin' to get somebody to pick up that professor's work. They all said it was nothin' but a bunch of crap, just like you." Jack hung his head. "Then Mary gets hit by a car…" He kicked up a little cloud of dirt. "I don't care what anybody says, that wasn't no accident."

Jack had always been a happy-go-lucky guy, which made it especially hard to watch him get so twisted up by these crazy notions. "Finish your beer and let's get some sleep," Lester said. "We can talk more about this in the morning."

"You think anything's gonna be different in the morning?" Jack stared over the fire at Lester. "Those Chirps will be drillin' in your ear while you're sleepin', tellin' you what a menace I am. By mornin' you'll be good and ready to kill me yourself."

"For Christ sake," Lester said. "Cut it out."

"Whatever." Jack drained his beer and threw the can into the fire, which caused the flame to sparkle briefly, then fade. "I'm gonna go take a leak."

Jack walked away from the light of the campfire, his image growing thin and fading into the blackness. The crackling of the fire was overwhelmed by the chorus of chirping that rose up out of the stillness. The volume seemed to increase as Lester thought about what Jack had said. Gradually, their piercing chitters seemed to be coming from inside his head.

Lester's anger grew as the highlight reel of events from the past few months rolled through his mind. Since Mary's death, Jack had alienated the few friends they still had. He'd become a laughing stock. Preaching his alien conspiracy nonsense, he'd been lampooned by a comedy news program with a video mash-up of his comments. It wasn't hard to see why Jennifer was ready to disown him. As Lester stared into the deep black of the forest, it was hard to see any hope of Jack pulling out of his nosedive.

Jack had been gone for a while when shouting pierced the dark from the other side of the campground. First one voice, then several, none of the words discernible. Lester stood on his boulder looking, listening for any details. More shouting rose up out of the distance. Blue and red flashing lights illuminated the canopy under the massive redwood trees.

Lester was about to head toward the ruckus when Jack emerged from the shadows. His annoyance returned. "What the hell, Jack?"

"Some guy's losing it. Pickin' up stuff and throwin' it at people in their camps. The park rangers are tryin' to chase him down." Jack held his hands skyward. "It's like I been tellin' you, the whole world's goin' crazy."

"I got enough crazy right here."

"You gotta wake up, Lester. You're gonna see that it's all true. And I hope when you do, it ain't too late to do somethin' about it."

Lester could feel the heat rising from his chest and face. The camping trip had been a terrible idea. The prospects of crawling into a tent to sleep on a skimpy little air mattress had him wishing he were home, rolling into his own bed. "I've heard about enough—"

The undergrowth crackled nearby with heavy footsteps. The shape of a man lurched into the light of the campfire. He stopped, glaring at Jack, then at Lester. He was big, red-faced and sweaty, with the crazed look of a man possessed. An axe dangled at his side.

"They've come for me, Lester." Jack turned toward the intruder. "You best stay out of the way."

The guy raised his axe with both hands. He charged at Lester with an awkward lope. Lester cringed behind the fire, ducking in anticipation of the attack. The man stopped, eyeing Lester. He mumbled something indiscernible and turned his attention to Jack on the other side of the campfire.

The crazed man lunged toward Jack, stumbling on the rocks around the firepit. His boot kicked up a shower of sparks from the coals. Dragging his leg across the fire, he clambered toward Jack with his pants ablaze. He raised the axe and took a wild cut, which Jack dodged, untouched. The man stumbled again, bending down to swat the flame off his leg.

More heavy footsteps pounded in from the woods. "Park Police!" A baby-faced officer, cheeks red from exertion appeared in the campfire light, his gun drawn. "Drop the weapon!"

The crazed man ignored the ranger, slapping furiously at his burning pant leg. Baby-Face pointed his gun at the man, arms locked stiffly in place, with a look of uncertainty. A winded middle-aged officer appeared at Baby-Face's side, waving his gun. "Drop it!"

With his flaming pants reduced to smoldering fabric, the wild man turned back to Jack. He raised the axe, and with a guttural scream swung the shiny blade at Jack's head.

Two gunshots echoed through the redwood canopy. The crazed man spun and hit the ground with a thud. The axe flew from his hand, falling harmlessly against a boulder.

The crazed invader disregarded his wound and scrambled toward the axe. Baby-Face tackled him while his partner trained his gun on the ruckus in a cloud of dust.

Jack fell to his knees, staring up at Lester with a look of wonder, or disbelief. Blood spurted from a red circle in his abdomen, running down over his crotch to a puddle on the ground. Lester rushed toward Jack, as he collapsed to the ground.

"No, Jack!" Lester fell to his knees and looked down at Jack lying in the dirt. "What can I do?"

The strain was now gone from Jack's face. "Nothin' you can do for me now. You best be careful." Jack coughed. "They'll be comin' for you next." Blood gurgled from the divot in his torso. The color drained from his skin.

"Help!" Lester looked around. Faces of other campers gathered in the dim periphery observing silently. "Somebody, help him!"

Jack pulled weakly on the fabric of Lester's shirt. "You got to take it up now, Lester. You got to speak up about them Chirps."

A stern-faced man stepped forward from the people gathered in the shadows. His tailored slacks and white shirt were starched and crisp. The man's hair neatly combed back, face free of whiskers. His eyes were steely and distant.

He knelt next to Lester and put a finger on Jack's neck. After a moment he turned to Lester. "He's gone."

Lester gazed in disbelief at Jack, who stared silently into the distance. Images of their younger selves flashed through Lester's mind as his vision began to blur.

"Was he trying to tell you something?" The man asked, not turning away from Lester.

Lester wiped away his tears and glanced at the slicked-back man. The unfocused eyes of the stranger sent a chill through his body. Lester returned his attention to Jack, reaching down to close his eyes.

"No." Lester sat back on his haunches in silent reverence, not looking up again. "Nothing I could understand."

2016 Short Story Third Place Adult Winner: The Birthday Story by Mikko Cook

A New York State Dairy Princess of 1978, Mikko returned to fiction after a twenty-year hiatus. A member of the WoWW writing group, as well as the Ventura Wednesday Writers, she channels her creative energy and neurosis into the made-up characters of her mind, thereby preserving the sanctity and sanity of the real-world characters of her family.

Delaney stopped picking at the skin on her pimply nose to give me the stink eye in the passenger visor mirror. She's Mom's accomplice, but after their fight this morning, who knows.

"Lily Bear," Mom said. "I can't believe you're nine years old today. Has your mustache started to come in yet?"

"Funny, Mom. No one gets a mustache when they turn nine years old. Especially girls."

Mom looked at me in the rearview mirror like I'd told her I had a cough or a splinter. "I can't believe Delaney didn't tell you. Ask her. Girl mustaches are silvery whiskers, sort of like a cat, you can sense danger with them. She made us shave hers off."

"Really, Delaney?" I said. She threw Mom a glare, then stuck her tongue out at me, which either meant Mom lied again or Delaney didn't want to tell me the truth. I hated Mom's lies. She added in enough truth, so I never knew what to believe. Like the time she told me my blue birthmark was a permanent ink stamp from when I arrived as a baby on a cargo ship from Madagascar. I'd never met anyone with a blue birthmark, not one with squiggle lines in the shape of a 3 and a W. Maybe I wasn't born in Connecticut, but on a mysterious island with friendly lemurs and those giant trees that look like carrots growing upside down. Sometimes I wished her stories were true.

"That's your idea of a birthday gift, Mom? Dragging her around Ventura for the hundredth time on your made-up history tour and freaking her out about facial hair?" Delaney said.

I closed my eyes, waited for Mom to comment. I heard Delaney whisper, "Fail." The car moved faster.

I ducked my head behind the front seat, pretended to pick something up off of the floor, touched my fingers to my top lip. Smooth like velvet. No prickly hairs. Liar.

"Get ready," Mom said, raised herself up in her seat. "We're coming up on the first stop of our Magical Ventura Tour." The groaning sound from the steering wheel made me think maybe the car didn't want to be on the tour either.

"Mom, can't we do something else for once?" Delaney said. "We know all of your ridiculous stories already. I bet Lily doesn't even want to be here and it's her birthday."

"Lily Bear is this true?" We sat curbside in front of City Hall, the engine coughed like a bear with a cold. Mom rammed the shifter into park, peeked around the front headrest at me.

I turned to the window. The weird smiling marble faces carved all along the front of city hall laughed down at me. *I hate birthdays. I wished Dad were with us.* "No, it's okay," I said. "Tell the story, Mom. Reminds me of when we moved here."

"Well, few people know this, but Ventura City Hall was built on top of an ancient Chumash burial site."

"Not true," Delaney said. "I asked my social studies teacher, he's from here. He said 'no'."

My stomach hurt. I thought about my cake in the fridge with my name written in blue cream cheese frosting. Dad and I both loved carrot cake.

"Mr. Carver?" Mom said, brushed Delaney's bangs out of her eyes.

"Yeah?"

"Honey, Mr. Carver drinks. He can't be trusted. Grab yourself some Midol from my purse. You'll feel better."

Mom turned back around to wink at me. Delaney sighed like a movie star, crumpled into a sulking pile.

"Anyway, Lily Bear, the city planners built City Hall on an ancient Chumash burial ground, then carved the faces of the Franciscan friars who founded the mission on the outside of the building. They did this to honor the men who wanted to civilize the native Chumash right out of their own culture."

"What's wrong with civilizing someone?" I said. Two girls in my class, Annabel and Janie, were in cotillion. When I asked, they told me they went to dances to learn how to be civilized. I tried to imagine the Chumash native's ballroom dancing together in grass skirts and white gloves.

"Depends on your definition of civilization. But the Chumash people got revenge. Know what they did?"

I did know, but I wanted her to tell me like she did every birthday. Mom started the Ventura "Her-story Tour" the first year we moved here, on my fifth birthday. In first grade, I had to write a special report after I told the class pirates put up Serra Cross, not missionaries. Mom made me a cross birthday cake that year, with vending machine toys baked inside.

"Nope," I said.

"They cursed the land. When the rare blue moon rises in the sky, those friars' faces come to life and tell all the secrets kept within the walls of City Hall!"

"When's the blue moon? Has anyone ever seen them come alive?"

I felt the familiar thrill rise up inside. My mother's magic held me.

"I have a question since you know about all things secret and mystical." Delaney's voice jabbed at our mother. My palms started to sweat. Unlike her usual pouty, dramatic self, a new Delaney voice came out. "Where's our father?"

Dammit, Delaney. It's my birthday! You need to do this now? Awesome.

"Excuse me?" Mom said, her voice like a policeman instead of a tour guide. She turned, faced Delaney head on.

"Our father. The one who used to live with us but one day never came home again. Where is he? And no more made up stories. How about some truth this time? Where's our father?"

I stopped taking full breaths, picked at the scab on my elbow. The sun poked out above the trees. I felt the beams burn on my shoulder, but unsticking my bare legs from the car seat meant ripping at my sunburn from yesterday, so I stayed still. I made a birthday wish that my window wasn't stuck closed. We never talked about Dad, just like we never talked about earthquakes, the great white sharks spotted around the river mouth or the drought.

"Your father is out to sea."

The car rolled away from the curb.

"For three years? How does someone go out to sea for three years?"

I can remember a lot from when I was six. I remember one time Delaney sat on top of me after I had eaten a bowl of mint chocolate chip ice cream, tickled me until I laughed so hard I puked all over her legs. I remember Tommy Leone from down the street threw my green Matchbox car into the sewer drain. And I remember when I won my goldfish, Percy, at the school carnival, even though he only lasted a couple of days.

But as hard as I try, I don't remember what Daddy's voice sounded like.

"He got on the wrong ship," Mom said. "He was supposed to be going out for an overnight fishing trip to Santa Rosa, but instead he got on a ghost pirate ship. This ghost ship was disguised to look like all the other fishing boats. Not his fault. Now he's sailing around the world."

We sat dangling at the stop sign on the top of California Street, below the sea stretched out like a silver blanket in front of us. Floating in the mist like scoops of whipped cream, were the Channel Islands. How fast would we have to go to fly out over the pier and the sea, to get to those islands?

"They say sometimes the ghost ships return to their original port, but I don't know if that's true. Your father always wanted to see the world. I guess this was a wish come true."

We moved down California Street, headed for the beach.

Aside from wishing the car window open, I had also birthday wished for a new bike, a puppy, and for Daddy to come home. I asked God to cancel the earlier three and put all my wish juice towards Daddy.

"No, Mom." Delaney's voice sounded stretched like a balloon filled with water. "The truth this time. We don't want any more stories. Please."

Mom yanked the car over to the side of the road, we skidded a bit when the tires hit the sand. Thrown into park the car jerked forward.

"What exactly do you want me to tell you, Delaney? What do you want the truth to be? Does it feel better to know City Hall is built on nothing more than dirt? The truth is cold and boring and doesn't ever go away. I don't know where your father is. He told me he was going fishing, a man who never owned a fishing pole mind you, decided to go on a fishing trip with a suitcase in his hand. Then I never saw him again. There. Does that feel better or any more real than he's on a disappearing ghost ship?"

Delaney burst out of the car, ran toward the massive sand dune in front of the water. Mom said the f-word, kicked her door open and marched across the sand toward Delaney.

When I caught up to them at the bottom of the dune, both of them sat in the sand.

A scrunched up Delaney sobbed in Mom's arms, Mom whispered into her ear, stroked her hair, rocked her back and forth. I wanted to pop the heavy empty bubble inside of me, so I squished myself in between them both.

We came up for air, a wet, snotty, sniffling mess and I birthday wished a box of Kleenex for us all.

"Come on," Mom said. "The sea wants to give a girl a birthday kiss."

2016 Short Story Adult Honorable Mention: Real Love by Dallas Woodburn

A Ventura High School graduate and recent Steinbeck Fellow in Creative Writing at San Jose State University has published fiction and nonfiction in Zyzzyva, Conclave: A Journal of Character, Fourth River, The Nashville Review, The Los Angeles Times, North Dakota Quarterly, *and* Monkey bicycle, *among many others. A three-time Pushcart Prize nominee, she won first place in the international Glass Woman Prize and second place in the American Fiction Prize. Her short plays have been produced in Los Angeles and New York City. She is the founder of Write On! For Literacy, an organization that empowers young people through reading and writing endeavors: www.writeonbooks.org.*

The good news comes on one of those falsely beautiful February days — sixty degrees, sunny, icicles melting off the eaves of every building on the block. I've been a Midwesterner for nearly thirty years, yet the blind California optimism still creeps into my thoughts on days like this—thinking maybe spring is here early, maybe this year it will just stay like this, warm and blue-skied.

"It's on!" Sam shouts. I press the down button on my cell phone volume. Sam never talks, only shouts. Before he started our Beatles cover band, he was a high school gym teacher. Then he retired and decided to pursue his teenage dream of playing the drums. "Lincoln Hall wants us!" he continues. "I'll give you the details at rehearsal tonight."

I yank up the blinds. Light streams in, making me squint. "Sounds great!" I hang up before he can try to talk to me about Bill. I don't trust Bill. I can tell he wants my role in the band. A woman once came up to me after a show and gave me a fierce, weepy hug, thanking me for bringing John Lennon back to life for a couple hours. It was one of the nicest things anyone's ever told me. The only problem was that Bill was packing up equipment right next to me, and he heard it, too. Ever since then he's been gunning for my spot.

I take my coffee out to my narrow balcony, looking down at the morning joggers and dog-walkers. My apartment is the top floor of an old house that's been split up into single-bedroom units. When I first moved in, I thought it would be a temporary place, just somewhere to store my boxes and catch my breath after the divorce. But it's been two years, and I'm still here. It suits me, I guess.

Puddles have gathered where last night was snow. The cold dampness of the wood seeps into my socks, but I stand for a few minutes longer, watching a group of kids laughing and jostling each other on the way to the bus stop, jackets unzipped and flapping. Unbidden I think of Sarah as a little girl, that bright pink headband she loved to wear, the way she'd run to give me a hug when I got home from work — as if I'd been gone weeks instead of hours. Faye used to be excited to see me, too. Or maybe that's too strong of a word, *excited*. But she was happy. Pleased. Pleased that I was home, pleased to sit down beside me on the couch after the dinner had been eaten and the dishwasher had been loaded, pleased to watch a couple hours of mindless TV side-by-side while the dishwasher hummed, and the dog snored and Sarah talked on the phone with friends up in her room.

I head back inside, unpeeling my socks and dropping them on the carpet just inside the doorway. I'll leave them there for days, because Faye isn't here to tell me not to. Two years post-divorce, it's still the small pleasures I cling to the most.

***

I first auditioned for the role of Paul, but I didn't get it. They wanted someone who could play left-handed. Sam is all about authenticity.

So leftie Rob got the role of Paul, I was chosen for John, and Bill was picked to be George. "If you're not serious, get out now!" Sam had barked at us that first rehearsal, in the basement of his house that had been converted to a music room. "This band is only for *real* musicians and *real* Beatles enthusiasts. We will not only play the Beatles, we will *become* the Beatles." Sam is our Ringo. He brings out the awkward middle-school student still inside me: eager to please, easy to shame.

"John!" he says, stopping us in the middle of "Come Together." He insists we call each other by our Beatle names. "You're flat. It's all building up to that chorus—you've really got to nail it, mate."

Bill smirks at me, eyes gleaming with hope. I grit my teeth and fiddle with my guitar, pretending to retune the strings. I'm not giving up my role as John. I've been playing him for nearly three years now. When I'm performing, the borderline between John Lennon and me fades away. I put on my long brown wig, all-white suit, and iconic round glasses, and I don't just look like John Lennon—I *am* John Lennon. For an hour or two, I bring him back to life. I won't let Bill take that away from me.

***

The night John Lennon died was a Monday, and I was sleeping on the ancient, musty couch in the basement of my college dorm. My roommate would barge into our shoebox of a dorm room with his frat guy posse, smelling of cheap cologne and cheaper whiskey, and he wouldn't even have to kick me out—I'd leave of my own volition. There was a piano in the basement I liked to play. It was missing three keys and severely out of tune, but it comforted me.

That night, for the first time in weeks, I went to bed happy. I'd finally met a girl who seemed to like me, too. We'd gone for coffee, and she hadn't seemed in a hurry to leave, and she hadn't seemed embarrassed to be with me even when I sloshed coffee onto my shirt. I fell asleep with her name looping through my mind: Faye, Faye, Faye.

The next day, I woke up with a stiff back that for once didn't bother me, and I may have even been whistling as I walked across campus to my morning class. It was there I found out about John Lennon. I thought someone was making a bad joke until I saw the newspaper headline. I stumbled back to my dorm, where I parked myself on the piano bench and pounded out every Beatles song I knew. Then I called Faye. As soon as I heard her voice, I started crying.

She didn't understand why I was so devastated over John's death.

"Because it's the end of something big," I tried to explain. "He was John Lennon. He was magic." How could I put into words what his music meant to me?

"It's sad," Faye said. "But you need to get a hold of yourself. He was a great musician, but he wasn't your friend. You didn't know him."

I probably should have known then that things between us would fall apart eventually.

***

A week before the big show, Sam decides in a caffeine-fueled frenzy to add a new song to our set list: "Real Love," a song John wrote post-Beatles. The remaining three came together and recorded it after his death.

"A song the Beatles were never able to sing together!" Sam shouts. "We will allow them to sing it now!"

A pit opens in my stomach. "Real Love" was the song Faye and I danced to at our wedding.

"John!" Sam barks. "Your voice should stand out more on the chorus! This is your song, mate!"

As we danced in the middle of the banquet hall, our friends and family watching, my arms solid around her waist, Faye met my eyes and whispered the words along with the song.

My voice cracks in the middle of the last note. A lump has welled up in my throat. The band stops playing. I can feel everyone's eyes on me.

Yearning for Faye expands inside me like it could crack my ribcage.

"Let's take a break," Sam says. I know he's disappointed. I'm not John Lennon today. I'm just me.

"You doing okay?" Bill asks. His eyebrows are two thick squirming caterpillars.

I shrug. "Just need a little water." I squeeze past him, walking up the steps from Sam's basement to his kitchen. Standing at the sink, filling a glass with tap water, I try to push Faye from my mind. I need to focus.

The day I moved out, driving to my new apartment, I'd scanned the radio for a Beatles tune, any Beatles tune, but found nothing.

***

Faye said joining the band was my version of a mid-life crisis. Maybe she's right. Turning forty makes you pause, lift your head up, look around. Take stock of things. This is what I had: a steady paycheck from a soul-draining job as an inventory analyst at United Airlines; a roommate-wife who passed me sections of the paper across the breakfast table and pecked me on the lips goodnight; and a teenage daughter who rolled her eyes whenever I opened my mouth and snuck twenties from my wallet. Not to mention the merciless monthly clockwork of mortgage payments, my ever-expanding potbelly, and the new ache in my left knee that seemed like some irreversible marker into the realm of Old People. I was sagging into middle-agedness, I was prepped for a crisis. And then one morning I popped into Starbucks and saw a flyer on the community bulletin board:

EVER DREAM OF BEING A BEATLE? NOW'S YOUR CHANCE! AUDITION FOR THE LIVERPOOL BOYS, A NEW BEATLES COVER BAND!

I tore off a slip of paper from the bottom and stuffed it into my pocket. Excitement buzzed in my chest for what felt like the first time in years.

I auditioned for the band that weekend. The guitar strings felt heavy under my fingers, and my voice was shaky. When Sam held up his hand to stop, I was sure he was going to tell me thanks, but no thanks. Instead, he asked if I could play "Strawberry Fields," and before I'd even reached the second chorus he clapped his hands loudly and said, "Yes! We've found our John!" Shaking my hand as we said goodbye, he added, "Welcome to the band. You're a natural."

***

I hadn't told Faye about the audition. She didn't care much for my guitar-playing. In the early days of our relationship I tried to use the guitar to woo her, stringing together love notes into melodies, but it didn't take me long to realize the smile she wore was forced, pasted-on. After we married, I only played my guitar in odd slivers of time when Faye wasn't home, or outside, late at night, when I couldn't sleep.

The first week of rehearsals, I tried making excuses about having to work late, but Faye could tell I was lying and confronted me. "Are you seeing someone?" she asked me point-blank, cornering me as I shaved after my shower. I'd wiped off a circle of the mirror to see my face; Faye's reflection was a fogged-up shadow.

"Of course not," I said. No plausible explanations came to mind, so I confessed the truth. I expected her to laugh it off. Instead, she seemed interested.

"Why didn't you tell me?" she asked.

"I wanted to surprise you," I lied. "We're playing our first show in a couple weeks, at Brewski's Pub."

Faye said she would be there, and in that moment, I was happy. But as the date of the show approached, a steadily worsening anxiety gripped my chest. I pictured Faye in the audience, her dark hair twisted up into a bun, her mouth set in a thin line. Judging. I knew that if she came, my fingers would fumble over the chords.

The day of the show, after a restless night of strumming to crickets in our backyard, I asked Faye not to come. Hurt leapt from her eyes, but she didn't push for an explanation. She never asked to come to another one of my shows.

***

Every other weekend Sarah's supposed to stay with me, but she seems to always have an excuse: a birthday party sleepover for one of her friends; a big science project requiring a complicated set-up at home. She never calls it her mother's house, just *home*.

I can't get a whole weekend with my daughter, but sometimes I take her out for ice cream. When she was little, she loved rocky road sundaes. Now she just gets a small scoop of vanilla, letting most of it melt while I ask questions about her studies and friends. When the silence bubbling up after Sarah's one-sentence answers becomes too unbearable, I usually end up talking about the Beatles. I watch my daughter stirring circles into her melting vanilla, no doubt counting the minutes until she is back home, while I ramble on helplessly about number-one singles and backmasking, hoping that something I say will spark her attention. It hasn't happened yet. But I keep trying.

"Hi Sarah, it's your dad," I say onto her voicemail. "My band is playing a concert next weekend, at Lincoln Hall, in the city. I got a ticket for you, if you want to come. If I don't hear back from you, I'll just leave it at Will Call."

***

We drive into the city for the show, our equipment piled in the back of Sam's van. It's a Friday and the roads are congested with traffic. We've been on the road for maybe ten minutes when the snow begins. Sam drives hunched over the wheel, knuckles clenched. One of the windshield wipers is coming off, a line of rubber dragging across the windshield, forward and back, smearing condensation around.

We arrive late to Lincoln Hall and everything is rushed, frantic. We only have time for a brief sound check before they want to let the audience inside the theater. In the dressing room, I button up my white suit, put on my long brown wig, straighten my round glasses. When I look into the mirror, John Lennon is staring back at me.

Sam ushers us upstairs and we wait behind the curtain, listening to the hum of people on the other side. There is a screech of feedback, and then the announcer's voice booms over the sound system. "Let's give a warm Chicago welcome for… The Liverpool Boys!"

The curtain rises. I pick up my guitar and stride onstage. The bright lights make my eyes water. I search for Sarah's smile in the crowd. I can't find her, but maybe she's out there.

Paul counts us in, *one two three four*, and then my fingers are strumming out a melody I know as intimately as my own heartbeat. I raise my lips to the microphone. The crowd is cheering my name, "John, John, I love you John," and I know it is not me they are cheering for, it is not me they love, but when I open my mouth to sing what comes out feels more true than anything else in this life I've made for myself, so I soak in the cheers and applause and giddy shrieks, "sing it John," and let myself pretend for a little while longer that it belongs to me.

2016 Short Story Adult Honorable Mention: Un-Miracle by Philip Brown

As a high school teacher, Phil is motivated by the power of words to change lives. He's inspired by his students, many of whom struggle to overcome difficult social and personal issues, and he believes the classroom is a place filled with brilliant and amazing stories. A VCWC member, Phil is a published YA contemporary fantasy author. Light Runner, Book One *in a trilogy, was published by Strange Fictions Press in 2016, The sequel,* Light Guardian, *has been completed and submitted to the publisher. Before he began writing fiction, he wrote a couple of astrology books.* Cosmic Trends *was published by Llewellyn Worldwide in 2006 and was a finalist for the Coalition of Visionary Resources Award. His widely read AstroFutureTrends blog was turned into the book,* On the Cusp: Astrological Reflections from the Threshold.

Desks rattled on the floor as the class assembled into groups, and Maddie found herself facing two other juniors. One was a boy she had a secret crush on, and she'd made sure to learn his name. Zack. Blond and muscular, he slouched in the desk chair, legs stretched out like he wanted to sleep, and closed his eyes. Dreamy.

Maddie didn't know the other student except for his weird name – Quentin. He was frail, thin, and kind of creepy. Not as tall as Maddie. And there was a hollow, haunted look about him, as though he spent too many hours alone playing *World of Warcraft* in the basement.

Zack pressed his tall frame into the chair, bending the plastic back support. Strong jaw, chiseled cheekbones. He opened one eye, looked at Maddie. "I like your hair," he said, then sat up straighter. "My sister streaked hers, too. Used a bleach kit, I think."

Maddie nodded and twisted a strand around one finger. Slow. Keep him focused. "I made it real light in just a few places, and then added the lime green streaks."

"Nice," Zack said, then looked down at the poem and shrugged. "This sucky poetry crap that Mr. K gave us – he wants us to come up with some kind of theme or whatever? I don't know about you, but the poem makes no sense. Some dude who's gone into the woods and can't figure out which path to take? How lame. Next time take a cellphone."

"Maybe he's not really confused," Maddie offered. "Just deciding."

"And what's *hence* mean?" Zack asked.

"The future." It was Quentin, who'd seemed lost, detached, hunched over his desk as he folded and unfolded a corner of the paper.

Maddie sank back into her seat, wishing it could be just her and Zack. Partners.

"Or therefore," Quentin added.

"Like you read a freakin' dictionary in your spare time?" Zack asked.

Quentin stopped fiddling with the paper. "There's this video game called *Fate* and—"

"As if that matters." Zack – arms crossed, sprawled in his seat – cut Quentin off with a look of disdain. He raised an eyebrow and turned to Maddie, then shifted his desk closer to her, away from Quentin.

Maddie's heart skipped a beat.

"Where you from?" Zack asked.

"San Diego," said Maddie. "My dad just got relocated here."

"You live with him?"

Maddie understood the subtext of the question – *not with Mom, right?* – and nodded, then stared down at her desk until her hair fell over her cheeks. When she brushed back the strands, she noticed that in the laminate surface of the desk, someone had carved a letter A with a circle around it. It made her think of her mother: Annette. "Me and my dad –just two peas in a pod," she said, and looked up with a forced smile

***

The courtroom. Mom and Dad had split up, and the judge was making it official, deciding who'd get the teenager. The jurist, a woman in a ruffled blouse, sat at the bench, a smile pasted on her face like this was a happy time for everyone.

Maddie sat beside her dad and felt the inescapable hardness of the courtroom walls, her chair, the judge's bench.

"So..." The judge glanced down at the file in front of her. "... Madeline. You will remain with your father. And you have indicated to the court, uh, to me that – that accords with your wishes?"

Yeah, Maddie thought, it accords. So cool that her parents were splitting up, that her mom would rather be with her new BF than with Dad – and Maddie. "Yes, ma'am," Maddie mumbled.

After the hearing, she'd hugged her mom and didn't know when she'd see her again.

Outside the courtroom, Mom and BF had walked down the long hall holding hands, receding into the distance. Dad and Maddie stood there and watched as though viewing the sunset ending of some home video.

He was cool: Mom's new BF. Better than Dad in some ways, Maddie supposed. He had his own business, a tattoo parlor. He even looked cool, with a scruffy goatee, big smile, and deep voice. The day he showed up with Mom in court, he wore a light blue cloth jacket with a pink and black yin-

192

yang symbol on the back. The sleeves had been cut off, revealing colorful arm tats. Marketing.

Mom once said she'd been saved. As in, "Sweetie, he rescued me from your father's drinking and showed me a better way. He's my miracle."

Which made Maddie feel like she'd chosen the losing team. The un-miracle.

***

Maddie slid the poem back and forth on her desk. She looked at the clock, then back at the page. Two paths. This dude chooses one just because it has more grass, is less worn. And then after he's been on it for a while, doesn't think he'll go back? The poem's words were simple, but the meaning seemed complicated, elusive.

"You like to party?" Zack asked.

"When I'm not grounded," Maddie said, smiling at him. "Which I am." Did he go for the bad girl? Her eyes flicked to the reclusive Quentin, who fidgeted with his pencil, and she wished she could make him disappear.

"No way," Zack said. "That's for middle school."

"You don't know my dad."

"What'd you do to deserve *that*?"

"Being grounded or my dad?" Maddie tucked one leg back, and curled her foot around a metal desk support. "Got home too late from school. Missed curfew just because I hung out in the park to practice some tricks on my board."

"You're kidding. You got grounded for that?" He chortled. "Does he make you wear a house arrest ankle bracelet?"

Maddie sighed. "He likes things tight, battleship tight, ever since—"

"So ... you're a brat." Quentin spoke in a halting, delicate voice, and blinked as though the fluorescent light bothered his eyes.

The word surprised Maddie. Away from the base and other military families, it was seldom spoken. Maddie nodded. "Every three years, a new home." The latest move, in the middle of her junior year, had been tough. Maddie's contact with previous friends was limited to Facebook, Instagram, an occasional text message.

"My dad's a swabbie, too," Quentin said, a note of soft apology in his voice as his eyes darted about the room.

Maddie looked at him and, for the first time, noticed the pendant that hung from a slim silver chain about Quentin's neck. A tiny navy anchor.

Maddie extended a fist towards him.

Quentin lifted his arm and reached out small knuckles to bump Maddie's fist. The backs of his fingers were slim, soft, yielding. They might have been a computer geek's fingers, but they reminded Maddie of her mother's.

She caught the disgusted look in Zack's eye and quickly withdrew her hand.

***

Maddie and her father took turns heating up leftover Mexican food in the microwave, then settled onto the couch. The apartment smelled of enchilada sauce, and a Netflix *Batman* movie droned on the TV.

Maddie got up, pulled a large bottle of Gatorade from the fridge and swigged it, then put it back.

"As soon as I finish dinner," her dad called to her, "I'm going to a Sober Steps meeting. Getting a six-month chip."

"That's good, Dad." Maddie stepped back into the small living room. Wait. One. Two. "This boy asked me to a dance." Casual. Like it happened every day.

"What's his name?"

It wasn't a no.

"Zackary. He's in my English class."

"And ... the dance is at school?"

Maddie nodded.

"But you're grounded."

"Just this one time, Dad! Please!"

"When's the dance?"

"Like ... two weeks."

"He drives?"

"Dunno." She'd forgotten to ask about that. But she imagined the two of them, her and Zack, Zack driving with one hand, his other arm around her shoulders. Her chest fluttered. "C'mon, Dad. He's cool. You'd like Zack."

He got up and ruffled her hair. "I gotta get going." He dropped the plastic plate into the sink. Before he got to the door, he turned around. "In two weeks, you won't be grounded anymore. So ... okay."

***

A week and a half later, on her way home from school, Maddie rode her skateboard on an asphalt path that cut through the park. The weight of her backpack forced her to stand straight, both feet planted on the board.

Loud voices sounded near a cinder-block restroom. She skated a short distance past the building, then skittered to a halt and looked back at a weed-filled dirt path which led to the restroom. At the end of the dirt path, someone was on the ground, another boy standing over him. A soft whimper. Quentin's voice.

Maddie wanted to skate away. Not her business, nothing she could do. Look the other way. Then she thought of her dad. Of Quentin's dad. Something clicked, and she stopped, turned around. "Hey! Leave him alone!"

She skated closer, and it was then she recognized the boy who stood over the fallen Quentin.

It was Zack, aiming a sneakered foot at Quentin's side.

She braked, thought of the dance, her head on Zack's broad shoulder. Her heart pounded.

For the first time, Zack appeared to notice her.

Maddie stepped off the skateboard. "No!" She rushed up and embraced Zack, using all her strength to pull him away. "Please don't." It wasn't the dance she'd imagined. "C'mon, leave him alone." Her voice shook. An image flashed through Maddie's mind: her mom's last hug before walking away with the miracle.

Zach put an arm around her. He was big and towered over her by at least a head. "The creep was going through my backpack." He pulled away and nodded at the backpack which leaned against the cinder block wall. "I set it down there while I was taking a leak."

Quentin got to his knees, and Maddie glanced down at him. A trickle of blood coursed down his forehead, his eyes pleaded, and she had to look away.

Zack clenched one hand into a fist.

"I-I was just getting my thumb drive you stole from me in computer lab," Quentin said.

Next to Quentin, a black flash drive lay in the dirt.

Maddie felt her heart pounding, and her hands trembled. Keeping an eye on Zack, she stepped over to Quentin and reached out a hand to pull him up. His hand felt soft, and she was once again reminded of her mother's hands, the way they'd felt one time when Maddie had fallen off her bike.

Quentin grabbed the flash drive, then rose and took off running, hunched over, spindly legs carrying him over the grass and towards the street.

***

"Bring it!" Maddie's dad yelled at the TV. He sipped from a can of Diet Pepsi.

Football. One team in orange versus another team in black, the cheering crowd a din of white noise. Someone ran with the ball, zig-zagging until he was tackled.

Maddie sat next to her dad on the couch. She looked down at her phone, tapped, and watched a silent YouTube video, a cat chasing its tail. She knew it was supposed to be funny and smiled because she thought she was supposed to smile. But no one else was watching, and besides it wasn't funny. Her mouth hurt, the smile faded, and she stared at the small screen, calico looping back on itself.

The football game cut to a commercial, and her dad turned to her. "Isn't that dance this weekend?"

"I-I'm not gonna go." She dropped the phone in her lap.

"How come?" Her dad arched an eyebrow. He fiddled with the remote, muted the volume, and turned on the couch to gaze at her.

She hesitated, then: "Turns out, he doesn't drive."

"No problem," her dad said. "How about if I take you, it'll be—" He stopped mid-sentence and studied Maddie, as though reading her expression.

She blinked once. Twice. Turned away.

The game was back, players on either side of the line. The ball was snapped.

But her dad didn't turn to look at the TV. He was still watching her. "There'll be others," he said. He ran a hand through her hair. "Guaranteed. Beautiful girl like you? They'd have to be crazy not to dance with you."

She looked at him, then snuggled up and rested her cheek on his shoulder.

2017 Memoir Honorable Mention: Red Dirt Fistfight by Philip Brown

A move to paradise upended my tranquil childhood. I was eleven when, in 1959, my father was transferred to Honolulu for a year to work on computer defense systems. My parents, three sisters, and I journeyed from Massachusetts – via United turboprop – to an older Hawaii that had not yet been transformed into a full-blown tourist mecca. There were relaxed buffet lunches at the pink Royal Hawaiian, weekend afternoons in Waikiki's tropical waters, and bodysurfing at famed Makapuu. It should have been an idyllic year in white sands heaven–but it wasn't.

I had begun junior high as an enthusiastic sixth grader at a progressive public school outside of Boston, along with the sons and daughters of accomplished professionals. The father of one of my classmates was a *Life Magazine* photographer, and my best friend's dad was a renowned cancer researcher at Massachusetts General Hospital. I'd grown up privileged and surrounded by an awareness of life's bountiful possibilities.

My Massachusetts school had been a blast. During math class, we'd literally jump out of our seats in excitement as we played the challenging game of Go. I performed in a Shakespeare play. There were animated class discussions and a degree of tolerance for well-intentioned student exuberance.

All that was about to change.

The move to Hawaii occurred too late for my parents to enroll me in the school they'd wanted. The only school I could get into was Kuhio, an inner-city Honolulu school. My first thought was, what difference does it make which school I attend? I'm just happy to body surf in waters that are a whole lot warmer than Cape Cod's.

Our home sat high on a hill overlooking Honolulu, with a view of Diamond Head in the distance. Each weekday morning, I boarded a city bus that took me from Saint Louis Heights down into the central city, where I got off near Kuhio.

I found myself in a tense, structured classroom silently using colored pencils and crayons to illustrate a map of our newest state – Alaska, followed by the wordless monotony of fractions worksheets. I felt like I'd been sentenced to repeat a grade, and my initial acceptance of a new school was soon replaced by resentment and disappointment.

Our school lunches consisted of canned La Choy Chow Mein, which I dutifully forked from a plastic plate. No burgers. No chocolate milk. No friends with whom to discuss the latest Red Sox game. Usually, I ate alone.

The students were mostly poor, and when I visited the home of an Asian classmate one day after school, I was surprised to find that his family's small, tin roof shack had a dirt floor. I silently recoiled, shocked at this stark, impoverished contrast with the colonial New England homes I'd grown up around.

Our teacher at Kuhio was Mrs. Liu. Hair fastened in a tight gray bun, she scolded us for the slightest misbehavior, working herself into a tirade as spittle flew from her lips.

"And when I went to school in the olden days, we had to stand up in front of the classroom to recite the lesson." A tight smile followed by more spittle.

I sat petrified, afraid to move.

"And if it was not right," she concluded, "we got hit with a ruler on the back of the hand!"

The class was eerily silent.

I frequently feigned sickness to stay home, a tactic my parents seemed to indulge for they never pushed me when I didn't want to go to school. In my pajamas, I played with model planes in our living room, filled with a sense of dread, knowing it was only a temporary reprieve. My life felt jarred, shaken, turned upside down.

One of our neighbors, Ernie, was an older, lanky boy whose father punished him by whipping him with a belt. When I first heard this, I inwardly shrank back: my father's discipline never amounted to more than a few strong words, and the thought of being whipped scared me. Ernie and I were casual friends, and he seemed to eye the world with a certain hardness. He never shared much about his life – other than his father's punishments, meted out for misdeeds that were never clear to me.

"I gotta go. Pops'll probably be waiting for me with the belt," was how he often ended our brief attempts at conversation, sending a shiver of apprehension down my spine.

One day after school, I was hanging out behind our house with a group of neighborhood boys. Birds-of-paradise and plumeria blossomed along the grass, and the ocean sparkled in the distance. Ernie said something that angered me, although I have long since forgotten what it was. But I still recall the anger, an intense, all-consuming rage that inflamed every nerve in my body. Under a lychee tree, I began attacking Ernie, egged on by the other boys. I'd never engaged in anything more violent than boyhood wrestling matches, but now found myself in serious fisticuffs with a boy who was bigger – and, I assumed, stronger and tougher – than I.

Long-simmering frustrations – the tyranny of Mrs. Liu's classroom, lonely chow mein lunches, faked illnesses – swept through me and I burst into a frenzied rage. Bottled fury poured out, and I pummeled Ernie with blow after blow, backing him up to the edge of an unfenced dirt hill that dropped down from our backyard.

Ernie landed a few defensive punches on me, but I didn't care. My goal was suddenly clear: I needed to send Ernie tumbling down the hill. I continued after him with a vengeance until he teetered on the edge, defenseless, as I rained blows upon him. I would have succeeded if Ernie's older sister hadn't leaned out their second story window and yelled at us to stop. The spell of rage was broken. When I backed off, Ernie – blackened eye, bleeding from the lip – sidestepped around me, and the fight was over.

After that, I was held in high esteem in the neighborhood. Another older boy told me that I'd beaten the "toughest guy on Peter Street." I took no pride in my supposed victory, however, and wondered about the invisible lever of fury that had so easily flipped inside of me. Ashamed of how quickly I'd lost control of my own emotions, I vowed to do everything I could to hide that troubling anger switch, the invisible circuit breaker of rage that had been tripped.

There were no more fistfights. We returned to our home in Massachusetts the following year, and I rejoined my old friends as we started seventh grade. I'd gained a tan, a closet full of aloha shirts, and a wooden *tiki* pendant. But underneath the casual, laid-back Hawaii persona was a new self-awareness, coupled with a lingering sense of lost innocence. In our backyard tropical garden, next to plumeria and passion fruit, I'd taken a bite of the apple. I'd triumphed in a backyard fight on the precipice of a red dirt hill, but it was a piece of myself – part of a simpler, more guileless boyhood – that had been forever knocked away.

2018 Poetry Adult Honorable Mention: The Kindnesses by Philip Brown

The slights, disappointments, and failures are outnumbered
in memory
by the kindnesses others have shown me: the aged Irish
landlady in London
who sang to me – a lonely, lost boy of 17. She stood in the
open doorway of my flat near Portobello Road and, before
bed time, sang sweet lullabies in Gaelic
with a smile of bad (and missing) teeth.
It's the off-notes one remembers most fondly.

The white-haired mechanic who kept my cab
running back when I drove a taxi
on L.A.'s desolate, nighttime streets and needed
someone to lean on
(he reminded me of my father, who also loved to
work on cars)
and roused himself from bed at three in the morning to tend to a busted
wheel bearing.
Mentally ill, once institutionalized, just before lung
cancer took him,
looked down at his Winchell's coffee, and said, "I don't feel like
I've been ripped off."

So many more- kindnesses stored up,
bulwarks against self-reproach,
each one a softening of sharp-clawed days, of cold and bitter nights
when I awaken, cannot sleep,
and turn to reach for something warm.

Short Story: Hot Cross Buns by Sheli Ellsworth

Sheli left her lucrative career as a guidance counselor for the Bohemian dream of becoming an author and humorist. She has authored three books for adults and co-authored/illustrated three children's books. She is also a freelance writer who has been published in the magazines: Auto Week, Spotlight on Recovery and Zone 4 as well as several newspapers. She is a regular contributor to the Ventura Breeze and teaches writing at the Conejo Valley Adult School. She designs books/covers, edits, and has been a book reviewer for 1776 Productions for eight years. You can find her award-winning short stories in the other VCWC's anthologies.

This is a story about Donald Williams, my co-worker at the *Lincoln County Gazette* (est. 1901). Don was my first friend at the paper. Our old metal, five-drawer desks sat across from each other in the corner of a capacious room filled with computers, copy editors and cobwebs. I remember Don's smile and large outstretched hand my first day at work as Artie introduced us. Sometimes males don't like the presentation of a new female to the pack, but Don was glad for the company. Before long, he could sense when I was one reactor short of a nuclear meltdown and would excuse himself, bring me back a Starbucks macchiato and tacitly place it on my desk.

Don, who'd been a newspaperman for decades, became my go-to for everything. My primary job at the paper was writing articles for the Living section and occasionally for the more-newsy front page. I tracked home and fashion trends, local artists and anything else I was assigned. He gave me contacts whenever I needed someone to interview or someone to pump for information or the story behind the story. He knew where the bodies were buried, and I was always looking for a shovel. Some people just don't want to talk to reporters, but Don had a way of convincing people it was their duty to contribute to community news.

Don covered the local sports news. He kept his job in perspective. He liked journalism because it had a definable objective: to inform. The literary crap associated with fiction writing or the research standards magazines have were not our concern. We just told readers what we'd been told. Our sources were their sources. Granted, we did so in a more organized and readable way than your average coffee shop conversation, but overall, we were just the go between. It was an honest living. No one at the *Gazette* was scooping stories or planning his Pulitzer acceptance speech.

One day in December, Don came in wearing a bluish-purple cashmere muffler with his dark gray woolen overcoat. The knitted scarf – a work of art. Its expertly matched shades were chosen with care and its maker had meticulously fringed it with all the colors intertwined in the sophisticated design.

"Nice scarf!"

"Thanks."

"No, really. It's a really nice scarf. Where'd ya get it?"

"Can't remember."

"It might look better on me."

"It's not your color." Don smiled. "Someplace in Meyersville. One of those little boutique shops in old town."

"Dude, I had no idea you were a fashionista." My dry attempt at humor was not lost on him.

"I was just over there on a story...."

One morning, I greeted Don and noticed his button-down shirt was untucked, the loose cuffs hung open at an oblique angle. But on closer inspection I could see that the shirt's hem had a split side, so it wasn't designed to be tucked into trousers. Since I wasn't aware of any dress code at the paper, it didn't really matter. Then he started wearing the Teva sandals. Yeah, it looked a little odd, but we were writers, not supermodels. Big guys might just need to be comfortable and while I wouldn't classify Don as huge – he was about the same size as the football players he interviewed. Then it happened again. A pair of baggy gauze beach pants caught my attention. Until then, a co-worker's personal style was of no concern to me. Don was still the same sweet guy, helping me when I needed it, keeping me from making a fool of myself. But where was he finding his clothes? A beach shop in Meyersville?

A skirt came next. The skirt itself was not without merit. It was a medium gray bias cut, tea length A-line. Probably rayon. Slimming without too much fabric; paired with a loose white crepe shirt tied at the waist, a clean style that looked good with Don's florid complexion and light hair. Artie, however, took a deep pensive breath when he saw Don. I could tell that of all the issues Artie had encountered in thirty years as managing editor, this was a first. Exasperation pained his face. Artie tried to play it off that first day – we all have off-style moments – but the second look Artie took while walking away told me Don had *crossed* a line.

In retrospect, to say that none of us were ever able to please Artie is an understatement. A typical editor, he always thought he could do everything better himself. I'm sure Artie would have chosen different dress for most of us. Newspaper writers aren't known for their sense of style.

I can't say that I understood Don's wardrobe proclivities, but I also can't say that I was as rattled as Artie. I didn't turn in his direction when I could avoid it and I tried not to stare or let my eyes wander over his wardrobe selection.

I wanted to mention something to Don. Or was it "Dawn" now? Something like, "Dude, you might have given Artie a little warning," or "Don, is this just a phase or do you want my hand-me-downs?" Actually, I didn't know what to say. What did Don's wardrobe transformation mean? Is he transitioning genders? Is he gay? From the way the rest of the *Gazette*'s staff was acting, no one else knew how to respond either. Unsaid words hung in the thick air like dust motes. Plummeting, dancing, a silent undetectable free-fall.

Everyone avoided our side of the room. Even the employees closest to us took the long, circuitous way, winding around through advertising to avoid Don's desk. When Don would initiate talk, the target of Don's words would avoid making eye contact. I even saw Artie have an entire conversation with Don in the break room, all the while his back to Don. Artie just kept adding sugar and creamer to his cup until it would hold no more, then he grabbed it and left.

The next day, Don wore another loose pair of pants – dark blue palazzos with a pale-yellow tunic. He really did have style. But come to think of it, if being female was just shopping for shoes, getting manicures, and buying lipstick – anyone could do it. No PMS, labor pains or breast-feeding. I wanted in. In fact, I wasn't surprised at the Caitlin Jenners of the world; I was surprised there weren't more of them. Why didn't Artie, Bob,

Monte, and the whole lot of my co-workers cross dress? From their perspective, it must look like fun to be a girl. We can wear bright colors, style our hair as outrageously as we want and change our minds at will. But what about the other stuff? Sure, we keep our hair, but we have to cut, curl and color it. And men may have to shave their faces, but compared to getting a Brazilian bikini wax, men are getting off light. And those colors – they change every fashion season – and some seasons there's not one color we like or look good in. The shoes, yes, we females have cooler shoes. Heels, boots and flip-flops in so many wonderful colors and styles that we have to keep a mental inventory of what is stored where – no guy could keep up with all that – they just aren't wired that way.

I know guys in many other cultures wear skirts. There are kilts in Scotland and men wear skirts in New Guinea, Albania, and Sri Lanka. But wasn't that different? Weren't those guys actually conforming to cultural norms? Maybe Don was just carving out a justification for his own bathroom. We have those little gender symbols: arrows for the men, crosses for the women. Perhaps, a question mark with an arrow for the Dons/Dawns of the world.

After a few days of me avoiding Don and digging in – getting more work done than I had in the entirety of the past six months – I thought it was time to invite him to lunch. I dreaded it, but I was getting caught up! In another few days, if Don and I didn't go back to our usual banter, I would have to volunteer for more assignments.

Where do you take your 230-pound cross-dressing lunch date who dresses better than you do? I was new to this. But, I remembered that I had dated a vegetarian once who had some out of the way restaurants he favored. So, I asked Don to meet me at Vegan's Paradise. If he got there first, I wouldn't actually have to walk in with him.

Well, Don didn't show up before I did. I sat there in Paradise wondering what to say: *So Don, have you always worn women's clothing and I just never noticed? Don, what's going on with your wardrobe, do you need to do laundry?* None of it sounded very compassionate. How about, *Don, is that a Kate Spade skirt?* Better.

When he showed up a few minutes later, he looked great. *Those blue-gray wedges set off that cream skirt and gray shirt perfectly!* I wanted to ask him where he bought them, but I decided not to. "Hey, Don, do you want some tea?" It was a start.

"Sounds good."

Looking across the room, I motioned to the waitress who immediately took pity on me. I didn't know what she thought, but I knew it wasn't, "Snagged yourself a *GQ* model, did ya?"

I opened the napkin and smoothed it out on my lap. "Hey, I've eaten here before. The lasagna is awesome."

"Sounds good. What does it come with?"

I finally made eye contact. "Buns and salad. Those little artesian hot cro—" *Oops.*

Don smirked. "It's okay. You can say 'cross' in front of me."

And then, I hate to say it, but we both cracked up. By the time the waitress brought our food, we had settled down some and were two friends enjoying a stellar meal. I finally asked Don if he was going to dress in skirts forever.

"*Et tu, Brute?*" he said with disdain.

"Sorry."

"Skirts are comfortable."

"I know! Skirts are the best. Although there was a time when we women couldn't wear pants and I do love my jeans."

"I love your jeans, too!"

We cracked up again.

"I don't want to be female. I do like women, though, I just don't want to be one," he confessed.

"So what kind of woman wants to share her clothes?"

"You'd be surprised."

"Really?" I immediately envisioned a plus size lady pulling out a credit card, telling herself that she was really shopping for two.

"Sometimes I wonder if they're normal . . . but they're out there."

"Don, is this a whole new thing?"

"It is. Sort of. After my wife died, I just couldn't get rid of her clothes. When I finally decided to go through her closet, I tried on her bathrobe, then a few other things. I realized that wearing her stuff made me feel sexy, for the first time in years."

"Well, you may have sent Artie right over the edge."

"Artie and I go way back. It doesn't take that much to send him off. He's a little high-strung."

"Maybe you should talk to him."

"And say what? Artie, I like wearing dresses and I'm going to keep doing it?"

"Umm ... maybe tell him the story about your wife."

"Artie just worries about the paper's reputation. He doesn't want people talking about the queers in the sports section."

"Isn't it queens?"

The edges of his mouth curved. "You know what I mean."

I smiled back. "I don't know. We all have to wear stuff we don't like. I went to a private school that required white button-down shirts and plaid skirts. I can't even drive by a Tilted Kilt sports bar without flashbacks."

That was the last time we had lunch together. A few days later, I came into work and found the beautiful purple knitted scarf on my desk. No Don in sight. "Hey, Artie. Where's Don?"

Artie nodded toward the scarf.

"He's gone. Left that for you."

2017 Poetry Youth First Place Winner Twelve & Under: Watching from God's Eye View by Grace Wynn

Grace is twelve years old and wants to be a writer when she grows up. This poem is inspired by virtual reality cameras that reveal a whole new world through technology.

I fit the camera onto my head,
The first thing I saw was white.
Pure, milky, bright white light,
As if I arose from the dead.

The blinding light had faded,
And from God's eyes view, I began to see,
A little man in a black and white striped uniform roaming free,
Quietly pacing as he waited.

The little man flicked up the latch,
On top of a stolen case,
What he pulled out made my heart race,
It was a glowing torch-like match.

The first flame leaped from the torch,
Up into the sky full of stars,
The constellation it illuminated was Aries, or Mars,
The god of the planet of fire's scorch.

The second flame went up,
To the blue constellation of stardust,
The constellation of the wolf Lupus,
A tiny little pup.

I watched from God's eye view, why did he not strike it?
He knew he was going to hell,
So he dropped the torch and it fell,
Down from the floating land, still unlit.

I saw from God's eye view, the Grimm Reaper,
Out in the mist,
Who took the little man into darkness without a wisp,
Into God's Death Keeper.

But he had let the match fall back down to the ground,
So its true owner could find it again, when he or she came around.

2017 Poetry Youth Second Place Youth Winner: The Skinny Deception by Reina Nadeau

Reina is a sixteen-year-old and has loved to write ever since she learned how to type on a computer. She attends the Thacher School, which is an academically-competitive boarding school in Ojai. This poem represents a time in her life that most teenagers go through, especially now in a media-crazed social climate. She says it is harder and harder for girls to love and appreciate their bodies when everything they see around them indicates otherwise. She hopes that through her writing, anyone who reads this poem, will feel less alone and understand that bodies are not for hating or for starving, but for loving.

I thought that if I lost weight and I finally became "pretty"
then I would stop feeling empty.

I'm always seeing celebrity health routines in the media.
They throw in the word "health" so they can encourage eating disorders
without actually having to own up to it.

"Love yourself," they say. "Every body type is beautiful."
And then they show celebrity health routines where celebrities,
if they're feeling frisky, might—and just might—splurge on half a cookie
where celebrities write cookbooks where meals are barely 500 calories
and they hide behind words like "organic" and "vegetarian"
when in reality
all they're doing is starving and they're telling us
—they're telling me—
that starving is beauty.

I thought that if I lost weight and I finally became "skinny"
then I would stop harboring so much self-hatred for everything.

But now my mind is like a machine
a calculator that never goes to sleep
a constant evaluator of how many calories are inside of me...
it makes me hate me.
I wish I could take a serrated knife and cut everything off that hangs on my
bones like limp jelly
even all the important things
even my muscles and even my kidneys
just so I can stop feeling
like I'm taking up
so
much   space.

2017 Poetry Youth Third Place Young Twelve & Under Winner: Mr. Xi by Lingyu Yan

Mary Yan lives in Shenzhen, China, and is currently a junior at the Thacher School. She enjoys writing poetry and short stories and has received recognition from the Scholastic Art and Writing Awards as well as been published on TeenInk.

Mr. Xi pours Longjing tea from teapots decorated with ivory
dragons; he makes dumplings from scratch – mixes the pork meat
with chives and pepper using his bare hands; he believes that
the number 4 brings death with its sharp corners and that the number
8 brings good fortune with its roundness, but he does not tell me about his
country, miles and miles away.

He tells me stories about Wall Street in the 1990s, about
the golden parties he dreamed of in color, the way the champagne bottle
popped and how the white foam frothed out like waves lapping a beach
line;
he shows me the dog-eared pages of Great Expectations by Charles
Dickens,
rests a hand proudly on Pride and Prejudice by Jane Austen; he speaks with
a quiet lisp, but
not in the language he must dream in.
I can imagine him as a boy: Xi, they would've called him, as he plowed the
field
with his old man, sweat glistening like marbles rolling off his back.
Xi, Xi, you must be good to your parents. You must stay here and look
over
the fields. I can imagine little-man-Xi coming to America and seeing
buildings instead of hay shacks and smelling the scent of coffee inundating
the air
and trading in himself for broad stripes and bright stars.

2017 Poetry Youth Twelve & Under Honorable Mention:
Simply Music by Leila Horton

Leila is a Junior at Besant Hill School and has been taking creative writing classes since September of 2016. She enjoys writing and this is her first time submitting to any form of writing competition.

Perspectives of the world,
Someone else's point of view unfurled.

The photographer,
Sees the world through a lens,
Like the autobiographer,
documenting their life.
Seeing the world in a different way than the painter
Caught by a camera
The flicker of a lighter.

The dancer sees the world according to dance.
The rhythm of a person,
The movement of nature at a glance.

The musician connects life to music,
The tap on a desk,
the wind in the trees,
the sound of a cricket,
Into a rhythm.
The sound of someone buying a ticket.
Everything simply music.

No one sees the world the same way.
Everyone is different.
Maybe someone's world is gray
But someone else's is the brightest color of today

2017 Poetry Youth Twelve & Under Honorable Mention: Daisy and the Dirt Below by Kaylee Sarah Slingluff

Kaylee (2017) was a High School Senior who says that poetry helps her reflect and process life. She has spent several years volunteering at a preschool, and recently, one of her students passed away. This poem is about her feelings in reflection on the child's passing.

I wear my rainbow bracelet every hour of the day,
I barely say the pretty things that you would always say,
I line up all your lyrics and I proudly count to ten,
But still my lips refuse to slip out those old songs again.

I lost my rainbow bracelet but I swear I wear it still,
Just like I always swore you'd make a great runway model.
Barely, but I hear you, in the movement of my smile,
Singing *Frozen* solos behind every happy child.

I saw my rainbow bracelet slip but somehow I was blind,
I barely saw your mother's eyes, she blankly looked behind-
The feeling of your dirt in hand- with too much pride to cry-
A plain black coffin disappeared with you submerged inside.

You barely raced to five years old but somehow you can't leave,
And years from now I'll see a dress marching down the street,
And I'll smile, and I'll barely think of you.
Again I'll feel my bracelet meet a dark and faceless place,
Barely made of colors anymore.

2017 Poetry Youth Thirteen+ Honorable Mention: Barbara, Marian, and the Elder by Nick Sweet

Nick lives in Shepherd, TX. He has been a freelance stage director since 1977 and has directed over 140 productions for theatre groups in Oklahoma, TX, Georgia, and Alaska, including the outdoor historical drama, Trail of Tears, at the Cherokee Heritage Center in Tahlequah, Oklahoma. He has written two children's plays and was named Senior Poet Laureate of Oklahoma in 2010 and of Texas in 2013 by the Angels Without Wings Foundation. His poetry and short stories have appeared in the Atlanta Review, Maine Review, Connecticut River Review, Rockhurst Review, Trajectory, California Quarterly, Nostalgia Press and the Oklahoma Centennial Heritage Collection. He recently co-wrote a musical with Nashville singer/songwriter, Becky Hobbs.

In a one room Amish schoolhouse, after recess bell had rung
Stood ten scared, hostage schoolgirls and a sad man with a gun

He lined them by the blackboard, all quivering with fear
Then screamed into his cell phone, "Get all cops out of here,

When I count ten, the killing starts," patrol cars kept arriving
Barbara faced her captor, with slim hopes of surviving

"Roseanna's only six" she said, "Naomi just turned seven,
That's the age of Mary Liz, but sir, I am eleven,

My life has been much fuller," she made her fervent plea,
"If there's to be a shooting, let it start with me."

Her sister interrupted, "I'm older than the rest,
I've had a rich and blessed life," Marian professed,

This enraged the gunman, in no mood to converse
But Marian persisted, "Please, sir, shoot me first."

Regrettably, she got her wish: the first of five who died
The others: badly wounded, the man chose suicide

"Bullet holes were everywhere," the sheriff said, aghast,
"Every desk and every chair, awash in blood and glass."

A newsman saw an elder who was stoic but heartsick
"You lost five precious souls," he said, the elder answered "six"

The reporter was astonished, he asked his solemn source
"How can you forgive someone who never showed remorse?"

Charley was our milkman," the elder softly said,
"It's not our place to judge him or speak ill of the dead,

Bless Marian and the others who bravely gave their lives,
Bless Barbara and the injured, we'll help them heal and thrive,

We'll reach out to the families of all who are deceased,
And Charley's is included, forgiveness brings us peace,

We'll not think evil of this man nor of his kids and wife,
Letting go of grudges is the Amish way of life."

2018 Poetry Adult Honorable Mention Decent/Descent by Nick Sweet

I'm stuck at a bad intersection, longest red light in town I absently tum the radio up and roll the window down

On the curb, six feet away, I try to process who I saw
Can't help thinking "Wizard of Oz," Scarecrow minus the straw

I know who he is without looking, flash back to our Little League days
When he was a slick-fielding shortstop, while I played a smooth second base

He' d chosen high-stakes poker as his highway to high-roller dreams Sadly he lost the ranch and his soul with debts he could never redeem

A diamond flush beat his two pair, triggered his steady decline
His bleak abstract: drugs and despair, WILL WORK FOR FOOD says his sign

Relieved he did not recognize me, I stare straight ahead and relax
But quickly recall how he intervened in a frightening schoolyard attack

He halted a battle I would have lost, allowed me to save face and skin James Taylor plays on the radio, reminding me You've got a friend

I hastily reach for my wallet, selecting my highest bill,
Extending my hand, averting my eyes, he takes it but stands very still

Finally he says, "Thank you, Larry," I reply, "You're welcome, Fred." As I wave, raise my window, hit the gas and run the red

2017 Poetry Youth Thirteen+ Honorable Mention: Objet D' Art by SR Grosslight

Mr. Grosslight lives in Playa del Rey and doesn't drive much anymore. He has been a packaging designer and consultant, a senior peer counselor, a student and teacher of epistemics, and a Sufi guide.

Bone-white china
Slim, fragile body
Swan's neck
She pours a constant stream
into his bowl.
Carefully.
He washed his hands,
His face—
Motioning impatiently
for more.

Drained,
she wonders about forever—
fears eternity in a glass case.
Desperate,
she dreams of the pure clay—
longs to feel again
intense heat

Short Story: Falling Down the Stairs by Terry O'Conner

Terrance, a psychotherapist who has treated people with multiple personalities, recently moved from the East Coast to Ojai. "Falling Down the Stairs" is excerpted from a novel in progress about a young and lonely psychotherapist from a dysfunctional family who meets the challenge of his life in Diana, a beautiful but tortured woman with multiple personalities.

Excerpt from *Falling Down the Stairs*, a novel in progress: It's late. Charlie, a young psychotherapist whose client has multiple personalities, has learned that she was so drowsy in his office earlier because she had overdosed on a nonlethal medication. Now she has filled a prescription for a lethal one, and she hung up when he called her. He rushes to her apartment.

***

After a heart-pounding minute, she came to the door, her dark hair spilling over the shoulders of a scarlet silk robe. She looked tired and exasperated but to his relief, she let him in.

"I'm sorry," he said, "I don't usually make house calls, but you overdosed. I don't want it to happen again, and I need the Imipramine."

She raised an eyebrow. "Feeling blue, are we?"

"I want the Imipramine."

"What you want. What you want. Is that what this is all about?"

"To whom am I speaking?"

"Hey, this is my house. To whom am *I* speaking?"

"I'm Charlie. I'm the guy who doesn't want you to give up. I'm the one who doesn't want you to die."

"Well, it's not your life, is it Charlie?"

She led him to the kitchen in her bare feet and motioned him to have a seat on one of the red-cushioned stools at the tall, white table. "What would you like?" she asked.

"I'd like to speak to whoever took the overdose."

She gave him a wry smile. "I meant coffee or tea?"

He smiled back, genuinely amused. "Whatever you're having."

"Tea, then."

She prepared the teas with her back to him, heating them in the microwave. On the counter closest to him Charlie noticed a sharp-looking paring knife. This was a decidedly different environment than his office. He couldn't see what she was doing with the tea, and he imagined her dumping a dozen Imipramine in his.

She set a steaming mug in front of him and sat on the stool on the other side of the circular table. The mugs were yellow, dotted with red ladybugs. They matched the toadstool shaped placemats covered with cute lady bug families. He was surprised by the domesticity. From what he had seen the place was quite neat, neater than an unexpected guest would have found his apartment.

"Okay," she said.

"Okay, what?"

"You wanted to talk to me."

"You're the one who overdosed on Serax?"

"It's not very good. The Imipramine, I hear, is better."

"More deadly. Can I ask your name?" Charlie asked.

"Fire."

"When did you come into the system, Fire?"

211

"A long, long time ago."

"As a child."

"As a wee lass."

"What part of the system are you from?"

"I'm a part of Azazel. I would think you'd know that."

At this point he didn't care how she fit in. He was feeling at a disadvantage on her home ground. He was asking the questions he usually asked of new alters to establish the same sense of therapeutic relationship in her home that prevailed in his office. She was, however, gradually leaning forward as they spoke, and with the neck of her robe open it was becoming an effort not to look down it.

"What's your function in the system?"

"What do you think it is?" Her tone continued to be slightly mocking.

He gave a casual shrug. "I don't think it's to knock yourself off."

"Not me, no."

"Then who?"

"Wimpy Diana." She pointed at him and smiled. "That would get rid of you, too, wouldn't it?"

"No," he said, "that would get rid of you. You share the same body."

"I don't think so. I don't think you know as much as you think you do. You worry about a little dog." She made a dismissive gesture. "It's nothing."

That stopped him. Lilith had sobbed that afternoon about her father brutally killing Blackie in front of her when she was a child. Just what in the hell was he into here? "Why do you say that?" he asked.

"Because it's true, honey-pie, because it's true."

With that she leaned forward enough he had to lean back and study his lady bug family. He began to realize how vulnerable he was, alone in the middle of the night in the home of a barely-dressed female client, a very attractive one at that. She wasn't the only one in danger here. "I think I need to speak to Diana."

"What's the matter, hon, I thought you wanted to talk to the one who took the pills? You don't even know my function yet. Don't you want to know my function?"

A voice inside him cried, *Don't ask! Run for the door.* "What is it?" he asked.

"I'm disappointed. We value intelligence, you know, and I was told you were bright. I thought you'd know from my name."

"Fire."

"Yes, can't you imagine why my name is Fire?"

"Why?"

"You don't want to use your noodle tonight, do you?" She scooted her stool back from the table, lifted her left leg and propped her bare heel on the red cushion, exposing her leg entirely. Dark pubic hairs curled around the edge of her robe. She pointed with two fingers on her thigh. "Because I was made to take it." At the base of her thigh in a neat row were three round scars, cigarette burns. "There are more. Would you like to see them?"

"No. Thank you for asking. Your father did that?"

"My father taught me I could do anything."

"Yeah, I guess that's quite a feat, to take those burns."

To his relief she lowered her leg. "I never made a sound."

"That shows what strength you have when you're determined. But you do have the scars. There's only one body, and it can only take so much. You can't hurt any of the others without hurting yourself."

"Oh, but I can." She stood up moved toward the kitchen with her arm out for the paring knife. "I'll show you."

His stool crashed to the floor as he raced her, but she got to the knife before he did. He grabbed her wrist with both hands and arrested the movement of the knife. For a few seconds there was a very real chance one or both would be cut, but he was stronger and once he secured her wrist, the outcome was not in doubt.

They struggled silently as he tried to disarm her without hurting her. At some point Charlie realized she wasn't fighting as hard as she could, and after a while it became a bit of a dance in which she was no longer trying to free herself, but was continuing to struggle, so he had to keep holding her wrist. She had reached around him with her right hand trying to pull his right hand off her left wrist. She had him in a hug from behind. He could feel the warmth of her breasts pressed against his thin shirt. She needs this contact, he thought, and I'm enjoying it.

"Fire, time to let go."

For the briefest of moments, she rested her head against his back, then the knife clattered on the floor.

"Thank you." He took her by the wrist back to the table, sat her on a stool and held on to her wrist while he picked up his stool. "Look," he told her, "for all the hell you've been through the world is yet going to have good things for you. If you let that happen." He fished in his pocket and came up with his pen. "Let me show you something. You value intelligence so let me mark 'IQ' right here." He wrote the letters on the back of her hand. "Now switch to some alter you want to hurt, just for a moment, and look through her eyes and come back and tell me what you see."

She closed her eyes. The switch took more than a minute. Her robe had opened in the struggle and was still open. Before he turned his head away, some adolescent part of him was compelled to sneak a peek. Her breasts were lovely. Here he was, late at night in the apartment of a half-naked, lovely young client holding her hand, trying not to look at her. If the downstairs neighbor heard the falling stool and the wrestling and came to investigate or called the police, this might be hard to explain. There could be an alter in there who would cry rape.

She opened her eyes, startled, and gave him a frightened, bewildered look.

"It's okay," he said, "you're safe. Look at the back of your hand. What does it say?"

"IQ."

"Okay, let me talk to Fire again."

She closed her eyes and Fire came right in.

"You see," he said, "if you had cut her wrist you'd be bleeding now."

She pulled her hand away. "That's just a stupid trick."

"Stupid? I thought you believed in intelligence. Use yours. I wrote it on you and it's on her, too, and it will be on all of you until one of you washes it off. And you can't wash off a knife wound or an overdose."

She refused to acknowledge the truth of it, but she couldn't make an argument against it. He'd made his point, so he moved on. "Just for the sake of argument suppose there was a way to get rid of Diana, what then? What would you do?"

"Then I'd be in charge. I would have the power."

"Power to do what, abuse yourself? Let other people abuse you? You've got power and determination, but being able to tolerate pain isn't enough to get you through life. If you'd team up with Diana you'd find new uses for your power."

"I don't want to be a **$#%ing commercial artist."

"I don't know that you have to. I'll support you in finding something that better suits you, something you and Diana might do together."

"I don't need her."

"How would you make a living? Diana pays the rent."

She insisted there was no end to the things she could do, but when he challenged her she couldn't come up with any experience or skills that would serve her. Finally, she said, "Men will pay money for lots of things."

Charlie was concentrating on her face and attempting to fuzz out his peripheral vision. He wanted to ask her to close her robe, but he was afraid if he did so she'd recognize his vulnerability and take it off. "So that's one of your skills, sexual service?"

"I'll get Lilith to do it."

"So rather than be a commercial artist you'll be a pimp. You'll sell Lilith back into slavery. That's a good plan. Look, you're talking about getting power by acting like your father, is that the kind of power you want? Putting yourself at the mercy of men? Diana may be struggling, but she had the guts to leave Ray. She's not dependent on any man. She doesn't have to be anyone's slave to be powerful. She's capable of love. But that has its limitations, too. If she could combine with your energy and your anger, the two of you would be a powerful combination."

She sat quietly on the stool with her head down. "I don't want to combine," she said weakly. "I want to kill her."

He touched the IQ on the back of her hand. "That won't work."

"Well, I want to kill someone."

"I would, too, if I were you, but you can't kill someone inside without killing yourself, and you can't kill someone outside without going to jail. Think about how you can use that anger — maybe protecting other little girls, or some other way of righting the wrongs of the world. This evil can be transformed. What we need is a little time — for you to think over what I've said, to consider the IQ connection. Give me time to keep working with the family."

After a moment she nodded. She agreed not to hurt the body again without first talking to him face to face and to think about what he'd said. She noticed her robe was open and tied it. He called for Diana. She came in quickly pulled at the hem of her robe and put her arms over her chest. She wouldn't look him in the eye. "It's midnight," she said.

"Did you get that? Were you watching?" he asked.

She glanced at the back of her hand. "I think so, most of it."

"Are you okay?"

She nodded. "I have to get up at six o'clock."

He stood. "I was just leaving." He picked up the paring knife and put it on the counter. On his way out the door she called after him.

"Charlie, here." She handed him a bottle of capsules. Imipramine.

214

2017 Poetry Adult Third Place Winner: Daphne by Camille Boudreau

Camille is a student at Moorpark College who has a love of poetry that started at a very young age. In her free time, she hikes with her dog Jasper and spends hours in the library reading.

My love, he kneels and pours water around my base
He sips from the sacred flask
Pursed lips and a quick bob of an Adam's apple
I am trapped in a tree
A relief carved of laurel
A sigh adrift in a swaying of branches
My love, he brandishes a pocket knife
His right hand poised, a warrior indeed!
Carving back the cowl enfolding my face
Revealing the veneer beneath,
Perhaps it will next be olive skin,
A stray curl?
My love, he is patient
He does not trip on the roots about his feet
Others may use an axe!
Not he, a steady hand and warm heart
Are the tools of his trade
To peel back my bark.

2017 Poetry Adult Honorable Mention: The House Cat by Susan Chambers

Susan lives in Minnesota and was a practicing attorney for over thirty-four years, served as the Blue Earth County Court Referee, a judicial position, and now has a full alternative dispute practice. Her manuscript Good Thunder, Blue Earth was published by RiverPlace Press in March of 2016. She won the National Federation of State Poetry Society's Grand Prize on two separate occasions. She is published in numerous anthologies and was a winner for three years running in the MnLIT poetry competitions and 2015 and 2016 poetry competition by The Crossings of Zumbrota. Susan resides on a country acreage in Blue Earth County, with her husband Henry and one old cat.

In all the flurry of the divorce,
he never requested you, cat.
For eleven years you favored him,
a soft comfort against his dark winters.
He never mentions that his lap
feels chill now as he watches the news.
He never talks about missing your
welcome when you scratched at the door;
nor recollects how your Maltese coat let you
blend into dusk, your delicate call
heard long before your slight body appeared.
He doesn't speak of letting you out when first
grey light lured you from the quilt by his feet.
You still sleep where his body no longer
dents one side of the bed. You seem
content with the new flat surface,
not having that small mountain
to rest your whiskers against.
Neither of us rolls over
to fill the empty space.
We just huddle down
into familiar positions
under a sighing moon.
You don't seem to mind
the gap his going opened;
and I guess he never asks
how either of us is doing.

2017 Poetry Adult Honorable Mention: But You Forgot by Nanci Woody

Nanci lives in Rocklin, CA. Her novel, Tears and Trombones, *recently won the Independent Publishers medal (IPPY) for "Best Fiction in the Western Pacific Region." The novel is based on the true story of a Depression-era kid who wants nothing more than to become a classical musician. His boozy father, however, has other plans for his son. She has published short stories and poems online and in print anthologies. She is also an amateur photographer and loves to draw and paint.*

My lovely mom, you left behind.
Behind. You left. My lovely mom
who never wore a golden band
who never held her husband's hand.

> My lonely mom, you left bereft.
> Bereft. You left. My lonely mom
> who longed for you, eyes wet with tears,
> who longed for you, heart filled with fear.

A bastard child you left behind.
Behind. You left. A bastard child
who never saw her father's face,
who never knew her rightful place.

> Your bastard child. Did you forget?
> Forget. Did you? Your bastard child
> who longed for love but had it not,
> who longed for you. But you forgot.

Poetry: Litany To Democracy by Maxine Landis

Maxine earned her Bachelor of Arts degree from Antioch University where she worked as a volunteer for Project InterAct at Morningside High School with the Inglewood School District. She has published nine chapbooks. While in the graduate program at CSULB, she was chosen for the Santa Monica Writers' Program and the previous year was accepted at UC Davis, "Art of the Wild" Writers' Program at Squaw Valley. She is a long-time member of the VCWC. She is married and has four grandchildren. She published a book called Wildflowers *and* Weeds, *as well as many anthologies and has a children's book, titled* Argonauts Adventures.

From this war that isn't a war daily they die, coming
home in body bags stacked to the sky.
0, freedom and democracy
do not forsake the human race.

From this war that isn't a war daily they lie, telling us
stand firm, don't cry.
0, freedom and democracy
do not forsake the human race.

From this war that isn't a war
daily we are losing billions of bucks, that could change luck,
feed the world, 0, freedom and democracy
do not forsake for the buck, the human race.

From this war that isn't a war daily we lose those
loved
what we can choose.
0, freedom and democracy do not lose the
human race.

From this war that isn't war, How do we as
humans wrest with this terrorist unrest?
0, freedom and democracy
do not forsake the human race.

2017 Memoir First Place Memoir Winner: The Brownie Pan by Judy S. Richardson

Judy lives in Richmond, Virginia and is published in The Penman Review, Persimmon Tree, Lowestoft Chronicle, *and* Stories Through The Ages: Baby Boomers Plus-2017. *She won second place in the Living Springs Baby Boomer story contest for 2017. Her current writing focuses on refugees, especially the Ethiopian family she had mentored for two years. As a professor of Education, she wrote numerous articles for academic journals as well as three textbooks. The professional articles she enjoyed writing most were in narrative style, so she could focus on the story behind the research.*

My husband had anger issues before Vietnam, but afterwards, he exploded on a regular basis. Today we call it PSTD but in 1972, we weren't that sophisticated. After he threw the car seat harness across the room — with one of our boys still latched in — I gave him an ultimatum. "It's counseling or this marriage is over."

But counseling didn't suit him. Ten minutes into the first session, he stood up and left the office. I sat there for a minute, thinking maybe he'd gone to the toilet. Then we heard the car screech away. "Thanks," I told the counselor. "I think he made his choice."

On his way to wherever he went, my husband cleared out our bank account, consisting mainly of my National Defense Loan. The university found me a scholarship, so I could continue my graduate studies. I rented a house in Victory Village. The tiny two-bedroom boxes had been barracks in World War II, donated to universities to house soldiers cashing in on the GI bill. Like everyone living in this complex, I had children and no money. Unlike everyone else, though, no father lived in our house.

As I packed for the seventh time in four years, I considered throwing out the battered pan that had been a wedding present in 1965. It looked as worn out as I felt. Since I couldn't afford a new one and still had to cook for three, I kept it. I baked sheet-cake, cornbread, strudel, and brownies in that pan during the years we lived in Victory Village. Brownie mix took the place of scratch ingredients, but my boys didn't notice, and my pan sure didn't care.

Rhonda, her husband and their daughter, Donna, lived four houses away. Our floor plans were, of course, the same. Barracks don't vary much. But Rhonda's house always sparkled while mine was a mess. I didn't have time to clean; I was a mother and a student. Rhonda was just a mother. She stayed home all day. What did she know about the juggling I had to do? She had only Donna, and the children she watched, including my boys.

Donna was almost four, my older son's age. She had beautiful large brown eyes and coils of blonde curls. Her clothes were pressed and clean, no rumpled jeans from the dryer and stained t-shirts. My boys were rowdy, bounding into Rhonda's living room each morning.

I hardly ever saw Paul at home. He stayed on campus till all hours, past Donna's bedtime. Sometimes I passed him as I hurried across the campus to the library. He was not hard to spot: same curly blond hair as his daughter's, winsome look but hard eyes. He might nod to me, or not. Essentially, Rhonda and I were both single parents.

Rhonda had intended to go to college on a scholarship. But instead, she became pregnant and quickly married Paul. She couldn't graduate with her class. Someone else got to be Valedictorian. Now Paul was the one studying for a PhD. His mother was footing his university bill, but she did not foot the bill for Rhonda and Donna, because they had come so close to ruining her son's brilliant future.

"Someday," I told her, "it'll be your turn." She didn't look convinced.

Since Rhonda's grocery budget was tighter even than mine, I offered to make brownies for Donna's fourth birthday party. But, by the time I had the boys in bed and studying done, I realized my pan looked none too clean. I should have scrubbed it. I convinced myself that the crustiness wouldn't show after the batter rose. At midnight, that seemed reasonable.

The morning of her birthday, Donna told me her daddy would be home in time for her party. I promised I would be too. I left my boys and the brownies and scurried off to campus. After class, I went by the library. Paul was lounging with friends on the steps. I halted, surprised. He looked up, nodded while lifting a lazy hand, then started to turn away. I asked if he had already been to the party.

"What party? Oh, crap. I forgot. Well, too late now."

"She'll be so disappointed."

"Who, Rhonda?"

"No, Donna will be disappointed. She was so happy, telling me how you would come home especially for her party."

"Yeah, well, can't help it now. Tell Rhonda my class ran overtime. I got busy studying for a test and forgot."

I stared. I wanted to punch him, the scumbag.

But all I said was, "I can't do that for you."

As I walked away, I heard embarrassed laughter from his friends. He drawled, "Doesn't bother me. She believes anything I say anyhow."

I was back by 5:00 PM, but the party was over. The house was quieter than it should have been. Rhonda met me at the door, peering beyond me.

"You haven't seen Paul, have you?" No way I was going to tell her.

She handed me the brownie pan. It sparkled. I told her she'd made a mistake. No way that could be my pan.

"No, it just needed a good scouring."

Now who was the scumbag? Rhonda was crying. I tucked the pan under my arm and stared at my feet. "I'm really sorry. I didn't mean to make extra work for you."

"Paul didn't make it to the party; I haven't even heard from him. She's just a little girl and she doesn't understand."

We sat together on the porch for a while. I held her hand. There wasn't anything I could say. I'd broken my promise to Donna. I wanted to punch Paul.

***

I packed the brownie pan when we moved out. I was headed to a good job teaching at a nearby college, a nicer house and a steady paycheck. To research for my dissertation, I often traveled to the university on Saturdays. Usually I stopped by to visit Rhonda and Donna. The time between trips lengthened until, one Saturday, they were gone. Moved out. I don't know where she went. I think of her often, keeping her life neat while she waited for her turn. I hope she is happy today. I hope she finally got her chance to graduate from college, with top honors.

I can't throw this brownie pan away. We are both relics now, having acquired dents and scratches over thirteen moves and forty-five years.

2017 Memoir Second Place Winner: Of Guns, Pigs, and Flies by Christina Steiner

Christina Steiner lives in Ventura, California. She spends her time away from the computer with her partner, two daughters, two grandchildren, four dogs and a horse. She introduces children through enchanting stories to the amazing natural world.

The shot rang through the air. I'd expected the first shot, but not the gunfire that followed.

Was there serious trouble other than the killing of one wild boar? The air stopped breathing. The birds halted their songs. An eerie silence settled over the vast expanse of the swamp and the fields beyond.

I looked through the screen door of the wooden hut on stilts, sixteen feet above ground. Flies settled and resettled on the mesh. Beyond the door, the balcony led to a rickety stairway. Though ramshackle, the hut had survived the Six-Day War of 1967 and eight months earlier the Yom Kippur War. The Golan Heights rose to the east.

When the birds resumed their activities, I returned to preparing breakfast for the Israeli crew. Each morning we brought fresh bread, eggs, and vegetables for breakfast. Dry food was stored in the refrigerator, not for the cold but to be safeguarded against vermin.

I sliced tomatoes and cucumbers and tossed them into the salad bowl. Physical activity always calmed my nerves. With my bare hand, I caught a stray fly that had snuck into the room and opened the screen door wide enough to set the creature free. The Israelis laughed, the first time they'd seen me catch and release flies.

***

Two months earlier, I'd joined a group of young people to volunteer in a kibbutz. At 20 years old, I'd finished my apprenticeship and wanted to travel before starting a career. Having little money, Israel was my best option. Working in a kibbutz meant free lodging and food. Israel sounded exotic. The country was rich in history and religion. It had two deserts, the Negev and the Sinai. I'd never seen a desert. The Sinai Peninsula was new to Israel. It had been captured during the Six-Day War along with the West Bank, the Gaza Strip, and the Golan Heights.

Kibbutz Ami-Ad, in the upper Galilee, was my assignment. The alfalfa fields this kibbutz managed were located 15 miles north of Ami-ad, banking the Jordan River. We drove there before dawn, passing grapefruit, avocado, and lemon orchards. Layers of clothes protecting us from the early morning chill were peeled off as the day progressed until we wore tank tops and shorts covered in sweat and dirt.

I'd gotten used to machine guns hanging on kibbutzniks' shoulders like extra appendages. During dinner in the mess hall, Uzis leaned on the chairs next to their owners, in cars they lay on the floorboard, and in homes, they graced the coffee tables like giant knickknacks - ready to be used at a moment's notice.

I was of the mindset that all violence should be avoided. My sympathies lay equally with the Arabic and the Jewish population. Mothers cry on both sides for their fallen children. That thought alone should be enough to eliminate war. I was young enough to believe that love cures everything.

This ideology was a touchy subject. Moshe, the kibbutz Casanova with his muscled body and two-inch afro, worked alongside me in the alfalfa fields. One evening, after dinner, his mood dipped into darkness. I asked him why.

"You wouldn't understand." His voice became abrasive. "You never had to collect pieces of your friends blown up by mines. Leave me alone."

I tried to hug him; he shoved me away and walked into the night. The next day, Moshe was his jovial self again.

These twenty-something men and women had seen and done things that were beyond my comprehension. Moshe and most young Israelis lived for the moment, taking advantage of every opportunity without thoughts of consequences. Their urgency to accumulate experiences stemmed from thinking that they lived on borrowed time with little chance for a future. War was in their blood, crowding their sleep with nightmares. They questioned why they walked this earth while their friends were dead.

On one of our early morning rides, a stray dog crossed the road. The van swerved. The driver hit the brakes and stopped. He grabbed his machine gun and killed the dog.

I dared to ask. "What did you do that for?"

"The dog should not be on the street."

"But why did you shoot it?"

"Because I can," Victor said. "Don't you worry about it!" His eyes were hard as steel. "If you've seen as many friends die in your arms as I have, you don't fret over the death of a mongrel dog."

The discussion ended; my response strangled in my throat. I'd grown up in safety. The wars had cloaked these young people's hearts in iron.

This morning, Moshe, Victor, and crew had discussed the wild boar wreaking havoc in the fields, flattening and trampling sections. They vowed to take care of the problem today. I didn't dare suggest a different solution and hoped the boar had moved on during the night. They'd told me to stay inside the hut, so as not to be in the line of fire.

***

Finally, I heard booted footsteps on the stairs. To my relief, the voices belonged to the crew. I dished out eggs, hummus, and salad. Victoriously they described the successful hunt. Not much of a hunt though. They surprised the wild sow ... and her six babies, all of them fast asleep after a night of foraging. That explained the multiple gun shots. They'd kept one of the piglets alive.

Later, I walked to where some of the dead pigs were hung to drain their blood. A few of them were skinned already, their stomachs and innards in a heap on a tarp next to their severed heads, sightless eyes clouding over, tongues limply hanging from their mouth.

***

Moshe's arms were buried in the body cavity of the sow, extracting the prime cuts. Victor finished skinning the next baby, an assembly line in an outdoor-makeshift butchery. Since the knives didn't have the sharpness to cut clean, the meat tore. The whole crew worked, oblivious to the grotesque sights and smells – a job to be done, nothing to be wasted.

The heat swelled with every passing minute. Blood and flies were everywhere. The sound of a hatchet cracking bones mixed with the buzzing of insects. The smell of death mingled with cut alfalfa and tractor grease.

I forced myself to watch. I loved to eat meat. I knew animals had to be slaughtered to fill my plate. But I ... I didn't have to kill them. Someone else did it for me. I'd never dwelled on the specifics. The reality was overwhelming, my hypocrisy undeniable. My stomach turned on itself, my legs weakened. I staggered behind the outhouse and retched and retched until nothing was left.

Jewish people consider pork unclean. Our Israeli crew gifted the meat to the neighboring town of Palestinians. Since Muslims don't eat pig meat either I assume they were Christians. The discards were left in the dump area for scavengers.

The live piglet was kept in the kibbutz, cared for and used as a teaching tool for the children.

***

That day haunts me. I'm baffled at my own desire to still eat meat ... but I do. The shock of seeing dead animals prepared for human consumption and my single mindedness that all life is precious even if it's just a fly seems conflicting. Humanity is full of controversy, ready to satisfy our own needs or wants. I learned life is never just black and white, rather many shades of gray.

2017 Memoir Third Place Winner: Money by Susan Jones

VCWC member Susan, writes under the name Susan Zannos. She has written biographies for children and young adults for Mitchell Lane publishers, a mystery novel for Walker and Co., and a study of human types for Samuel Weiser. These books are available on Amazon.com. Susan Jones is a retired college English instructor.

The summer I was thirteen, I picked tomatoes in Sammy Blair's tomato field down on the flat rich land near the river. Sammy was a Scotsman with the legendary parsimonious nature of his countrymen. He was a hunting and fishing crony of my father, who mentioned that his friend was hiring young pickers. I begged to be allowed to work for Mr. Blair. There weren't a lot of employment opportunities for thirteen-year-old girls, and I was desperate to earn some money.

My parents could not, or at least certainly would not, buy the clothes I absolutely had to have when school started. I had to have at least one pleated skirt, and I had to have cashmere sweaters. Some items, such as Ship 'n Shore white cotton blouses, were in a price range that I could convince my mother to buy, but cashmere sweaters were completely out of the question unless I could somehow earn the money myself.

My father tried to discourage me by pointing out how difficult the work was, how pickers had to bend over, and how hot it would be, and how few rest breaks there would be, and how I wouldn't be shown any favoritism because he was Mr. Blair's friend, but I wouldn't give up insisting that I could do the work. Finally, my father gave in, under one condition: "If you start," he said, "you have to finish. There'll be no quitting when you get tired of it."

And so I began a most curious three weeks in August. My father got me up at 5:00 AM, and I got into my work clothes, jeans and boots and a ragged shirt, took the lunch my mother had packed in an old tin lunch box, and was standing out on the corner by 5:30 when the truck picked me up. The other pickers were from the west end of town, so I was the last one picked up and we were in the field by 6:00.

There were only six or seven pickers, not the same ones every day since many quit, some without making it through even one day. Sammy's employees were for the most part not experienced field workers, who would have asked higher wages than he offered. One of my colleagues was there every day, however, an older German woman who spoke only broken English and not much of that. She must have been at least in her late fifties, and maybe over sixty, and she never stopped working. No matter how hard I tried, I couldn't keep up with her.

The days had the oddly timeless quality of nightmares in which one struggles against some unsolvable dilemma, a monster that has one trapped, a pit with slippery sides that lean in, a row of tomatoes that stretches endlessly into blinding, burning sunlight while sweat runs in itchy rivulets down the back and under the arms and the pain in the back grows gradually worse. And all through those days the only indication of time passing at all was the sight of the German woman's broad rump moving gradually farther and farther ahead of me as we both picked tomatoes, filling flats that were left in the rows for the foreman to mark with our initials and stack for the tractor to pick up.

On the second day three high school boys gave it up after our lunch break and started a tomato fight, pelting each other and shouting and jumping across the rows. That was the last we saw of them. They didn't even get a ride home in the truck but had to hitchhike back to town. Without even stopping to watch the altercation between boys and foreman, the German woman kept picking and got even farther ahead of me. Three times each day I got to start even with her: at 6:00 in the morning, at 9:00 after our fifteen-minute morning break, and at noon after lunch. My preoccupation with the German woman was a kind of rope that pulled me on through the days. There was no question of quitting, of course, no agony of heat and pain that could cause me the shame of breaking a promise made to my father. And I didn't quit.

The three weeks of picking ended at last and Mr. Blair confessed his surprise that I had lasted the entire time. I made $50 and started ninth grade with an acceptable wardrobe.

That fall a movie, *Rock Island Trail,* had its premiere in the Quad Cities. Movie premieres were not frequently celebrated in these mid-western cities; I suspect this was an isolated instance. The film combined the format of a western shoot-'em-up with the history of the Rock Island Lines railroad, or so the reviews indicated. The movie was not particularly successful, and I never saw it.

The premiere was of interest to the students of Sudlow Junior High School because the celebration included a window painting contest, and the participants would get an afternoon out of classes to decorate store windows downtown with scenes that we imagined might be in the movie. In art class we drew lots to determine which store window each participant would paint.

I drew the side window of Abraham's Women's Clothing Store on the corner of Third and Gaines Street downtown. The afternoon that we had for painting was a cool October day, and since I was painting on the side window, the wind from the river blew in gusts up Gaines. I took frequent breaks to walk along Third Street to see what others were painting, join the small groups that were gathering to critique paintings, take breaks with others to have Cokes at the lunch counter in Woolworth's. Nonetheless most of us got a window painting more or less completed.

My painting was of a cowboy on a rearing pinto horse, with railroad tracks running along in the background and a train coming in the distance. The horse wasn't bad. I was crazy about horses and spent a lot of time sketching horses rather than taking notes in classes. The train wasn't good. If it hadn't been for the tracks and the steam coming out it would have been hard to identify as a train rather than, perhaps, a wall, or a line of low buildings. But the painting was finished after a couple of hours of alternately painting and enjoying downtown Davenport, and we were all herded onto the bus to go back to the school.

A week later the prizes for window painting were announced in *The Daily Times.* I won first prize. The prize was $50.

I had not yet studied logical fallacies, so I did not recognize the trap of hasty generalization that my thinking fell into. And I don't know that it would have made any difference. The fact that these two very different experiences resulted in exactly the same amount of money, that the three weeks of suffering from heat and sweat and dirt and aching back while picking tomatoes yielded $50, and two hours of play with paints yielded $50, seemed to be an important message about work and money and time. The message was about the advisability of doing what is fun to do and letting the practical details take care of themselves. I never changed my mind about that basic precept.

2017 Memoir Honorable Mention: I Can Do This! Or Can … I? by Shawn Simon

We are all different. But some are extra different. Shawn Simon is one of those. She was born with one arm. Living in a world designed for two hands has not been easy, but she has learned to rise above. Now she wants to share her stories of challenges and triumphs to help others with differences on their journey. She believes this thing called life is more enjoyable when we realize we are not alone.

"Oh, hell no!" I said to Lisa as I looked up at the enormous waterfall in front of me. Panic crept in, making my scalp tingle and my skin shiver. My hand shook and sweat. Climb that? All the way to the top? No way!

We were in Ocho Rios, a little port town in Jamaica. Lisa and I were on a cruise to the Caribbean, and one shore excursion was an opportunity to climb this waterfall. I have no idea how Lisa talked me into this. Adrenaline junkie is not me, even as a child. People often assumed I couldn't achieve great feats because I had only one and a half arms. But the truth had little to do with that. Yes, having one arm added to my fears because it did make doing things harder. But for the most part the fear and trepidation resided in my head. Here I stood, in my twenties, and not much had changed. I trembled as the roar of the water deafened me.

On the cruise ship, Lisa and I heard about the Dunn's River Fall, a terraced 180-meter mountain waterfall that roared to the river below. That's almost two football fields high! People actually climbed to the top of this waterfall. Climb a waterfall? I'm afraid of water. I love to look at it and be near it, but I'm not a big fan of going in it. "No, no! It's not so bad." The passengers said, waving their hands in the air, brushing away my silly fears. "It has wide steps on either side, built into the rock. It's perfectly safe!" Sure it is. As I looked up at the rush of water spilling over big boulders, snaking its way around the mountain, I thought, *No way! Not gonna happen.* But here I stood in front of this pounding water, and I knew I couldn't chicken out.

I watched as lines and lines of people, all holding hands in single file, slowly climbed up the steps on either side of the cascading water pouring down into the lagoon below. *Wait! Holding hands? How's that going to help me? I can only hold hands on one side! One side would be all on its own, left to fight for itself.*

I pictured myself falling on one side, with no way to hang on to anyone nearby, while Lisa held on to my one hand for dear life, trying desperately to pull me back on to the steps.

This is the craziness fears conjure up. I shared my irrational thoughts with Lisa who came up with a perfect solution. She knew I would never ask a stranger to hold my half arm, so she said she'd wrap her hand around my upper half left arm, and I would hold hands with a stranger.

I let out a deep breath and looked again at the people slowly making their way up the waterfall. I noticed all the middle-aged people and all the young kids, and I chastised myself for my anxiety.

Taking a deep breath, I said, "Okay, let's do this!"

Lisa and I found our place in line and waited for our turn to start the treacherous climb.

As we got closer, anxiety crept in again. I shoved it aside, reminding myself that children and old people were making this climb. I felt ridiculous. I stuffed my fears down and inched forward.

When I stepped on to the first step, covered in water, surrounded by trees, I thought, *This is fun! It's not slimy or slippery at all. My water sandals are gripping the surface of the rock steps. I can do this.*

We inched our way up the sides of the waterfall, splashing through the trickling water, with trees brushing against us as we trudged onward. At the cliff, I shook from head to toe, and I laughed out loud. I wanted to shout to the world, "I did it! I survived!" Pride burst inside me.

I stepped off the top of the waterfall, onto solid ground, and saw the cruise ship employee waiting to congratulate each of us before we headed to the bus and back to the ship. Bouncing on my toes like a little girl, I announced, "I did it! With only one arm, I climbed all the way to the top!"

"That's great!" he said. "Just last week a guy did it with one leg!" And just like that my feelings of triumph were deflated. With one leg? And here I was so scared, so fearful? I stared at Lisa, mouth hanging open, with no clue what to say to that. I could see her stifling her laughter, and then we both burst into peals of laughter.

It's all relative, isn't it? One leg, one arm, no arms, no legs, one of each. A reminder that things can always be harder and more challenging. We are all on our own journey, and for me, climbing that waterfall was quite an accomplishment.

2017 Memoir Honorable Mention: Summer of Love? by Bob Calverley

Bob has worked as a newspaper reporter, writer, editor and public relations consultant. He is the author of a Sixties novel, Purple Sunshine: Sex & Drugs, Rock & Roll, War, Peace & Love, *and a murder mystery,* Hyperventilated Underwater Blues. *He lives in Newbury Park, CA.*

Summer, 1967, the summer I graduated from Michigan State University, the Summer of Love.

I had to take two courses in summer school because I'd switched my major to journalism from pre-med, shattering my parents' dreams. But I was determined to make a living as a writer. So it wasn't until mid-July on a sunny Sunday afternoon that I was finally rolling down I-96 in my brand new forest green Plymouth Barracuda Formula S on my way to Detroit to start work the next day as an editor at the American Concrete Institute. Okay, it wasn't my dream job. Horrific boredom loomed, but it paid well. I had car payments.

Oh yeah, I'd been assured that the publications I'd be editing were so vital to the nation's building codes that I'd be exempted from the draft. I really wanted to believe the manager who told me that. Every morning, the *Detroit Free Press* had more front-page stories about the Vietnam War. And the TV evening news was even worse. Before switching to journalism my reading tended to J.R.R. Tolkien and Philip K. Dick. My only TV was *Star Trek*. I'd been paying attention to the news for the journalism classes. We were comparing television and print news and discussing how pictures changed emphasis. My professors thought TV was more volatile and superficial. They said you had to read newspapers to get the real story. But the pictures seemed real to me, too real, and I was starting to worry. My student draft deferment had ended.

Since then, I've learned that it was far worse than either newspapers or TV told me in 1967. According to the American War Library online database, 449 Americans were killed in action in Vietnam during June 1967, followed by 458 in July, 466 in August, and 460 in September.

Some Summer of Love.

In 1967 all I knew was that a lot of my friends had been drafted. That meant the Army, usually the infantry, or even worse, the Marines. Some guys enlisted in the safer havens of the Navy or the Air Force, or they joined the National Guard. A few lucked out and failed draft physicals. That summer, I suddenly discovered a new appreciation for building codes. I pondered ways to add poetic verve to dry technical descriptions of concrete creep and shrinkage. After learning that you couldn't edit in Levis 501s, I acquired a suit and tie from J.C. Penney.

Approaching Detroit, a column of thick black smoke rising over the city drew my attention from the rock and roll on the radio. It was a great time for rock and roll. The Doors, Jefferson Airplane and Van Morrison had hits that July. But it was the Beatles who provided the soundtrack for the Summer of Love. *Sergeant Pepper's Lonely-Hearts Club Band* was released at the end of May. A month later, the Beatles, clad in their iconic Sergeant Pepper regalia, recorded the final take of "All You Need Is Love" in the first worldwide live television broadcast. The single, which wasn't on the Sergeant Pepper album, rocketed up the charts in July. John Lennon's universal message of love resonated with me then, and still does today.

With the smoke looking more and more serious, I skipped around the radio dial for news. A violent civil disturbance had erupted in Detroit early that Sunday morning triggered by the police raiding an unlicensed inner city drinking establishment where people had gathered to celebrate the return of two soldiers from Vietnam.

Luckily, when I got to the apartment I'd rented, there was no sign of trouble other than the acrid smell of smoke. Next day, my new co-workers, all of whom were white, angrily complained about their declining property values and "those people" they saw on TV. None saw any of the violence first hand. No one knew any of 43 who died or any of the more than 1100 who were injured. After it was over, a few of us drove down to 12th Street to where it had started. Ten years later when I was working for the *Free Press*, you could still find the charred rubble in garbage-strewn vacant lots where many of the 2,000 burned buildings once stood.

Not a Summer of Love in Detroit.

My first work assignment was to edit several dozen Japanese technical reports on concrete that had been poorly translated into English. My supervisor said that the institute wanted to publish a special edition of the collection as soon as possible. I got to work. I bought another suit. I made my first car payment.

There was trouble in other cities that summer. Only a week before Detroit's civil disturbance, 26 people died in Newark. During that long hot summer, there were well over 100 "race riots," as they were termed at the time. President Lyndon Johnson established the Kerner Commission to investigate the causes. I was only vaguely aware of this. I'd stopped watching the news on television, listening to records on my stereo instead. I could finally afford to buy more albums. Cream and Jimi Hendrix played the Grande Ballroom. The Detroit Tigers flirted with winning a pennant. I was in love with a girl on the other side of Michigan, a couple of hours away on the freeway. Gas was 35 cents a gallon.

Near summer's end, I was ordered to report for my draft physical. My supervisor, the same manager who'd said I'd be exempted from the draft, was quite upset. But he told me not to worry; he was going to write to my local draft board. At least I got to take a day off to go to Fort Wayne for the physical. I'd finished with the Japanese papers, but a fresh batch had arrived, enough for a second volume.

Summer ended. The Tigers faded to second place. The fall colors around Detroit were spectacular. So was my health according to my draft board. I was told to report for induction in spite of the danger this posed to the nation's building codes. Standing in line to receive my service number, Johnny Cottrell taps me on the shoulder. We'd gone to school together for two years at Michigan Tech in the Upper Peninsula. Both of us were drafted the same day. We entered the U.S. Army one serial number apart and had adjacent bunks in basic training. He opted to re-enlist for an extra year and take the "shake 'n bake" course for sergeant's stripes. With a pregnant wife, he needed the extra pay. On his first combat mission in Vietnam, an errant rocket from a helicopter gunship took his life. The Army sent me to an assault helicopter company where a dozen more of my friends would die in my year in Vietnam.

Turned out that the most important skill I'd learned in sixteen-years of schooling was how to type. I became the company clerk. And my professors might have been right about television. By the time I got home, many of my co-workers, along with thousands of others, had fled Detroit. The *Free Press* won a Pulitzer Prize. Somehow, I managed car payments on Army pay.

If few of us actually went to San Francisco to weave flowers in our hair, we still tried. For one glorious summer we pushed back with love against the violence and bigotry.

We could use another Summer of Love today.

2017 Memoir Honorable Mention: Boys and Girls by Gail Field

Gail grew up in Colorado where the air smells of pine and snow in winter is a welcome invitation to build snowmen on the front lawn. Now Gail is a Co-Organizer of the Conejo Valley Writers, a Meetup.com group that convenes monthly in Thousand Oaks.

At the table over tonight's dinner, I put my hands on my growing belly and talk about this new one coming. My husband Kenny looks up from his crab salad. "Well, it's only about a month more, isn't it?"

"Yep." I nod and smile at him, happy to be having a child.

"I do hope it's a boy," he says. "What do you think?"

"I do, too, if that's what you want."

Kenny leans back in his chair, looking satisfied and takes a bite of the salad.

My mind wanders, considering the future. I'm not sure how I would do with a little girl. All my life I was surrounded by boys – father and two brothers, Gary and Tim, doing their boy things – whooping it up, going to ball games, fighting to see who was the strongest. Mom and I were not a match for them. It seemed that whenever a decision was to be made, one of the boys or Dad made it. My mother held back, tentative as she usually was, and the boys had their way as if it were promised them at birth.

I learned to do as my mother did – to take the back seat, to say "no, thank you" when offered the last piece of cake, to go to a ball game instead of to the city for shopping. The boys always held sway. They learned to express themselves, take chances, abandon caution, and assert their position. Mom was on the side of acquiescence, of keeping the peace. In those days I followed in her footsteps as the only way I knew for a girl like me.

In summertime we took our vacations in the Rocky Mountains, an hour's drive from our home. We loved the brisk mountain air, the aroma of the pines and the clear blue skies. The year I turned thirteen, we rented a cabin next to a rushing stream in Estes Park. My dad loved to fish and often came home with enough for a good trout dinner.

"Come on, guys, we're going fishing," said Dad, waving his hand to include me.

I looked at Mom and she nodded. "Go ahead. You all have fun!"

Dad, my brothers and I took off in the station wagon and made a stop at the bait shop. "Fish are biting this year," they told us. We bought live worms and shiny lures designed especially for trout.

"We're all set," said Dad. "Let's catch us a good dinner!"

Dad found a flat spot alongside a rushing stream where we stopped and unloaded our fishing gear. My brothers and I prepared our rods with the bright trout lures and worms and chose our positions along the stream.

I planted myself on the bank and watched the glistening water as it rushed over the boulders. When I threw my fishing line out over the water, it wavered in the breeze, then settled down into the current. I watched and waited. When there were no nibbles, I tried again and again.

Finally, I felt a tug, saw the pole dip, and my father called out, "You got one! Pull it up! Pull it up!" Dad rushed over to track every movement of my line. I held tight and pulled the line just enough to make sure the fish was hooked for good.

"Bring him in! Bring him in!" Dad shouted.

I gripped the pole and reeled in the line till I could see the fish come out of the water. It writhed on my line, my hook in its mouth, its rainbow scales shining.

"Good girl," my father said, beaming and puffing up as if he had caught the trout himself. The boys each caught one, too, but I smiled to myself; mine was the biggest one. At the end of our day, we proudly showed off our catch to Mother. She ooh-ed and ahh-ed like it was the first time she ever saw such a catch, and we basked in the glory of our successful expedition.

Mother and I were left to clean the fish and fry it over the old stove while Dad read the local paper and the boys took up their comic books.

My mother laid out the three fish on the cutting board. "Oh, these fish are beautiful," she said, "and this one is so big!"

"That's the one I caught," I tell her with a note of pride. I waited for her to ooh and aah some more, but she just shook her head. "Here, slice them open. Be careful of the knife."

I sliced each fish along the bones and cleaned all of them, while my face burned in shame. Should I not be bragging?

I handed the cleaned fish to my mother and she fried them up on the iron stovetop. At dinner we sat around the small kitchen table and Mom set down a plate of freshly fried fish in the center next to the potato salad.

Dad set his cowboy hat aside and looked at Mother, grinning. "A fine catch, wouldn't you say, Helen?"

"A fine catch indeed," she said, beaming across the table at my brothers. They drank it all in, each nodding and taking another bite.

Nobody mentioned my part in the expedition, so I kept my sense of satisfaction to myself. *That's the way it should be.* A girl has got to learn what it is to coexist with the boys, to balance herself on the tightrope between pleasing them and holding her own. Hanging tight and not falling.

I glance at my husband, rub my belly again and lean in. "Kenny," I say, a bit louder than necessary, "if we have a girl, she's going to keep up with you boys."

He looks at me a little puzzled, then nods and takes a swallow of wine. "What's for dessert?"

In Memoriam

Remembering VCWC Member Peter Pohl

By Nancy Aronson, step-daughter

Born in Austria in 1922, Peter and his mother were allowed to leave Nazi-occupied Austria after the death of his father because his mother's nurse's uniform had a swastika on it. In his 70s, Peter learned that all of his grandparents were Jewish, and they had converted to hide from the Nazis. Peter was 17 when he arrived in Los Angeles and moved in with relatives including his aunt, author Vicki Baum, who wrote a number of books, including *Grand Hotel*.

Peter entered the U.S. Navy and taught at the officers' school in Monterey. After the Navy, he attended UCLA where he received his degree in physics. He married Florence, who died in 1992 after 40 years of marriage.

He worked as an engineer until he was in his 80s, retiring more out of choice than necessity. In 1993 Peter met, Irene, who had also lost her husband in 1992. Peter was always busy. He wrote stories often and loved the VCWC. He read daily about current events and watched political news shows. He refused to use an e-book and insisted that a real book felt the way a book should.

He loved classical music – as a child in Austria, the teacher asked which one of the Strausses were still alive. Peter replied, "Richard Strauss." The teacher asked how he knew. He replied, "We had dinner with him last night." He also told the class that Thomas Mann had a mean dog.

Peter always had a sense of curiosity and wonder about the world which is probably why he lived so long. Even at the end, his mind was still sharp and aware. When it was decided that he should stop driving at night – he was still driving during the day – his step-daughter volunteered to drive him to his Writer's Club meetings. He was so excited about her participating in his Tuesday night monthly event that she didn't have the heart to tell him that she was just his driver and not a budding club member.

Peter lived almost 96 years. One of his doctors said his body could not keep up with his brain. Peter always had a smile and a story. When he started a story by saying – this is true, everyone knew it was going to be an untrue, but funny, story. He had a true love for life and shared it with all who were graced with his presence.

Peter's love for life will stay in our memories long after we have said goodbye to him.

2015 Memoir Third Place Winner: Freedom by Peter Pohl

Vienna, Austria was my home. When I was five years old we moved to Mairhofen, a small village in Tirol. The scenery was from *The Sound of Music*. Blueberries grew in the meadows, mine for the picking. In the forest, mushrooms grew near tree trunks. Cooked they were delicious, but you had to know the edible from the poisonous. This was farming country. Most farms had cows for milk and pigs for meat. When a pig was butchered we had bratwurst. In season, venison and game birds were available. Trout filled the streams.

My father was an engineer, working for a multinational construction firm. They built tunnels, bridges, and hydroelectric power plants. At the time, my father's job was building a power plant at the Achensee, a lake north of Mairhofen. His jobs always lasted a few years, then we had to move to a new location. We were always renters, not owners. One farm had a bedroom with bath for rent. We shared the living room and kitchen. My mother was an outstanding cook. The farmer's wife provided the food my mother cooked. We ate well.

Mairhofen had dirt roads. We walked everywhere. In the winter, the roads were covered with snow. Skis got us to school faster. Everybody skied in our valley, the Zillertal (Valley of the Ziller River). For the die-hard skiers there was the Hintertux glacier, with year-round snow. It reached the Italian border at the lofty Dolomite Mountains.

At age eleven, I skied well enough to join other teenagers in the Christmas celebration. On Christmas Eve, a horse-drawn sleigh took us up the mountain behind the church. We carried burning torches while skiing in serpentines down the mountain to church for midnight mass. Baked apples warmed our hands and souls.

My father's work at the power plant finished in June 1934. His new job was in Styria. Graz, the capitol, the Chicago of Austria. The "Erzberg" (Ore Mountain) had open-pit mining for iron ore. My father designed grading for tracks, bringing ore carts to the bottom of the mountain. The nearest village was Deutschlandsberg, a mining town with plenty of rentals.

In the summer of 1935, my father died after a long bout with cancer. My grieving mother decided to move back to Vienna. She had two older, married sisters with children my age. She needed family around her.

Sunday, March 12, 1938: The bloodless Anschluss of Austria by Germany was completed.

Monday, April 25th: Jewish students were ceremoniously kicked out of my school. Students and teachers stood at the exit calling out the Jews' names. Long-time hatred turned to physical violence. The kids were beaten while laughing teachers cheered. I could hardly believe when my name was called. Neither could my friends on the soccer team. They walked with me past the aggressors. I had been baptized in a Catholic church at birth. I knew my relatives were Jews, but I was a Catholic. Nazis didn't give a damn about my religion, only my heritage. By tracing back my parents' birth certificates, they found their Jewish grandparents.

While school was in session, I stayed in our apartment. I couldn't take the risk of being arrested as a truant. After school, weekends or vacation, I was on my bike around town as usual.

My mother worked as a nurse at the local hospital. They stamped a swastika on her diploma, a sign of acceptance. They never checked her lineage. Neighbors in our apartment house knew us as a young widow and her kid. We were safe for a while.

Our California relatives filed affidavits with the US government, guaranteeing that we would not become financial burdens if we emigrated to America. This was required for entrance into the US. The Nazi government did not allow emigrating Jews to take money or valuables out of the country, but Hitler wanted to get on good terms with Mussolini. He allowed us to pay for passage on Italian ships. We could afford only third class.

Three nights before our departure there was a knock on our door. I opened it and stared at an SS officer. He asked to see the furniture we advertised for sale. Our knees stopped shaking. He said he and his wife just rented an unfurnished apartment. They needed furniture. He liked ours and paid cash. We were allowed to use the money to upgrade our tickets on the cruise ship 'Rex' to first class. What a treat!

Our first glimpse of the Statue of Liberty brought tears of joy. We hugged each other. My Uncle Ernst Lert, who lived in NYC, met us at Ellis Island. We spent two days with him and Aunt Emma. Then came a long train ride to Los Angeles.

The Lert family owned a mansion in Pacific Palisades. Richard Lert was the conductor at the Hollywood Bowl. His wife, Vicki Baum, retained her maiden name which she made famous as a writer. Her novel *Grand Hotel* won an Oscar as Best Film of the year at its 1932 debut. They had plenty of room in their house for my mother and me. Their sons, Wolfgang, twenty-one and Peter, eighteen taught me to speak English and to drive a car. All our cars had manual transmissions: "three on the floor." I was an apt student.

In the fall of 1938, I started school at University High School in West Los Angeles. In the junior year, the college offered electives. I chose Print Shop. I set type one letter at a time. It broadened my vocabulary and improved spelling.

At the start of the second semester, my classmates bestowed on me the honor of leading the Pledge of Allegiance at every assembly. They chose me despite my faltering English, or maybe because of it. I was an immigrant, so appreciating the freedom I found, the love for America shined through my poor English and brought tears to many eyes.

One night at a party a man played the piano beautifully. He played Mozart's opera scores from memory, like a concert pianist. My mother sang the lyrics. He tried to trip her up by changing to a different opera. She followed him no matter what he played. He was a Viennese refugee. Love and music triumphed. He married my mother and together they moved into a small rental in Los Angeles.

I decided to stay with the Lert family. By fall of 1938, I received my driver's license. It was a long drive from Pacific Palisades to the Hollywood Bowl. My uncle hated driving. I was glad to drive. His car was a dark blue 1936 Packard Roadster, a classic.

Prominent artists and actors came to visit Vicki Baum. Legendary filmmaker Fritz Lang, Nobel Prize winning novelist, Thomas Mann, Greta Garbo, leading actress of *Grand Hotel*, villain actor, Peter Lorre and many more. I liked Peter Lorre.

One hot day in June after mowing the lawns, I decided to go for a swim. As I strolled out to the pool, I noticed a woman already swimming in the shallow end. I jumped into the deep end but kept bumping into the pool walls. I didn't open my eyes under water because the woman was naked. Eventually, I opened my eyes wide, exhaled slowly, and came up for air.

When I broke the surface, I said, "Hello," and Marlene Dietrich smiled at me.

And that's how I learned to open my eyes under water.

Poetry: Joy Dreams and Songs by Alvin Bernie Barnes

Alvin "Bernie" has authored three books and currently has other books in process. He is a WWII veteran (US Navy), and a former industry and consumer corporation sales person. He keeps active with hobbies, gardening, and family relationships. He is father of four, grandfather of six, and great grandfather of five.

Men, through the years, have penned
Sad thoughts of dim twilight;
Mourning loss of day's end
And comfort of daylight.
From sadness of lost day,
To turn heart's reveries,
They search for Spirit's way
And happy memories.
Would that they write of dawn.
Emotions of evening's
Melancholy withdrawn,
By joy, in the morning.

Poetry: Kingdom of Light by Alvin Bernie Barnes

Dawn broke suddenly,
like underwater swimmer breaks the water surface,
and then it cast bursts of light upon hills and waters;
first light reveals long tree shadows and crawls up higher
till it flashes against windows of lofty homes there.

The awakening
of the new day inspires me to be ready to start
and savor the gift of bright new page of life ahead;
every shadow now light filled, set and ready places
to begin life building in great day opened to me.

In bright light wonder,
my soul brought in humble awe of choices afforded
finds sense of creative ways and ideas of service;
my feet on firm ground and eyes lifted to highest view,
I see an awesome new day in my Kingdom of Light.

Short Story: The Fast Forward by Alvin Bernie Barnes

Athletic Director Bert Mason stood in the locker room of Highland College's football team. "Coach, you won't like it, but we are required to put Gil Meyre on the football roster and that's that," Bert said.

"I don't want to be responsible for injuries to someone that skinny and I won't play Meyre in a game," Coach Condi said.

"I sympathize with you," the AD said. "It's part of a scientific study headed up by Mrs. Meyre for a dissertation she is working on for the college and we have to do it. I received a memo that Mrs. Meyre will deliver Gil to practice and to home games."

Coach Condi frowned. "I'll get the gear and uniforms ready for Mrs. Meyre to pick up."

***

My name is Nicholas Dinth, known to the team as "Nick." I heard that unusual conversation I've related because I was assistant to coach Bob Condi and in charge of team conditioning, practice drills, and time trials, as well as the auditing of our playbook. Our team had been so-so in the past, but we hoped to continue a winning streak for Highland College this year. We were undefeated in the first four games that season, but we expected to have a real test the following week when we went up against Portage in an away game.

In the meantime, our team had given the tall, lanky player a new nickname. They call Gil Meyre "Bencher" because Coach had yet to call Gil's number.

Gil was not on any travel squad for away games. I asked Coach about that.

"Nick, I'm afraid to risk injuries unnecessarily," Coach said. "This is my first year at Highland. I'm trying to live down what happened at my last school where there was a nasty situation concerning an injury. In fact, I have a civil lawsuit hanging over my head right now. It was the second year the rule change came through allowing girls to compete in our conference's football games. I had one girl on the team. She was our kicker. In one game, she twisted her leg on a kick and ended up in the hospital."

"Some say she was hit by an opposing player, but the films did not show that. The parents charged me with criminal negligence, but the suit was thrown out because it was shown to be false. Next, they brought a civil suit and that hasn't been settled yet. So, Nick, you see if I risk putting a player out there who is thin and long-legged like Gil against those big beefy players, and there's an injury, I'll get all kinds of flak and may lose my job."

"Well," I said, "I want you to know that if there is a time you need a fast runner, Gil can outrun any player. When I timed the races, no one matched the speed and quickness."

Our bus broke down on the way to the big Portage game and by the time we got another bus, we were about a half hour late for our pre-game practice. I noticed Coach Bob wasn't feeling well and it began to rain.

Portage was perhaps the strongest team we were to face all year, but we realized that the rain also fell on them. However, both sides managed to hold on to the ball. That was until we fumbled just before halftime. It was a tough battle and the score was Portage 7 and Highland 0 at halftime. Both sides couldn't run well on the wet grass and many passes were dropped in

237

the second half. We went home with our tail between our legs, swallowing our first loss on that gray afternoon. Coach Bob lay in the back of the bus, his illness had gotten the better of him. He slept all the way home.

I took the blame for our loss because I felt I might've done more. I began working on a few ball control exercises I could use in practices. The coach felt better the next day and worked on a tighter defense and we began devising new lineup stances.

We both knew Portage could be beaten, and we would have another chance when we met again in four weeks. If we could go undefeated for the rest of the season, we could play in the championship game. Highland College hadn't done that in years.

Gil didn't take the nickname "Bencher" personally and didn't seem to mind that there had been no playing time in a game, but I knew hope was there for future playing time.

***

"I've made diagrams of most of the teams' defenses," Gil said.

"How could you have done that when we haven't played some of them yet?" I asked.

"Well, Mom took me to games of future opponents and I made notes of their plays."

"Did you tell the coach about that?" I asked.

"No, because I was afraid I'd spout off to him about riding the bench all the time."

"It's great that you made notes on opponents. I want you to meet with me and Coach Bob to go over what you discovered. That's valuable information for him."

Next, we went over Meyre's materials and organized it by team and down situations and even what weather might be expected. The information was crucial to Bob's offensive tactics and he went right to work devising his plans for the next games.

"Nick, I have news. I want you to know I'm off the hook. The civil suit was thrown out and I don't have to deal with that anymore," Coach Bob said.

"Good, now we can concentrate on new plays and ways to gain more yards per play."

"Do you have suggestions on how we can utilize Gil Meyre's speed?"

"Quarterback Green can hand off or shovel pass to Meyre on either end where no player will be able to keep up."

"I like both ideas," Bob said. "I have another idea. What about a long pass down field after Gil outruns the defender? Green is a great passer and can throw long."

"Can I tell Gil we're considering a play with a speedy run?" I asked.

"Sure, but let Bencher know we must keep it under wraps."

The next day, after practice, I saw Mrs. Meyre and asked why Gil came to practice already suited up and never showered with the team. She said it is part of the study and she would answer all the questions later. I was still mystified by the unusual circumstances.

The Highland Panthers won the next three games easily with an improved defense and a good running game. Our running backs had recovered from injuries and were healthy again. The team made efforts to practice harder with renewed vigor. Coach still didn't use Bencher.

The Portage game was a home game and a large crowd was assembled for a shoot-out with undefeated Portage. The night seemed colder in the crisp white lighting on the field. What was important to me was that the field was dry and in good condition.

At halftime, the score was again Portage 7 and Highland 0. Portage defense stopped all of our attempts to put up points. At the end of third quarter, the score had not changed. At the start of the fourth quarter, the Portage right tackle fell awkwardly and was replaced by a big freshman. Bob called timeout and instructed the Highland line to double team that position. He told me to go to Gil with the play previously set for such a situation. The ball was snapped and handed off to Gil.

Bencher jumped through the opening and outran all the defenders. The touchdown tied the game.

Bob yelled, "Bencher was as fast as the wind!"

Tears came to my eyes. I saw our team completely change with a new energy sparked by the knowledge they could win this game. Bob made the surprising decision to try for a two-point conversion. It was successful, and the score was now 8 to 7, Highland over Portage.

After Highland kicked, Portage ran the ball back to the 50-yard line. Coach Bob called time and notified the team that three minutes remained in the game and our defense must stop the Portage offense. Thanks to an eleven-yard loss when the Panthers sacked the Portage quarterback, we were successful. With less than two minutes left, Highland had the ball again. Expecting Highland would run the ball to run time off the clock, Portage didn't watch for a pass play.

Bob called for Gil to run fast down field and go under the ball at about the goal line. Gil ran past the defender, catching the ball in the end zone.

Final score: Highland 15, Portage 7. That win gave Highland the conference title because Portage had lost one previous game.

Coach Bob had a new goal and not an easy one. That was to win our division and go on to the state title game next month. He decided he was going to have to exploit his secret weapon, Gil Meyre. We had a new star player. Students planned a big entourage to attend the playoff game.

The toughest game of the year confirmed Coach Bob's pregame talk when he said, "The best defense wins games." Neither team had scored by half time. Bob's speech encouraged the team to be quicker and do what our opponent, Rangle, was not doing. That was to focus on the ball and read the quarterback's eyes before he released the it. On offense, Coach used runs by Meyre and I had those plays ready for the second-half.

The surprise plan called for the return man to run toward the right sideline, then, he would stop and lateral the ball to Meyre who was to run to the left. The defenders would be going to Highland's right while Gil would run down the left sideline in front of the nearest safety.

On defense, Bob elected to double team Rangle's star receiver and use Meyre to cover the other two receivers in case they were targets of a pass. He counted on Gil's speed to cover either one who might get the ball thrown to them.

One defender was to stay behind the main receiver and the other defender was to step in front and bat the ball down. The play worked so well that the second man intercepted the ball and Highland had possession on their own forty-eight-yard line.

On the following play, Meyre was to be a pass receiver. Putting all this in motion worked well because Meyre outran the defender and gained thirty yards. Two running plays later, our halfback made it into the end zone. After the extra point was made, the score stood at Highland 14, Rangle 0. The rest of the game became a defensive battle with both teams scoreless.

Celebrations went on all night beginning with chants everywhere, "MY-R, MY-R, MY-R." Though Rangle was thought to be the best team, it was Highland earning its way to the championship. It took all the next week for Coach to realize his team was actually slated for a chance to be state champions. He also knew his plays using the incredible speed of Gil Meyre were known to his opponents.

He and I worked on that problem for days. I didn't know whether the fans were coming to the championship showdown because of a chance to be state champs or to cheer for Gil Meyre. I felt it was the latter reason. It took my breath away to see Gil run. It never grew old.

Thousands of fans across the state and the nation honored our new star. The championship game was played in the largest stadium available, and yet there was standing room only. Kick-off came sooner than I was psychologically ready for, but soon I was engrossed in the details of play calling. I hoped our preparation was good enough to win.

We traded punts as both teams went three and out. Then, we recovered a fumble and our running back scored a touchdown at the end of the first quarter. Soon the Eagles were in our end of the field, but I was proud of the defense as they limited our opponents to a field goal. We knew the game would pit two of the country's best defensive teams in the second half. So, it was no surprise that the score was still 7 to 3 in the fourth quarter.

Bob looked comfortable and calm when I reminded him there were ten minutes left in the game. That's when he sprang another surprise. Of course, it involved Meyre. I couldn't believe he'd try that play on the fifty-yard line. Bob had noticed a defensive back got up with a slight limp and ordered a pass play over the middle to Meyre in front of him.

Meyre easily outran everyone and scampered to the end zone. The Highland defenders continued to shut out the Eagles and earned the victory. Highland College was the new state champions. But, the fans took the successful defense for granted and gave the credit to Meyre, shouting, "MY-R, MY-R, MY-R." This time the celebrations lasted for days.

I wound up my assistant coaching career as part of a state champion team, telling everyone I believed we won the trophy because of the outstanding performance of Gil Meyre.

Greater than a state championship, greater than Coach Bob Condi, and greater than all previous running records; Gil's name goes down in sports history as the greatest *woman* athlete in history. Yes, we will always remember Gilliam Meyre and our part in *her* life.

2018 Poetry Youth First Place Twelve & Under Winner: The Mist by Elizabeth Kate Baer

Elizabeth is a ten-year old writer from Atlanta, GA. Her best friend is her cuddly dog Coco who inspires her to do silly stuff. She has been writing poems ever since she can remember. Besides writing, Elisabeth loves to sing, play the violin and the piano. Music gives her the tempo and inspiration and helps transport her to the places that she writes about.

The icebox of the morning

Chilling the gallant, crystal

Air that roams wildly around.

t rouses shyly over

The timid River, slyly

Greying the tamed atmosphere

Shielding us from the angered

Sun.

2018 Poetry Youth Second Place Twelve & Under Winner:
Reincarnation by Mathew Sun

Mathew is a twelve-year-old boy who attends Medea Creek Middle School. He enjoys reading and most of all daydreaming. He does extracurricular activities, like swimming and piano. He has been a resident of Oak Park for seven years and lives a quiet life. Matthew has always liked writing, poems especially, but this is the first writing competition he has ever entered.

I looked from the sky, in heaven's domain
And could not see the ants I once knew
When I saw such ants that seemed invisible from the sky
I related to their steady lives.

The ants walked as if they were a string of thread
Swarmed the grass in search of land
They grew and grew and built until their end
And I stood and watched from God's hand

Yet even though I had seen
What I did not need to see
I leaned even further, towards the ants
The land within grasp, as I fell.

Down through the clouds
Falling out of heaven's hole
Rid myself of divinity, then welcomed to the ground
In curiosity of this reminiscent world, my eyes could not be lulled

The world around was unlike the clouds
It had life and it was teeming
Dew was always dropping
And spiders were always weaving

So, as I sat there looking at the blank sky
I had no regrets, for I did not fall into hell
Yet I only thought:

If Angels praise
And Demons punish
Then I think heaven was quite a haze
From other, better things

2018 Poetry Youth First Place 13 to 17 Winner: The Performance by Daniel Filz

Daniel is fifteen years old and is currently a tenth-grade student at River Oaks Academy in Westlake Village. He excels in language arts, computer science and math. He loves music, especially playing the piano, writing and reading, movies, and hanging out with his friends and family. He was inspired to write his submission while pursuing his poetry studies this year, and writing poetry has now become a favorite creative outlet.

I sit in solitude,
in silence, asleep;

Until the fingers swiftly
touch my ivory keys,
black then white.

I am awake!

The rhythm gently builds.
Vibrations stir the air,
as the warm scent of devotion
whirls around me.

The sounds of joy, passion,
and sadness inspire me
to reach great mountains,
and explore deep valleys.

I taste the sweetness
of the music,
as it fills the room
with swirls of golden, glistening,
notes.

The treble and bass clefs
Dance hand in hand
to the composition.
Finally, the last note hangs in the air.
I try to catch it – I miss.

Silence.

The darkness closes in once more.
I wait, dreaming
of my next performance.

2018 Poetry Youth Second Place 13 to 17 Winner: Daughter by Mable Ji

Mabel is a seventeen-year-old student living in Sugar Land, TX. Aside from writing, she loves making art, discovering new music, eating snacks, and hibernating in the winter. She hopes to inspire others through writing. She aspires to further her creative writing career in college and become a successful writer.

A woman who raised me
Watches me turn into a woman
And I can't tell if she's

Happy with what she's created,
Or disappointed—
maybe a bit of both.

When I was little, I always wanted to be old.
I told my mother I wanted to be a mother, Until I realized I didn't want
to do the work—

Mothers have got to do – now,
she tells me that I'm too
Lazy, too laid back, too unmotivated—

That I need to start looking forward Instead of looking down at my
phone That I need to believe in myself

And become something worthwhile.
I need to be something, she tells me, Or I'm just a waste of potential.

I hate to listen to her,
But she's right- I just don't really know
What to be anymore.

All we had were
Memories of when things used to Be simpler, happier,

When she was satisfied with Me just being me
A sleepless child dreaming.

But soon I'll leave her, Or she'll leave me,
And then all we'll have are

Unfulfilled expectations.

2018 Poetry Youth Third Place 13 to 17 Winner: A Black Bird by Shakti Dutt

Shakti is a freshman at Foothill Technology High School, Ventura. In 8th grade, her Language Arts teacher introduced her to the art of poetry. That is when she fell in love with poetry and has been writing ever since. The first poetry book she read was "This time called life" by Walter Rinder. His work made her realize how beautiful Mother Earth is. "All other poets, Anne Bradstreet, Edgar Allen Poe, Rabindranath Tagore, and other great poets have helped me understand the wonders of writing and express who I am as a human being!"

Looking in the waters
With ants by my side
The reflection of my scars
Is still frozen as ice

The beauty around me is still beautiful
Until the blood moon reminds me of my past
That still lasts

Run!
The voice in my head screams
Louder than my own thoughts
And here I took a flight
Breaking my cage and the locks
I fly and fly like a black bird
Under the starry sky
Alone with the sound,
The sound of fear
That draws me back to the ground

And here I am
On my feet against
The ones who love me

All I can say
Is
I am who I am
For you, I am who you want me to be.

2018 Poetry Youth 13 to 17 Honorable Mention: One Man by Lola Crane Flores

Lola, fourteen, is attending the Multimedia Arts & Design Academy at Santa Barbara High School. She enjoys singing, playing piano, guitar, volleyball and spending time with her friends and family. Lola is also involved in drawing and the performing arts. She has been writing poetry, prose, children's stories with illustrations and songs since a young age. Poetry in lyrical form, she realized, is an interest in which she could potentially pursue a career.

It took one man
to stand up and be a leader.

It took one woman on a bus
to say "no".

One law causing great destruction.
One school girl to swim in a fountain of color.

Many battles to break the chains.
Many people who gave their lives for freedom.

It took thousands of people to march.
It took one President to sign a law.

One person to make a difference.
One man to start it all.

Imagine what would happen if we all decided to stand up.
Imagine what would happen if we all took a rainbow path.

It took one man to have a dream.
It took one dream for all of us to live as one.

2018 Poetry Youth 13 to 17 Honorable Mention: My Half Shell
by Peter R. Appleby

Peter is a local young writer eager to share his work with others willing to hear. Writing, in his opinion, is an incredible gift, tool, and skill which is fueled by one's imagination and experience.

For that half shell, Of its lustrous wonders
Found in the piercing eyes of the Osprey on perch, Yet always in my
quest exists that present blunder.

Submerged, its arcane shine cast All too late in quick revelry for my eyes,
Enveloped by Poseidon's cloudy tides, too fast, But the tides, by
existence, don't unfold the lies.

For tides roll in and fall out,
Washing pebbles of thought and memory across the shore, But even
they, when reading the messages, are cast into doubt,
Of fate's untimely foretelling, yet not knowing who for.

Whyever in truth, unlocking ease Do those sirens sing,
Of vivid young life gone away in age on my voyage?

So stars, hide your fires, and please
Cover the world from my deep ephemeral desires, The search in me for
my half shell never tires,
Or fades deep, below the temporal sand.

2018 Poetry Youth 13 to 17 Honorable Mention: In The Mirror by Haley Fisher

Haley lives in Mississauga, Ontario, Canada. She enjoys writing poetry, short stories and plays. She has had her poetry "Explore Your Life", "Fear to Flight", "Fun in the Sun" and a short story "Hello, Future", selected to be published. As well, her play "Rosie Evergreen's Nightmare" was chosen to be performed. Haley likes to inspire others and hopes she does so through her writing.

Staring into the smudged mirror briefly she sees, What she wanted to be,
A strong and confident girl,
Instead, she looks like she went through winds that swirled.

Her tired eyes are puffy and dark, Tears dripping down her face,
Being shamed for who she truly is, A girl
should never feel this way.

She does everything in her power,
To try to convince herself she is alright, But her hopes are pushed deep down again, It feels like in her soul there is only rain.

Then someone comes and comforts her, Now she realizes that this
is the cure,
No matter what she is strong in every way, In the mirror now she clearly sees.

Short Story: Beyond Belief by Connie Mukherjee

Constance, the 2017/2018 President of the VCWC, also held the position of First Vice President, arranging programs during the 2016/2017 term. She is the author of Nanibala's Belief, *a cross-cultural and inter-generational work of creative non-fiction released in 2015 by Balboa Press. Connie holds a Master's Degree from Indiana University, and practiced medical Speech-Language Pathology for forty years before her retirement. She now loves to travel, play bridge and pursue her passion of writing. Connie resides in Oxnard with her husband, Ajit.*

My husband, Ajit and I walked through the door of our home after a thirty-seven-day trip to India at 9:00 AM on Saturday, January 30, 2016. He stayed up trying to shake the daze of jet lag. Exhausted, I fell into bed and drifted into deep sleep. Before long, I heard our son, Misha, and our family dog, Maddie, burst through the front entrance.

"We're home!" Misha yelled.

Maddie's loud joyous cries of hello carried into our bedroom, followed by Ajit's delighted laughter. Our beloved pet darted into the bedroom and to my side of the bed.

"So happy to see you!" she whined at me.

Tears of joy came to my eyes. I climbed out from under the covers to hug her.

I knew right away. Maddie's nightmare had begun.

***

Ajit, Maddie, and I moved to our California condo in 2010 to be close to our only child, Misha, who resided in Los Angeles. I never wanted to miss witnessing Maddie's joyous greeting for Misha when he arrived for weekend visits. Whether an absence of a few hours or a few weeks, Maddie's welcome warmed each of us to the core.

Maddie seemed the happiest when the four of us spent time together; sitting in the living room watching TV, or eating takeout on our patio. On Saturday and Sunday mornings, we piled into the silver Volvo and headed to the park or the ocean for walks. Despite Maddie's preoccupation with sniffing, if one of us lagged, she stopped and waited for us.

When she was satisfied we were safe from the big bad Chihuahuas and all else she deemed a threat, Maddie continued her exploration of the world.

Through the years, we began to notice lumps under Maddie's skin. They appeared to be doggie fat tumors, but the veterinarian strongly advised removal of one particular hard round lump on her leg. Maddie's first surgery was on December 12, 2012. The vet's suspicions were confirmed when the lab reports returned with a diagnosis of mast cell cancer.

Maddie underwent four more surgeries in 2013 to remove tumors. As soon as she healed from one surgery, another lump would appear somewhere else on her belly or legs. She came back strong each time, seemingly invincible. The vet's nickname for her was Miss Personality; we called Maddie a survivor.

In April of 2015, a large, rapidly growing tumor appeared under Maddie's right ear and into her cheek. We asked our new veterinarian to perform the surgery. Labs revealed cancer in the margins of the tissue he removed, but the anatomy of her face prevented cutting deeper. We all knew it would be impossible to predict the exact course of her health, but the vet urged us to consider chemo and radiation.

Driving Maddie to Los Angeles for treatments would have been an act of cruelty for both Maddie and for us. I knew I was signing her death warrant when I told the vet six cancer operations was enough. We were not going to put Maddie through more surgeries nor take lifesaving measures. I told Maddie not to worry, I would not let her suffer.

***

Far away in India, Ajit's great niece became engaged. The astrologer recommended January 27, 2016 as an auspicious date for the marriage. My husband had not been to his homeland for 12 years and I had not visited for 24. Ajit was 76 years old; we decided to make the trip while we were healthy.

Ajit took a semester off from his adjunct teaching duties at the community college. Misha wanted to join us, along with his girlfriend. However, they could only take vacation time over the holidays. My husband and I planned a 37-day trip to India to accommodate both our son's schedule and attend the wedding.

During half of our visit, we explored Rajasthan, Goa, and the holy cities of India. The remainder of the time we spent with family. The trip was incredible, but wrapping my head around the dichotomy of the country took effort. The emotions of visiting Ajit's family after such a long time were intense. We experienced bouts of stomach issues and coughed incessantly from the pollution and assorted bacteria we caught along the way. Mentally and physically, the trip took its toll.

Meanwhile, my brother and sister-in-law stayed in our condo and doggie-sat Maddie. She played on the beach like a puppy with her 18-year-old doggie cousin. When they returned to Indiana, our kind and competent neighbors kept Maddie for five days. El Nino rains restricted Maddie's time outside and as much as our neighbors loved and distracted her, she became obsessed with licking her elbow.

Misha and his girlfriend returned home to L.A. on January 10 and took Maddie to their apartment. Through emails we received while in India, Misha let us know Maddie developed what he termed, "sores."

To keep her from incessant licking, Misha was forced to put a cone on her. He took Maddie to a veterinarian who gave him a topical spray to anesthetize the areas and also recommended a visit with her regular vet when we returned. Ajit and I left Kolkata on January 30, flew through Hong Kong, and thanks to the International Date Line, arrived in Los Angeles the same day.

***

Before we left for India, I felt small lumps on Maddie. She was old and had cancer, and I feared the worst. Ajit also felt the lumps, but because her behaviors remained stable, wishful thinking allowed him to believe she would live for six months after our return. He argued with me when I predicted two months. I told Maddie to stay strong while we were away.

When I got out of bed and hugged Maddie that fateful morning of our return, I discovered the huge horrible open mass which grew from the side of her neck. Five cancerous tumors had burst through the skin, oozing fluids, pus and blood, all the while continuing to grow. Maddie reeked of cancer. While we were spending our last few weeks in India, Maddie was waiting for us before she died.

Saturday evening, I lay on the floor with Maddie, hugging her spoon style. I began to weep uncontrollably. I got up, hugged my son, and told him Maddie would soon die. I asked him if he was free the next weekend if the vet recommended we put her to sleep.

"Stop being so melodramatic," Misha said.

At that point, Ajit too struggled to accept the obvious. "If we ever needed to put Maddie down, I will have a heart attack."

I worried about him. I knew I had to be the strong one for Maddie and for my two men. I repeated my vow to Maddie and myself; I would not let Maddie suffer.

Ajit and Misha needed to progress through the stages of acceptance on their own terms. Within days, five tumors bursting through Maddie's skin increased to eight. One on her foreleg grew larger and began to interfere with her mobility. To keep blood from dripping to the floor, I wrapped her leg. Although Maddie didn't appear to be in pain, if we removed her cone for a second, she began to lick furiously.

Midweek, Ajit acknowledged Maddie was losing her spark. Yet he kept saying, "Let's wait to hear what our vet says on Thursday morning."

At my insistence, my husband and I held a frank discussion. "I admit we can't let Maddie suffer. We will inform Misha, and he too must realize the time has come to let Maddie go."

We were all devastated.

Maddie was a friend to all three of us. She gave us parting gifts in the year before her death, making sure we would be fine. Ajit came to a natural acceptance of her death. Misha fell in love with a remarkable woman. In 2008, Maddie had inspired me to write *Nanibala's Belief*, and she once again had rekindled my passion for writing.

The week between our return home from an amazing trip to India and Maddie's looming death was one of the most difficult weeks of my life. The cataclysmic clash of grief and joy, while being physically drained and emotionally strong, shocked me into a heightened awareness of the mystery of life.

Everything Maddie did, everything she and I did, or everything the family did together, took on special significance as "the last time." On walks in all her favorite places, she was not as fast nor could not go as far, but she explored and smiled as if she had not a care in the world.

The evening before her death, she rested on the floor with her cone on and spotted her squeaky friends lying nearby. She began to whine at them, a mournful soulful whine, as if saying goodbye to them for the last time. I cried like a baby.

I talked to Maddie. "Feel my love and take it with you. Spread it to the ancestors and all the other souls with you in the cosmic energy."

On Saturday afternoon, February 6, 2016, Misha, Ajit, and I petted Maddie lying on a blanket on the floor of the veterinarian's comfort room. She lay with her head at Misha's feet like she had so very often in her life. We stroked her as the vet injected her with propofol, then sodium pentobarbital. She took her last few breaths, her heart slowed and stopped, and she died.

It was hard for me to leave her. I followed Ajit and Misha to the door, but I turned back, walked to her and petted her soft fur for the last time. I told Maddie that her light would live on.

***

A few days following Maddie's death, my sister, Candy, came for her annual February visit to California. Ajit, Candy, and I drove down the Pacific Coast Highway to a rocky beach near Malibu. I built a rock stack in the shape of Maddie to honor her energy. On Valentine's Day, a black velvety moth appeared on the ceiling above our bed. It visited every evening after that for days. Maddie had come back to thank us for being there for her when she needed us most. She returned to show her love for us.

On February 21, Misha spent the day with us. I filled a Tupperware container with some of Maddie's gravelly ashes. In another box, I placed dried yellow roses from a bouquet we received when Maddie passed. The three of us went to the park, the ocean and the common spaces of our housing community. We spread her ashes on the places she loved, along with a single rose. At home, Ajit performed a Hindu celebration of life. He placed her picture, a candle, incense, and her favorite "foodie" on her placemat. He silently prayed, and all of us took bites of her human foods.

After watching my sister board the shuttle to the airport a few weeks later, I walked to the mailbox and found it empty. Sadness and grief overcame me, prompting me to take a walk in our neighborhood following the path that Maddie preferred. When I passed the front gate, a chilly breeze made me decide to cut my walk short. Instead of continuing to the corner of our gated community along the eucalyptus fence row, I started back toward our condo. I crossed the street toward a neighbor's lawn where Maddie liked to rest under the shade tree.

Maddie's spirit intervened in my plan. She pulled me back toward the corner row of towering trees. She talked to me, roaring loud in the silence. "Go where Maddie would make you go." The multiple meanings of the phrase struck me. Indirectly, Maddie had previously taken me along the path to spiritual wisdom. Now, she was telling me if I listened, I may become brave as a writer and in life, leading me to even deeper wisdom.

On the way to the corner, a green and red hummingbird hovered in the tall stalks amidst the bird of paradise flowers. When I stepped on the first paver to the back corner, I remembered the last time Maddie and I walked there together...a few days before her death. Through her big smile she told me, "I'm going to check everything out once more. Make sure all is right in my kingdom." I knew she was going to die soon. I let her go wherever she wanted to go for as long as she wanted to be there.

Her behavior confirmed she also knew she was going to die. Born from that thought came the next revelation from Maddie on my solitary walk. She lived until the last moment; we should live our lives until the very last moment.

Maddie's favorite tree on our neighbor's lawn now beckoned. I stood on various spots in the shade staring down at the grass. I remembered how Maddie loved to lay there and watch her world. How she moved closer to me for affection. How she smiled. Oh, how I loved her smile.

I stepped to the curb where I often stood to look at her. I stared down at the spot where she usually rested. I couldn't believe my eyes. Grass was mashed in her shape as if she were there.

Maddie *is* still with me, with us. Someway, somehow, I feel her. She is teaching and protecting. She is making me feel and helping me be brave. Her light will live on.

2018 Poetry Adult First Place Winner: (lover) by Caroline Erickson

Caroline is currently studying Creative Writing at Wichita State University, Wichita, KS. In 2017, she received a national silver medal from Scholastic Writing Awards for her senior writing portfolio, and her poetry took First place in 2014 and Second place in 2016 in the Kansas Voices Annual Writing Contest. She is incredibly excited to continue her writing career into college and beyond, wherever it might take her.

You want to be buried in that room.
The duvet, its small blushes of cherry blossoms
spread across the powder sky, the pillows
mismatched white or blue-striped, the rough wood frame of the window,
the pale non-light soft from the grey sky – oh god, you want especially
to be buried in the light.

This is the only perfect moment no word spoken, no telegraph lines
thrown out across your shared skins. You are alone in the room,
except for his silence.

He's sitting
on the opposite edge of the bed.
You can feel his weight in the dip
of the mattress. A visualization of gravity,
an object bending a two-dimensional plane so all satellites spiral
around it. The model is flawed. You want him out
but you want him here forever,
just a weight, a well in space time
to remind you that you're not alone.

How you want
to be buried in that room.

2018 Poetry Adult Second Place Winner: Cutting on the Bias
by Marcy Wingard

Marcy lives in Newbury Park, California. She worked in the field of Human Resources/Employee Benefits for most of her career but began writing short stories and poetry while attending Miami University in Oxford, Ohio where she studied English Literature. After marriage and children, writing took a back seat to life. She started writing poetry again in earnest after her husband's death. Now retired, she is very active in the local and online poetry communities.

Billowing reams of cotton
cover the kitchen table
mounded in folded piles
spilling down onto the floor delicate clouds of material

When I examine it
the hidden pattern appears softly
regular and even I am fascinated

Wrinkled bony hands feel the fabric porcelain doll arms absently work
the unbroken lengths

Deft from years of practice
gossamer silk moistened by thin pursed lips she threads the sharp needle
surely, with no hesitation I hear her whisper

Straining, I try to catch her words those words of ancient
importance she shares
"Always cut cloth on the bias
it provides more give"

2018 Poetry Adult Third Place Winner: Stepping Back by Warren Argall

Warren at age seventy-eight, is married to Linde. They live in Sydney, Australia and have eight married children and numerous grandchildren. Warren retired from Medical Practice in 2017. They have travelled to Europe several times, usually visiting the Czech Republic where Linde was born. They also went to St Louis in 2016 for the marriage of a granddaughter, and then toured the spectacular Canyonlands. They share a passion for music and reading and are regular members of a local protestant church congregation.

on the ragged edge of time we stand
the family shadows

tracing their pathways love, pain, labour distance and discovery

once we could hold and mend listen and talk
and be there at the borders of their land
edges beyond our reach were always there we watch together
my arm around your shoulder your head at rest on me

longing for all of them to find that time at morning light when children sigh
and stir
where trust and gentleness are limitless while minutes slip away